San Diego Christian College
2100 Greenfield Drive
El Cajon, CA 92019

The Development of Giftedness and Talent Across the Life Span

The Development of Giftedness and Talent Across the Life Span

Edited by
Frances Degen Horowitz, Rena F. Subotnik, and Dona J. Matthews

American Psychological Association • Washington, DC

Published by
American Psychological Association
750 First Street, NE
Washington, DC 20002
www.apa.org

To order
APA Order Department
P.O. Box 92984
Washington, DC 20090-2984
Tel: (800) 374-2721; Direct: (202) 336-5510
Fax: (202) 336-5502; TDD/TTY: (202) 336-6123
Online: www.apa.org/books/
E-mail: order@apa.org

In the U.K., Europe, Africa, and the Middle East, copies may be ordered from
American Psychological Association
3 Henrietta Street
Covent Garden, London
WC2E 8LU England

Typeset in Goudy by Circle Graphics, Columbia, MD

Printer: Edwards Brothers, Inc., Ann Arbor, MI
Cover Designer: Mercury Publishing Services, Rockville, MD
Technical/Production Editor: Tiffany L. Klaff

The opinions and statements published are the responsibility of the authors, and such opinions and statements do not necessarily represent the policies of the American Psychological Association.

Library of Congress Cataloging-in-Publication Data

The development of giftedness and talent across the life span / edited by Frances Degen Horowitz, Rena F. Subotnik, and Dona J. Matthews.—1st ed.
    p. cm.
  Includes bibliographical references and index.
  ISBN-13: 978-1-4338-0414-4
  ISBN-10: 1-4338-0414-X
  1. Gifted persons. 2. Developmental psychology. I. Horowitz, Frances Degen. II. Subotnik, Rena Faye. III. Matthews, Dona J., 1951-

  BF412.D49 2009
  153.9'8—dc22

                       2008026715

British Library Cataloguing-in-Publication Data

A CIP record is available from the British Library.

Printed in the United States of America
First Edition

CONTENTS

v

CONTRIBUTORS

Christa J. Anderson, University of Kansas, Lawrence

James E. Birren, PhD, University of Southern California, Los Angeles

Otilia M. Blaga, PhD, University of Kansas, Lawrence

John Colombo, PhD, University of Kansas, Lawrence

Carol S. Dweck, PhD, Stanford University, Stanford, CA

Adele Eskeles Gottfried, PhD, California State University, Northridge

Allen W. Gottfried, PhD, California State University, Fullerton

Sandra Graham, PhD, University of California, Los Angeles

Diana Wright Guerin, PhD, California State University, Fullerton

Frances Degen Horowitz, PhD, The City University of New York Graduate Center, New York

Kathleen N. Kannass, PhD, Loyola University, Chicago, IL

Daniel P. Keating, PhD, University of Michigan, Ann Arbor

Lynn S. Liben, PhD, The Pennsylvania State University, University Park

Dona J. Matthews, PhD, University of Toronto, Ontario, Canada

D. Jill Shaddy, PhD, University of Kansas, Lawrence

Rena F. Subotnik, PhD, American Psychological Association, Washington, DC

Ellen Winner, PhD, Boston College, Chestnut Hill, MA; Project Zero, Harvard Graduate School of Education, Cambridge, MA

Frank C. Worrell, PhD, University of California, Berkeley

FOREWORD

CAROL S. DWECK

This most exciting volume offers a deeply thoughtful, modern perspective on giftedness and talent. It represents a tremendous advance over past perspectives that simply categorized people as gifted or not gifted, that (erroneously) portrayed giftedness as a stable characteristic, and that sought more to measure giftedness and talent than to develop it. This volume, in stark contrast, recognizes that talent is often very specific, that it can wax and wane over time, and that one of the most exciting questions facing researchers today is how to encourage and sustain talent—across cultures and across the life span.

THE NATURE OF GIFTEDNESS

The 1985 predecessor of the current volume focused throughout on the gifted, whereas this volume talks about giftedness in a way that allows for specific gifts and talents as well as changes in them over time.[1] To their credit, many of the authors talk about talent less as a pure gift and more as something

---

[1]Horowitz, F. D., & O'Brien, M. (1985). *The gifted and talented: Developmental perspectives*. Washington, DC: American Psychological Association.

that develops and reaches fruition through dedication and learning. They capture the fascination and long hours of engagement that typically go into developing an exceptionally high level of skill, and they note that even in prodigies, talent is accompanied by a tremendous zest for the skill domain and by sustained engagement with it.

This fact is important because the old view of "the gift" blinded people to the important role of psychosocial factors in the development of talent. Indeed, when talent withers on the vine, it may often be because the passion and engagement are lost, not because the gift is somehow inadequate. To the extent that young people believe they simply have a gift that makes them intelligent or talented, they may not put in the work necessary to sustain that talent. Moreover, the gifted label that many students still receive, and that their parents relish, may turn some children into students who are overly cautious and challenge-avoidant lest they make mistakes and no longer merit the label. These may be precisely the circumstances under which talent fails to grow.

Thus, the present volume, by portraying talented students as advanced learners rather than gifted people, has done a great service.

GENE–ENVIRONMENT INTERACTIONS

People often want to know whether talent is born or made. Another great advance evidenced in this volume is the sophisticated understanding of gene–environment interaction in the development of talent. It addresses the question, How do constitutional factors work together with environmental factors to create unusual ability? However, a further contribution of this volume is to open up new possibilities and present more options than had previously been considered. For example, it might be that genes and environment work together to create not simply the ability itself but also the psychological factors that are prominent in geniuses and that foster the development of talent over time, such as specific fascinations, sustained attention, the love of challenges, the enjoyment of effort, and resilience in the face of setbacks. If so, then this would take the field even further from the "some people have it and some people don't" mentality and even closer to understanding how to foster talent. I will return to this point—and, in particular, the importance of motivational factors—in a moment.

DEVELOPMENTAL, LIFE-SPAN, AND CULTURAL PERSPECTIVES

A prominent view in this volume is a developmental perspective that holds there are key points in a person's development at which talent may be derailed or may flourish. Sometimes these may be points at which the skill demands change in important ways. For example, instead of just getting good grades, a student needs to design an original experiment, or instead of playing against other high school students, an athlete now must compete with professionals. However, as several of the authors point out, sometimes these may also be points at which motivational factors come into play. For example, adolescents may not want to practice as much as before, their peers may disapprove of academic effort, or students who had coasted along before may be afraid of the new challenges and turn away from school. Older adults, in contrast, may find that they now have the time to pursue long-held passions or to try different things and see what might take hold.

A focus on motivational or psychosocial factors in the development of talent may also yield ways to foster academic or intellectual ability in underrepresented cultural groups. As pointed out in several chapters, many of these factors are teachable, but there has been little systematic effort to teach them. Yet several recent studies with minority populations both at elite universities[2] and in working-class public schools[3] have shown that simple motivation-relevant interventions can significantly boost school engagement, grades, and achievement test scores. These interventions have taught students about the malleable nature of intellectual ability[4] or affirmed students' sense of belonging in their academic institution.[5] Following these interventions, students valued and enjoyed their schoolwork more, studied more, made greater contact with their teachers, and did substantially better. Are environments that send these kinds of messages the ones in which talent is likely to emerge?

WHY DOES IT MATTER?

When the study of giftedness was chiefly about identifying and describing the gifted few—about sorting people into categories—it was an enterprise of somewhat restricted interest. One of the great strengths of this volume is that it reveals that developing and sustaining talent is one of the most important and exciting areas of study. In this form, the enterprise is not limited to

---

[2]Aronson, J., Fried, C., & Good, C. (2002). Reducing the effects of stereotype threat on African American college students by shaping theories of intelligence. *Journal of Experimental Social Psychology, 38,* 113–125; Walton, G. M., & Cohen, G. L. (2007). A question of belonging: Race, fit, and achievement. *Journal of Personality and Social Psychology, 92,* 82–96.
[3]Blackwell, L., Trzesniewski, K., & Dweck, C. S. (2007). Implicit theories of intelligence predict achievement across an adolescent transition: A longitudinal study and an intervention. *Child Development, 78,* 246–263; Good, C., Aronson, J., & Inzlicht, M. (2003). Improving adolescents' standardized test performance: An intervention to reduce the effects of stereotype threat. *Journal of Applied Developmental Psychology, 24,* 645–662.
[4]Aronson et al., 2002; Blackwell et al., 2007; Good et al., 2003.
[5]Walton & Cohen, 2007.

a small set of researchers studying a small set of gifted people. Rather, it encompasses many researchers studying many abilities, how they develop, and the factors that can promote them. And, as an enterprise, it takes as its target many people of diverse cultures and backgrounds and ages. It is a field that has become less about *who* and more about *how*. What could matter more than understanding how people can fulfill their extraordinary potential?

PREFACE

What is known about giftedness and talent development across the life span? What is known about identifying and supporting promise and possibility during childhood, adolescence, or adulthood? At a time when there is a great deal of emphasis on pathology and widespread concern for all manner of social, political, economic, and environmental problems, the focus of this volume is on human development gone right.

In the early 1980s, the American Psychological Association, with the support of the American Psychological Foundation's Esther Katz Rosen Fund, commissioned the book *The Gifted and Talented: Developmental Perspectives*.[1] The purpose of that volume was to engage psychologists to think about, from the perspective of their own work, the development of gifted and talented individuals. These psychologists were selected on the basis of their expertise and the fact that they had not previously conducted research with gifted populations. Contributors were also invited to provide historical perspectives, to discuss policy issues, and to review implications for gifted education. Frances Degen Horowitz and Marion O'Brien concluded the volume with a chapter

---

[1]Horowitz, F. D., & O'Brien, M. (1985). *The gifted and talented: Developmental perspectives*. Washington, DC: American Psychological Association.

challenging readers to think seriously about the implications of viewing gift-edness and talent from a developmental perspective. The volume had a seminal impact on the field of giftedness studies, gifted education, and talent development, encouraging researchers working on giftedness and talent to incorporate developmental frameworks into the course of their work. It also influenced some of the contributors to address issues related to giftedness and talent development in their own research.

Continuing the work of that 1985 publication, the American Psychological Foundation funded a small invitational conference in 2005 involving developmental psychologists who, again, had not focused their own work on exceptional high-level development. But this time, in the interest of strengthening the bridge between developmental psychology and the field of gifted education, psychologists doing research on giftedness and gifted education were also invited and, in some instances, asked to reflect on the presentations. In light of the increased importance of life-span perspectives, the conference contributions covered giftedness and talent among infants, the aging, and age groups in between.

The present volume evolved from the conference. Some chapters originated as presentations, and other chapters originated as commentaries on these presentations. Still other chapters were added to address two important developmental junctures: the transition from childhood to adolescence and the transition from adolescence to adulthood. The volume was designed to provide a focus on recent scholarship in the study of giftedness and talent as they relate to traditional and new emphases in the field of developmental psychology and to explore implications for research, educational practices, and public policies.

The major themes and challenges in considering the development of giftedness and talent have not changed since 1985, but they are currently discussed at a more complex and sophisticated level as a result of intervening years of research and theory generation: Can predictions be made about giftedness and talent development? How should giftedness and talent be thought about in relation to specific ability domains? What accounts for the absence of diversity among those served in many gifted and talented programs? What is the role of psychosocial factors as they contribute to the emergence of gifted and talented behavior over time? How high should the bar be set for identifying those with extraordinary abilities? The knowledge that child prodigies may not be exceptional as adults, and that extraordinary adults may not have been exceptional as children, raises theoretical questions with practical implications about continuities and discontinuities in development. The gaps in the literature that would explain these inconsistencies have yet to be filled, but it is our hope that this volume will inspire developmental psychologists and others to move the field forward.

As was true with the 1985 volume, this volume addresses the topic of gift-edness and talent in an exclusively American context. We are quite aware that educators around the world are grappling with similar questions and concerns,[2] but in the interest of keeping our focus to a manageable size, with this volume we chose to consider these topics as they apply to the United States. We trust that those more familiar with other contexts can best gauge how to apply the conclusions and recommendations of this volume to their own situations.

This volume is organized by developmental period. Chapter 1 introduces the reader to themes that emerge from the discussions in the following chapters as well as to current considerations of giftedness and talent from a developmental, life-span perspective. Looking at giftedness through the dynamic lens of developmental processes, Horowitz raises questions related to continuities and discontinuities in development, the role of social context, expectations, and issues of diversity.

Part I, which consists of chapters 2 and 3, addresses infancy and early childhood. In chapter 2, John D. Colombo, D. Jill Shaddy, Otilia M. Blaga, Christa J. Anderson, and Kathleen N. Kannass present intriguing data to suggest that very early measures of cognitive behavior in infants may be useful in identifying individual differences at the high end of the spectrum of cognitive performance. In chapter 3, Allen W. Gottfried, Adele Eskeles Gottfried, and Diana Wright Guerin question the ability to predict and identify giftedness early, citing data from their landmark longitudinal study.

Part II, which consists of chapters 4 and 5, addresses childhood. These chapters focus particularly on giftedness in the spatial domain. Evidence of giftedness in extraordinary spatial understanding is described by Lynn S. Liben in chapter 4, and artistic exceptionality is discussed by Ellen Winner in chapter 5. These two chapters challenge the reader to think about giftedness and talent in a variety of intelligences that are not measured by traditional IQ.

Part III, which consists of chapters 6, 7, and 8, addresses adolescence. In chapter 6, Dona J. Matthews discusses the critical transition from childhood to adolescence and the factors and variables that impact continuity and discontinuity in the development of giftedness and talent. Sandra Graham, in chapter 7, and then Frank C. Worrell, in chapter 8, tackle underrepresentation of adolescents of color in traditional gifted and talented programs. Graham challenges the validity of standard measures and the resultant exclusionary effect on populations of color for admittance to gifted and talent programs, whereas Worrell argues for improving educational opportunities for all children as the pathway to increasing opportunities for minority populations in gifted and talented programs.

Part IV, which consists of chapters 9 and 10, addresses the transition to adulthood and the later years. The topic of transition is revisited in chapter 9

---

[2]Balchin, T., Hymer, B. J., & Matthews, D. J. (Eds.). (2009). *The Routledge International Companion to gifted education*. Abingdon, England: Routledge; Heller, K. A., Mönks, F. L., Sternberg, R. J., & Subotnik, R. F. (Eds.). (2000). *International handbook of giftedness and talent*. (2nd ed.). Oxford, England: Elsevier Science.

by Rena F. Subotnik, who considers the challenge of continuities and discontinuities in gifted and talented behavior from adolescence to adulthood. She notes the increasing rigor of criteria used to identify gifted and talented behavior in adults, as compared with children and adolescents, and the increasing and changing demands on individuals as they make this transition. The chapter provides a keen analysis of some of the factors that decrease or increase the likelihood that those identified as gifted in childhood or adolescence will make the transition to giftedness in adulthood. Then, in chapter 10, James E. Birren discusses whether, and to what extent, previously unexpressed gifts and talents may be developed among the elderly population.

Part V, which consists of chapters 11 and 12, ties together the rest of the book and lays out conclusions. In chapter 11, Daniel P. Keating suggests a developmental framework for thinking about giftedness and talent. He provides a history of the developmental approach and the work in giftedness research and points out the historical incompatibility between these two approaches. He then addresses how evidence-based perspectives in both areas are changing in a way that makes developmental approaches increasingly compatible with studies of giftedness and talent development. The resulting framework that emerges in this chapter reinforces the rest of this volume, enhancing the book's usefulness for future researchers in the field. In chapter 12, the editors—Matthews, Subotnik, and Horowitz—discuss the implications of this volume for research, policy, and practice.

We invite you, the reader, to dip into this volume, to learn from it, to ask more questions. We hope we have contributed to your understanding of the importance of developmental and life-span perspectives for providing a firmer foundation to scientific understanding of the development and expression of giftedness and talent.

The editors wish to express their deep appreciation to the American Psychological Foundation for supporting the invitational conference that served as the basis of this volume and to the American Psychological Foundation's Esther Katz Rosen fund for generous support of this endeavor.

We also want to recognize the hospitality provided by the Graduate Center of the City University of New York in hosting the scholar forum that served as the basis of this book.

The Development of
Giftedness and Talent
Across the Life Span

1

INTRODUCTION: A DEVELOPMENTAL UNDERSTANDING OF GIFTEDNESS AND TALENT

FRANCES DEGEN HOROWITZ

"What is it about the creative geniuses of this world that makes them special? Is their genius inborn, or is it something that can be developed and enhanced? If so, what are the environmental factors that have the power to encourage creativity?" Thus began a review of a biography of Isaac Newton (Shoshani, 2007, n.p.). Shoshani's questions are the generic questions that have characterized the long history of the debates about individual differences and giftedness and talent: How much in development is attributed to nature, and how much to nurture?

These questions are explicitly and implicitly threaded through almost all the chapters of this volume. Only recently has the simplistic juxtaposition of nature and nurture been replaced by more multifaceted formulations that rest on a growing understanding of the complexities of genetic expressions and their possible contributions to behavior, on the significant increases in knowledge of organismic plasticity across the life span, and on a more subtle and textured analysis of the components of environmental experiences (Churchill et al., 2002; Gershoff, Aber, Raver, & Lennon, 2007; Hess, 2005; Johnson, 2007; Simonton, 2005).

The consideration of giftedness and talent in a developmental perspective requires an understanding of the current issues in developmental theory with respect to the origins of individual differences and prediction across the life span—from infancy through the adult years. In this chapter I discuss these matters along with changes in the definition of giftedness and talent, the emerging themes in the developmental discourse on giftedness and talent, the role of cultural contexts and matters of diversity, and the implications of all of these issues for setting the research agenda in the field.

DEVELOPMENTAL THEORY, INDIVIDUAL DIFFERENCES, AND PREDICTION

The issues related to the roles of genetic, organismic, and environmental variables in determining developmental status at any point in time have been central to the discourse since the early days of the field of developmental psychology (Horowitz, 1987, 2000). Over the years and most recently, as developmental psychologists' understanding of the expression and role of genes in behavior, disease, and disability has deepened, it has been clear that genes and chromosomal anomalies, at the low end of a distribution, can have a direct and significant impact on development. Consider the evidence for the chromosomal basis for Down's syndrome, or the identification of the biological basis of the phenylketonuria (PKU) deficiency. The inability of an infant to metabolize phenylalanine, which is at the heart of the PKU deficiency, leads to severe mental retardation. Instituting a rigid early dietary intervention erases the inevitability of that outcome (see chap. 11, this volume) and normal development can proceed. At the other end of distributions for intelligence, creativity, and talent, there is currently no comparable evidence for a one-to-one correspondence in genetic or biological determination or any simple intervention such as dietary modification that can produce gifted and talented behavior. Even as heritability estimates suggest genetic influence on IQ, the degree of that heritability appears to be influenced by environmental factors (Turkheimer, Haley, Waldron, D'Onofrio, & Gottesman, 2003). And it is known that environmental experience has an impact on both brain structure and brain function across the life span (e.g., Churchill et al., 2002; Diamond, 1988; Rueda, Rothbart, McCandless, Saccamano, & Posner, 2005; Zangel & Mills, 2007). However, the present lack of evidence for a simple, direct genetic or environmental influence on the emergence of gifted and talented behavior does not mean none will be forthcoming.

Although there is no unequivocal evidence of the singular, unalloyed effect of the naturally occurring environment or of environmental interventions on development, there is good evidence that environmental factors and managed interventions affect the expression and development of complex behavior (Duncan, Brooks-Gunn, & Klebanov, 1994; Feldman, 1986; Hart & Risley, 1995; Hill, Brooks-Gunn, & Walfogel, 2003). As Colombo and his colleagues (chap. 2, this volume) and others have demonstrated, a good deal of evidence indicates that a stimulating home environment advantages early cognitive behavior. And as Feldman (1986) noted, without the provision of a violin, even the potentially most gifted violinist will not become a violinist.

Understanding the earliest capacities of human infants and early individual differences in temperament, learning, and other behaviors is not possible without considering the organismic contribution to the equation of organism and environment interactions and transactions that determine developmental status at birth. In the gestational journey from conception to birth, alongside and interacting with the genetic expressions and inheritances that dictate some of the characteristics of the fetus during this period are variables such as maternal nutrition, smoking, the ingestion of prescribed and nonprescribed drugs, and contracted illnesses—all of which are environmental in origin (Horowitz, 2000). At birth the human infant is the sum total of all these influences, and for this reason it makes sense not to juxtapose genes and environment as the sources of discrete interacting factors when discussing infant status and subsequent development. Rather, taking into account the variables of environmental origin that affect biological structure and function, one should refer to the interacting and transacting factors influencing development as constitutional and environmental—not genetic and environmental. And it should be noted that environmental influences can change constitutional characteristics and status subsequent to birth. Some are obvious: illness or injury that results in blindness or deafness; accidents and abuse that produce various disabilities; irritants that contribute to biologically enduring sensitivities. Others are likely subtle and yet to be described. The fullest understanding of development will thus require an account that includes variables of both constitutional (including genes) and environmental origin.

How, one might ask, does this affect the way in which one views the developmental models and theories that purport to account for developmental outcomes and their relevance to individual differences, to the development of giftedness and talent, and to the development of the behaviors that define giftedness and talented? Genetic—constitutional factors have been seminal in explaining individual differences in some theories of development, but not at all in others. The empirical study of individual differences and the research on development and developmental processes has oddly historically been almost orthogonal. As is made clear in a number of the chapters in this volume, the study of individual differences has been, until relatively recently, largely concerned with categorical classifications, psychometric analyses, testing, and prediction.

At the same time, developmental theories have existed quite separately from the field of psychometrics and have not been particularly attentive to individual differences. Developmental theories have been more focused on explaining the development of universal, normal behaviors than on trying to explain individual differences. When individual differences have been considered by developmental theorists, they have been treated simplistically. Gesell (1954) attributed individual differences to innate factors. The behaviorists, to the extent that they had a developmentally oriented theory, attributed most individual differences to the history of individual learning experiences (Baer, 1976). Freudian theory was individualistically oriented without being concerned, theoretically, with the origin of individual differences except in the context of individual psychodynamic histories (Freud, 1905/1953). Piaget (1952, 1972) assigned advanced intellectual progress to a difference in rate of development—presumably genetically controlled.

Nonpsychometric attention to individual differences or "individuality"—such as temperament—has been more oriented to innate origins than to experiential origins. In sum, none of the historic grand-sweep developmental theories have had much of a focus on understanding individual differences, much less the origin of giftedness and talent. These grand theoretical traditions, however, have passed and no longer hold sway. In their place are a plethora of mini-theories oriented to particular behavioral systems, some of which, like attribution theory (Blackwell, Trzesniewski, & Dweck, 2007; see also chap. 7, this volume), habituation and attentional systems (Colombo & Cheatham, 2007; see also chap. 2, this volume), multiple intelligences (Gardner, 1983; see also chaps. 4 and 5, this volume), and cultural ecological theory (see chap. 8, this volume), can be applied to giftedness and talent development but are not essentially developmental theories.

Although not grand in the sense of the historic developmental theories, the most currently popular uses of developmental theory draw on versions of systems theory (Horowitz, 1987, 2000; Spencer et al., 2006) that can be applied to any domain and across the life span (e.g., Granic & Patterson, 2006; Schöner & Thelen, 2006) and that can be used to think about transitions across developmental periods (see chap. 6, this volume). Horowitz's version (1987, 2000) is more specifically applicable to the development of giftedness and talent. It posits interacting roles of constitutional and environmental variables that change in their dynamical interactions over time. And it accounts for both continuity and discontinuity in development.

The issues of prediction and of continuity and discontinuity in development have, of course, been central to the discourse about the development of giftedness and talent. It is taken up in every chapter of this volume and (along with domain specificity, diversity, and psychosocial factors) is one of four themes addressed in the final chapter of this volume. The evidence is that there is no accurate prediction across the life span as to who will be gifted or talented; there is no evidence that once a person is identified as gifted or talented such a status will necessarily endure. In theory, from a dynamical systems perspective, there is no reason to expect early identification of gifted and talented behavior to be necessarily predictive over the long term.

Horowitz (1987) addressed the general issue of continuity and discontinuity in development by positing nodal points in development where relationships between and among relevant variables affecting behavior and performance are reorganized, new variables potentially introduced, and the salience of other variables possibly enhanced or diminished. In theory, it is at these nodal points in development when the expectation of discontinuity might be highest. And it is at these nodal, or transitional, points when intervention might be particularly effective. In chapters 6 and 9 (this volume) Matthews and Subotnik consider this possibility in the context of the transition from childhood to adolescence and the transition from adolescence to adulthood, respectively. Thus, in the ongoing processes of dynamic combinations and recombinations involving assembled and emerging skills and behaviors, the introduction of new variables, influenced by constitutional and environmental factors, status changes (discontinuities) for many are to be expected whereas stability (continuity) may be the norm for some. Making the matter even more complex, nodal points or points of reorganization and recombinations do not necessarily occur at the same age point for all individuals. Because of the dynamic nature of development, there is no reason, a priori, to expect continuity—especially across the most dynamically active periods of development. Although not expressed exactly in these terms, there is remarkable agreement with respect to this perspective among most of the contributors to this volume. This agreement is a signal advance when applied to the field of research on giftedness and talent development, and to the field of gifted education in terms of both practice and policy.

Such perspectives are also relevant when considering giftedness and talent development from a life-span perspective. Although a life-span perspective is not a theory or necessarily theoretical, it engenders a set of theoretical propositions that encourages more complex thinking about development than does focusing on a particular age period or a particular behavioral domain (Baltes, 1987; see also chap. 11, this volume). It encourages a more sophisticated approach to the issue of prediction and nonprediction with the sometimes surprising appearance in middle and older ages of gifted and talented behavior that was not evident earlier. Still, as has been noted, with age gifted and talented expressions become increasingly domain specific and have differential likelihoods in different domains. In many instances, new interests and skills in adults and in the aging can be admirable and creative without rising to the level of the extraordinary that is typically a hallmark of gifted accomplishments. Nevertheless, by increasing one's understanding of the possibilities inherent in late adult development one may begin to understand the nature of the emergence of creativity and of gifted and talented behavior during adulthood and the later years (see chap. 10, this volume).

CHANGES IN CONCEPTIONS AND DEFINITIONS
OF GIFTEDNESS AND TALENT

As a successor to the 1985 publication *The Gifted and Talented: Developmental Perspectives* (Horowitz & O'Brien), the current volume reflects a number of changes with respect to both the field of developmental psychology and the study of giftedness and talent. In the more than 20 intervening years, developmental psychology has evolved to encompass increasingly sophisticated theoretical models. Perspectives gained from the neurosciences have been incorporated. The importance of life-span perspectives—from infancy (and preinfancy) to the years of aging has been recognized. Also, in this volume, mirroring the basic change in how giftedness and talent are thought about, nomenclature differs from that of the 1985 publication. The title of the 1985 volume and the terminology used throughout referred to *the gifted and the talented*, conferring an inherent and permanent status on those so identified. Following Matthews (chap. 6, this volume; Matthews & Foster, 2006), the title of the present volume and the referencing terminology throughout is *giftedness* and *talent*—indicative of the understanding that giftedness and talent are expressions of high-end abilities, behaviors, and performances that are not necessarily inherent or enduring characteristics.

Beyond the matter of differences in title and terminology, in this chapter and in the chapters that follow, I and my fellow authors encounter the current challenges of defining giftedness and talent and of how best to discuss giftedness and talent in a life-span developmental framework. We concern ourselves with the traditional issues of individual differences and prediction as well as with the less traditional focus on context and cultural diversity in fostering the development of giftedness and talent. We discuss implications for the research agenda in the study of giftedness and talent and, in the final chapter, the gaps in the research agenda identified by the contributors to this volume. Above all, in this chapter and in this volume, the focus on a developmental perspective for thinking about giftedness and talent across the life span is intended to stimulate a conversation among developmental psychologists, students of giftedness and talent, and those who care to cultivate for harvest the vast contributions to American society that can be realized by nurturing human potential.

The definition and strategy for identifying giftedness in the United States was framed in the 1920s when Lewis Terman initiated long-term, longitudinal studies using the then relatively new Stanford-Binet intelligence scale for selecting high-functioning children. Terman established a 140 IQ cutoff criterion (the top half of the top 1% of the population, although he sometimes lowered the cutoff score to find more subjects; Shurkin, 1992), and followed them through adolescence and into adulthood (Terman & Oden, 1959). As described and discussed by Keating (chap. 11, this volume), the work of Terman and his colleagues and of the investigators who followed the sample further (Holahan, Sears, & Cronbach, 1995) revealed, over time, continued high-level competence as the children grew into highly productive adults but little evidence of extraordinary achievements at what might be thought of as the highly gifted or genius level.

Increasingly and especially in the past 20 years, the very definition of giftedness and talent solely in terms of IQ scores has moved considerably beyond the table that Terman and his colleagues had set for the study of "the gifted" toward greater refinement, both conceptually and in relation to what some have suggested is a needed paradigm shift (e.g., Borland, 2003, 2005; Cross & Coleman, 2005; Feldhusen, 2003; Feldman, 2003; Gagne, 2005; Matthews & Foster, 2006; Rogers, 2003; Subotnik, Olszewski-Kubilius, & Arnold, 2003; VanTassel-Baska, 2005). This paradigm shift involves relinquishing a reliance on categorical definitions—one individual is labeled permanently gifted; another, without any label, is assumed permanently not gifted—and adopting a developmental understanding that takes into account individual differences in developmental trajectories whereby a child may demonstrate gifted behavior and talent at one point in development but not necessarily at another point in development, or may exhibit gifted behavior in one domain but not necessarily across all domains (Borland, 2005; Dai & Renzulli, in press; Horowitz, 2000; Lohman, 2006; Matthews & Foster, 2006; Subotnik & Jarvin, 2005; see also chaps. 3 and 11, this volume).

These new perspectives deemphasize the notion that giftedness is innate, permanent, and mysterious. Matthews and Foster (2006) described this shift as a move from a categorical "mystery model" to a "mastery model" with concomitant implications for developmental theory, identification, and educational practice. From a mastery model perspective, the identification of individuals as having gifts and talents is determined by the presence of high-end, exceptional behavior in specific domains with an initial emergence of these behaviors possible at different points in development and, once in evidence, not necessarily a stable characteristic of the individual's behavioral repertoire.

Further complicating the picture of the development of gifted and talented behaviors is the fact that there is no universally agreed on consensus about where and how to set the bar for defining behavior as a manifestation of talent, giftedness, or exceptionally high-end performance. The traditional definition of giftedness set by Terman and continued by others rested on the evidence of high academic ability as determined in the assessment of IQ or its surrogate, the standardized achievement test. In this framework, giftedness was typically designated by a cutoff score such as an IQ over 140 (as used by Terman) or a score achieved by only the top 2% or 3% among test-takers. But there has not been any kind of agreement in specifying where the cutoff scores should fall, that is, what cutoff score should be specified—whether it be for theoretical purposes, for research, or for educational practice. Designation of the gifted range has varied from the top 25% to 30% of the population (Renzulli, 1986) to the top one half of 1%, as with Terman's specification.

With regard to more domain-specific definitions of giftedness and talent, the IQ score may or may not be relevant. In some domains such as reading comprehension, scores on standardized achievement tests are highly correlated with IQ, and gifted behavior can be defined by a score on the test as performance in the top 1%, 2%, or 3% of the population. However, in other domains, such as spatial understanding, music, art, or writing poetry or fiction, there are no widely used standardized assessments with population norms against which to identify performance in the top percentiles.

As well, across the life span, especially in the adult and most mature years, there are no robustly normed domain-specific instruments that can be used to test the maintenance or emergence of high-end exceptional behaviors. One may know a "Grandma Moses" when one sees her but little is known about all the other comparably gifted adults who do not achieve late-appearing fame in any systematized or publicized manner. The work being done to better understand cognitive decline, including the prediction and onset of dementia and of Alzheimer's disease, is contributing to the development of standardized instruments for adult evaluation. But these tests are designed to distinguish low-end from "normal" performance and not really applicable to identifying exceptional high-end capabilities. The focus on giftedness and talent in aging populations has not been systematic, nor is there much in the way of funding for relevant research questions. Although Birren (chap. 10, this volume) can point readers in the direction of issues related to the maintenance and enhancement of performance in older years, the fact is that the research cupboard on giftedness and talent among elderly persons is, relatively, quite bare.

In this volume several of the contributions focus on going against the grain of what is standard practice to date. Colombo and his colleagues (chap. 2, this volume) offer the possibility that widely used measures of infant cognitive behavior might be turned to the purpose of identifying early cognitive giftedness. Liben (chap. 4, this volume) and Winner (chap. 5, this volume) draw our attention to gifted and talented behavior in school-age children in the spatial and artistic domains. Wrestling with the issues of underrepresentation of children and adolescents of color in gifted programs, Graham (chap. 7, this volume) and Worrell (chap. 8, this volume) question the usefulness of standardized assessments for gauging achievement in these populations. Subotnik (chap. 9, this volume) addresses psychosocial and other contextual factors implicated in the nurturing, emergence, and maintenance of exceptionally high-end abilities. But even in going against the grain of general standardized high academic ability definitions, it becomes clear that there is no agreement on where to set the bar for identifying giftedness and talent in many domains of competence and ability. Complicating things further, standards are not dependable over time: By adulthood, the criteria for gifted and talented behavior are often different and more rigorous—in the same domains—than they are in childhood and adolescence.

Although discussion of categorical definitions, cut-scores, and domain specificity were not much in evidence in the Horowitz and O'Brien volume in 1985, a number of other issues raised in 1985 continue to pose challenges: How should the origins of gifted and talented behavior be thought about? How are individual differences considered in developmental theories and in relation to gifted and talented individuals? What about the matter of prediction from early to later ages? How can the challenge of increasing the diversity of those identified and selected for gifted programs be understood? What, now, are the questions that should define the future of the research agenda?

The major themes that emerge in the developmental consideration of giftedness and talent are no different than issues long standing in the field of developmental psychology: How predictable is developmental progress and outcome? How domain-specific are the principles of development? What accounts for different developmental trajectories in diverse populations? What role do psychosocial variables play in determining developmental outcome? Although here discussed discretely, from a developmental perspective, these are not discrete topics. They interrelate on a variety of levels not only in matters of research, but also with respect to educational practice and opportunity and to public policy. They involve issues that arise repeatedly in the context of different theories of development.

CULTURAL CONTEXTS AND DIVERSITY

Any discussion of cultural contexts and diversity, of necessity, casts a broad net. Included in this net are topics related to culturally different populations, to alternate approaches to identifying giftedness and talent, and to the variety of behavioral domains in which gifted and talented individuals are found. As several authors of chapters in this volume have noted (especially Winner, Graham, and Worrell [see chaps. 5, 7, and 8, respectively]) culturally different populations in the United States are significantly underrepresented in educational programs designed to serve the academically gifted and talented when *academic* is defined by the major areas of the elementary school curricula: reading, writing, mathematics. Gifted and talented programs have generally omitted or ignored the other multiple intelligences (Gardner, 1983), leaving the nurturing of those with extraordinary artistic, musical, and social–emotional gifts to the chance events of opportunity and the availability of mentors both within and without family and school. The one exception has involved sporting activities, especially in the adolescent and young adult years when athletic abilities become increasingly prized for the purpose of competitive school sports.

There are many reasons why educational programs to nurture giftedness and talent have been so focused on the core academic subjects. For one, psychometric criteria for identifying gifted levels of behavior are well developed in these areas. Another reason is that these subjects are the core of the curriculum on which teacher and student effectiveness is judged. The twin aspect of heavy dependence on both psychometric criteria and teacher judgments for identifying giftedness and talent, along with the restriction to core curricula subjects, has the effect of narrowing the neck that exceptional students must pass through to get to programs designed to serve those labeled as gifted and talented. And that narrowed neck is further exacerbated by extraneous factors. In the case of psychometric evaluations, test-taking smarts, stereotype threat, attitudes, and motivation come into play—often to the disadvantage of poor and minority students. In the case of teacher judgments, stereotypes and cultural unfamiliarity are hypothesized to contribute to reducing the diversity of students in gifted and talented programs.

Furthermore, because those who exhibit gifted and talented behavior in nonacademic areas are not likely to be evaluated or served by gifted education programs, little is known about the distribution of giftedness and talent in these domains. And it follows that there are rarely strong pressures to serve giftedness and talent in these other intelligences. Small studies of spatial and artistic giftedness (see chaps. 4 and 5, this volume), were they to be extended to larger samples and inclusive of minority and poor children, would be informative. It is interesting that unsystematic observations of talented individuals in the fields of sports and music give evidence of a great deal of talent in minority communities. Commercial market interests and socially driven selection strategies in late adolescence and early adulthood are likely at work in successfully identifying giftedness and talent among minority group members in these domains. A review by Subotnik and Calderon (2008) suggested that when viewed from the perspective of talent development rather than gifted education, actual performance in writing, conducting scientific experiments, and mathematical problem solving are more content-valid alternatives to psychometric evaluation. Such forms of "audition" could be used for a variety of domains in a developmental context. Because these strategies focus on high performance in specific domains rather than standardized tests with all their inadequacies, they hold promise as strategies for increasing the diversity of those identified as gifted and talented.

It is relevant to consider, when thinking about the underrepresentation of minority populations in gifted and talented programs, the mechanisms that suppress or amplify abilities across the life span. They are only beginning to receive systematic research attention. Of some of the suppressor variables that work against the expression of high abilities in the core academic subjects, especially during childhood and adolescence—poverty, racial discrimination and stereotypes and lower expectations, family dysfunction, abuse, psychological and psychiatric problems, peer distraction and devaluing academic pursuits, limited parental education, and the absence, often, of stimulation and experiences most relevant to robust development in the earliest years—only broad outlines are known. Advances in the neurosciences are beginning to shed some light on the specific effects of poverty on neurocognitive development in children (Farah et al., 2006) and a large body of evidence reveals the deleterious effects of poverty on developmental outcomes (e.g., Brooks-Gunn, Duncan, Klebanov, & Sealand, 1993), but little is known about the specific mechanisms by which many of the suppressor variables work individually or in combinations. The fact that many of these factors are disproportionately at work in minority communities may account for some of the absence of minority students in gifted and talented programs. However, as Steele (1997) has demonstrated and as discussed by Graham (chap. 7, this volume), suppressor variables such as stereotype threat, lower expectations, and racism also appear to affect more advantaged minority populations. This phenomenon likely contributes further to reducing the presence of minority students in school-based, psychometrically driven gifted and talented programs.

Something is known about some of the amplification variables that encourage the expression of high academic abilities; these variables include higher levels of socioeconomic status and economic security, more years of parental education, someone taking a special interest in a child or teenager, family stability, and living in advantaged neighborhoods. But, again, not much is known about the mechanisms by which these influences do their work except in the most general sense that the provision of highly stimulating environments increases the probability that those affected will be increasingly "at promise" for exceptional achievements (Horowitz, 2000). Nor is there a good understanding of the forces of resilience through which an individual deals or learns to deal with adversity and acquires the drive to succeed.

The knowledge base about suppressor and amplifying conditions is better grounded with respect to childhood and adolescence than the later years. The ability to account for the first-time expression of gifts and talents in adult years—including old age—is less well developed (see chaps. 10 and 11, this volume). It is interesting that the probabilities of exceptional talents first appearing at the adult and aging stages of development seem to be differentially distributed by area: rarely mathematics or music; less rarely in writing and art (Feldman, 1986) or in diplomacy (see chap. 10, this volume). Advances in the neurosciences with respect to (a) the interaction of the suppressor and amplifying variables associated with experience and motivation and (b) brain plasticity across the life span may well contribute to researchers' understanding of these phenomena.

The challenge of being more inclusive in identifying giftedness and talent is significant—empirically, theoretically, and for the future health of America's increasingly multicultural society. Although anthropologists have typically been descriptively sensitive to subtle aspects of cultures and subcultures, developmental psychologists have traditionally been less likely to incorporate these variables in their work. Super and Harkness (1986) suggested considering the role of what they labeled the "developmental niche"—the physical and social settings in which the child lives, including customs of child care and child rearing along with the psychology of the caretakers. To the extent that different developmental niche environments result in distinct, culturally shaped behavior patterns, traditional techniques for identifying giftedness and talent may prove to be wide of the relevant marks. Graham (chap. 7, this volume), Worrell (chap. 8, this volume), and Matthews (chap. 6, this volume) touch on these issues.

In America's increasingly global society, more attention to understanding the culturally subtle and sometimes not-so-subtle factors affecting development and behavioral patterns will be needed to maximize the identification of giftedness and talent and address the concomitant learning needs.

IMPLICATIONS FOR THE RESEARCH AGENDA

In the chapters that follow, it is clear that the research agenda going forward will be one that advances the understanding of the development of giftedness and talent by way of a life-span development orientation. New investigative techniques and strategies will need to be embraced in combination with some of the old standards, and a commitment is needed to broaden the ways in which high-end exceptional behaviors are defined.

New approaches using standard techniques. Colombo et al. (chap. 2, this volume) describe techniques and studies of young infants that hold a great deal of promise for expanding knowledge about cognitive behavior, learning, individual differences, and early markers of advanced development. Colombo and his colleagues also demonstrate the value of short-term longitudinal studies for detecting those early markers. Those studies, along with the longer term longitudinal strategy described by Gottfried et al. (chap. 3, this volume), should enable the development of a more functional understanding of the dynamic developmental processes that produce developmental continuities and discontinuities. However, a better understanding of which chunks of time are the most informative for framing longitudinal studies is needed. In the early years, when developmental change is especially rapid, what measures over time will provide the most useful evaluations in longitudinal analyses and in experimental analyses of individual differences? Pursuing these questions will permit going beyond the traditional descriptive studies of predictive validity in recognition of the fact that, theoretically, there is no reason to expect that any early markers of advanced development will be predictive of advanced development, giftedness, and talent over a lifetime. But there is reason to expect that early markers will illuminate some of the processes that contribute to continuities and discontinuities in exceptional development. As well, advances in the neurosciences and an increased use of techniques for neural imaging across the life span will open up fruitful research paths for tracking and understanding the characteristics involved in individual differences that relate to high-level performance in a variety of domains.

Application of new research techniques. Several of the chapters in this volume demonstrate the utility and importance of research that uses measurement and evaluation strategies different from some of the standard psychometric techniques. Included are the experimental studies of early individual differences in learning and cognition that offer alternative definitions of intelligence (see chap. 2, this volume), a focus on performance-based evaluative strategies (see chap. 9, this volume), and increased attention to the development of exceptional skills and talents in the domains of the various multiple intelligences (Gardner, 1983; see also chaps. 4 and 5, this volume). The definitions of high-end exceptional behavior in some of these domains differ from study to study. What benefits might derive from more standardization within domains and across investigations? How does one encourage greater and more equal attention to giftedness and talent in the noncognitive domains?

The role of personal/psychological factors. Mentioned with some frequency, but less understood and less a part of the research agenda to date, are the personal characteristics and behaviors that have been described as important in the achievement of exceptional high-end behavior in various domains: the "rage to master," a kind of intensity of focus and sustained interest that leads to a development of expertise that is deeper and more advanced than would normally be expected (chaps. 5, 6, and 9, this volume). These descriptive characterizations of those exhibiting gifted and talented behavior need to be better understood. How constitutionally based are they? What is the role of parental, mentor, and teacher encouragement? To what extent is the rage to master distractive in terms of performance on the psychometrically standardized evaluations? Is such intense focus more typical of high-end performance in some domains than in others?

Attention to framing the research agenda. Important as well are sensitivities to how the research agenda is framed—from the use of terminology (e.g., referring to *giftedness* and *talent* rather than *the gifted and talented,* as suggested by Matthews, chap. 6, this volume) to considerations of cultural nuances (see chaps. 7 and 8, this volume) and the *social affordances* (those institutionally and culturally constructed contexts that foster or suppress giftedness and talent; see chap. 11, this volume). It is also important to note that the research agenda for understanding the development of giftedness and talent must take into account the pivotal importance of transitional junctures, whether it be from childhood to adolescence (see chap. 6, this volume), from adolescence to the adult years (see chap. 9, this volume), or from the middle adult years to the later years (see chaps. 10 and 11, this volume).

A focus on promise. In both developmental psychology and education, as Graham (chap. 7, this volume) notes, there has been a great deal of funding for and interest in studying those at risk for below-normal development: objects of study have included the factors that contribute to putting an individual at risk, that result in retardation, delayed development, and disability; the interventions that will be ameliorative; and the conditions that will be preventive. Without diminishing the importance of these efforts, I hope that this volume and the growing interest in giftedness and talent will increase awareness of the potential for maintaining and enhancing a robust, developmentally oriented research agenda designed to better understand the factors that contribute to situating an individual to be "at promise": the dynamics that foster the emergence of high-end exceptionality across the increasing length of the life span and the interventions that will be facilitative of the emergence of giftedness, talent, and promise among those in the variety of cultures in America's increasingly rich and diverse society.

REFERENCES

Baer, D. M. (1976). The organism as host. *Human Development, 19*, 87–98.

Baltes, P. (1987). Theoretical propositions of life-span developmental psychology: On the dynamics of growth and decline. *Developmental Psychology, 23*, 611–626.

Blackwell, L. S., Trzesniewski, K. H., & Dweck, C. S. (2007). Implicit theories of intelligence predict achievement across an adolescent transition: A longitudinal study and an intervention. *Child Development, 78*, 246–263.

Borland, J. H. (2003). *Rethinking gifted education.* New York: Teachers College Press.

Borland, J. H. (2005). Gifted education without gifted children: The case for no conception of giftedness. In R. J. Sterberg & J. E. Davidson (Eds.), *Conceptions of giftedness* (2nd ed., pp. 1–19). Cambridge, England: Cambridge University Press.

Brooks-Gunn, J., Duncan, G. J., Klebanov, P. K., & Sealand, N. (1993). Do neighborhoods influence child and adolescent development. *The American Journal of Sociology, 99*, 359–395.

Churchill, J. D., Galvez, R., Colcombe, S., Swain, R. A., Kramer, A. F., & Greenough, W. T. (2002). Exercise, experience and the aging brain. *Neurobiology of Aging, 23*, 941–955.

Colombo, J., & Cheatham, C. L. (2007). The emergency and basis of endogenous attention in infancy and early childhood. In R. Kail (Ed.), *Advances in child development and behavior* (Vol. 34, pp. 283–321). New York: Elsevier.

Cross, T. L., & Coleman, I. J. (2005). School-based conception of giftedness. In R. J. Sternberg & J. E. Davidson (Eds.), *Conceptions of giftedness* (2nd ed., pp. 52–63). Cambridge, England: Cambridge University Press.

Dai, D. Y., & Renzulli, J. S. (in press). Snowflakes, living systems, and the mystery of giftedness. *Gifted Child Quarterly*.

Diamond, M. C. (1988). *Enriching heredity: The impact of the environment on the anatomy of the brain*. New York: Free Press.

Duncan, G. J., Brooks-Gunn, J., & Klebanov, P. K. (1994). Economic deprivation and early childhood development. *Child Development, 65*, 296–318.

Farah, M. J., Shera, D. M., Savage, J. H., Betancourt, L., Giannetta, J. M., Brodsky, N. L., et al. (2006). Childhood poverty: Specific associations with neurocognitive development. *Brain Research, 1110*, 166–174.

Feldhusen, J. F. (2003). Beyond general giftedness: New ways to identify and educate gifted, talented, and precocious youth. In J. H. Borland (Ed.), *Rethinking gifted education* (pp. 34–45). New York: Teachers College Press.

Feldman, D. (1986). *Nature's gambit*. New York: Basic Books.

Feldman, D. (2003). A developmental, evolutionary perspective on giftedness. In I. J. Broland (Ed.), *Rethinking gifted education* (pp. 9–33). New York: Teachers College Press.

Freud, S. (1953). Three essays on the theory of sexuality. In J. Strachey (Ed. & Trans.), *The standard edition of the complete psychological works of Sigmund Freud* (Vol. 17, pp. 123–246). London: Hogarth Press. (Original work published 1905)

Gagne, F. (2005). An imperative but, alas, improbable consensus! *Roeper Review, 27*, 12–14.

Gardner, H. (1983). *Frames of mind: The theory of multiple intelligences*. New York: Basic Books.

Gershoff, E. T., Aber, J. L., Raver, C. C., & Lennon, M. C. (2007). Income is not enough: Incorporating marital hardship into models of income associations with parenting and child development. *Child Development, 78*, 70–95.

Gesell, A. (1954). The ontogenesis of infant behavior. In L. Carmichael (Ed.), *Manual of child psychology* (pp. 335–373). New York: Wiley.

Granic, I., & Patterson, G. (2006). Toward a comprehensive model of antisocial development: A dynamic systems approach. *Psychological Review, 113*, 101–131.

Hart, B., & Risley, T. R. (1995). *Meaningful differences in the everyday experiences of young American children*. Baltimore: Brookes Publishing.

Hess, T. M. (2005). Memory and aging in context. *Psychological Bulletin, 131*, 383–406.

Hill, J., Brooks-Gunn, J., & Walfogel, J. (2003). Sustained effects of high participation in early intervention for low-birth-weight premature infants. *Developmental Psychology, 39*, 730–744.

Holahan, C., Sears, R., & Cronbach, L. (1995). *The gifted group in later maturity*. Stanford, CA: Stanford University Press.

Horowitz, F. D. (1987). *Exploring developmental theories: Toward a structural/behavioral model of development*. Hillsdale, NJ: Erlbaum.

Horowitz, F. D. (2000). Child development and the PITS: Simple questions, complex answers, and developmental theory. *Child Development, 71*, 1–10.

Horowitz, F. D., & O'Brien, M. (1985). *The gifted and talented: Developmental perspectives*. Washington, DC: American Psychological Association.

Johnson, W. (2007). Genetic and environmental influences on behavior: Capturing all the interplay. *Psychological Review, 114*, 423–440.

Lohman, D. F. (2006). Beliefs about differences between ability and accomplishment: From folk theories to cognitive science. *Roeper Review, 29*, 32–40.

Matthews, D. J., & Foster, J. F. (2006). Mystery to mastery: Shifting paradigms in gifted education. *Roeper Review, 28*, 64–69.

Piaget, J. (1952). *The origins of intelligence in children*. New York: International Universities Press.

Piaget, J. (1972). Intellectual evolution from adolescence to adulthood. *Human Development, 15*, 1–12.

Renzulli, J. S. (1986). The three-ring conception of giftedness: A developmental model for creative productivity. In R. J. Sternberg & J. E. Davidson (Eds.), *Conceptions of giftedness* (pp. 53–92). Cambridge, England: Cambridge University Press.

Rogers, K. B. (2003). A voice of reason in the wilderness. *Journal for the Education of the Gifted, 26*, 314–320.

Rueda, M. R., Rothbart, M. K., McCandless, B. D., Saccamano, L., & Posner, M. (2005). Training, maturation, and genetic influences on the development of executive attention. *Proceedings of the National Academy of Sciences, 102*, 14931–14936.

Schöner, G., & Thelen, E. (2006). Using dynamic field theory to rethink infant habituation. *Psychological Review, 113*, 273–299.

Shoshani, Y. (2007). World enough, and time [Review of the book *Isaac Newton*]. *Ha'aretz*, n.p. Retrieved from http://www.haaretz.com/hasen/spages/871262.html

Shurkin, J. N. (1992). *Terman's kids: The groundbreaking study of how gifted children grow up*. Boston: Little, Brown.

Simonton, D. K. (2005). Genetics of giftedness: The implications of an emergenic-epigenetic model. In R. J. Sternberg & J. E. Davidson (Eds.), *Conceptions of giftedness* (2nd ed., pp. 246–279). Cambridge, England: Cambridge University Press.

Spencer, J. P., Clearfield, M., Corbetta, D., Ulrich, B., Buchanan, P., & Schoner, G. (2006). Moving toward a grand theory of development: In memory of Esther Thelen. *Child Development, 77*, 1521–1538.

Steele, C. (1997). A threat in the air: How stereotypes shape the intellectual identities of women and African Americans. *American Psychologist, 52*, 613–629.

Subotnik, R. F., & Calderon, J. (2008). Developing giftedness and talent. In F. A. Karnes & K. P. Stephens (Eds.), *Achieving excellence: Educating the gifted and talented* (pp. 49–61). Columbus, OH: Pearson Education.

Subotnik, R. F., & Jarvin, L. (2005). Beyond expertise: Conceptions of giftedness as great performance. In R. J. Sternberg & J. E. Davidson (Eds.), *Conceptions of giftedness* (2nd ed., pp. 343–357). Cambridge, England: Cambridge University Press.

Subotnik, R. F., Olszewski-Kubilius, P., & Arnold, K. D. (2003). *Beyond bloom: Revisiting environmental factors that enhance or impede talent development.* New York: Teachers College Press.

Super, C. M., & Harkness, S. (1986). The developmental niche: A conceptualization at the interface of child and culture. *International Journal of Behavioral Development, 9,* 545–569.

Terman, L., & Oden, M. (1959). *Genetic studies of genius: Vol. V. The gifted group at mid-life.* Stanford, CA: Stanford University Press.

Turkheimer, E., Haley, A., Waldron, M., D'Onofrio, B., & Gottesman, I. I. (2003). Socioeconomic status modifies heritability of IQ in young children. *Psychological Science, 14,* 623–628.

VanTassel-Baska, J. (2005). Domain-specific giftedness: Applications in school and life. In R. J. Sternberg & J. E. Davidson (Eds.), *Conceptions of giftedness* (2nd ed., pp. 358–376). Cambridge, England: Cambridge University Press.

Zangel, R., & Mills, D. L. (2007). Increased brain activity to infant directed speech in 6- & 13-month-old infants. *Infancy, 11,* 31–61.

I

INFANCY AND
EARLY CHILDHOOD

2

HIGH COGNITIVE ABILITY IN INFANCY AND EARLY CHILDHOOD

JOHN COLOMBO, D. JILL SHADDY, OTILIA M. BLAGA,
CHRISTA J. ANDERSON, AND KATHLEEN N. KANNASS

Chief among the attributes of *giftedness* is the expression of exceptionality in one or more domains of talent or ability, and most commonly this exceptionality is expressed in the domain of cognition. In this chapter, we address issues pertaining to the concept of such high ability within the period of infancy and early childhood, and we do so from both the empirical and theoretical realms. In the empirical realm, we present new data on the prediction of high cognitive ability (HCA) from infancy and early childhood. In the theoretical realm, we outline a recent significant advance in the field of early cognition and its implications for how intelligence is thought about.

Preparation of this manuscript was supported in part by National Science Foundation Grant NSF0318072 and National Institutes of Health Grants DC005803 and HD41184. Collection of the data reported in this chapter was funded by Grant HD35903. Address correspondence to John Colombo, Department of Psychology, 1415 Jayhawk Boulevard, 426 Fraser Hall, University of Kansas, Lawrence, KS 66045 (colombo@ku.edu).

PREDICTING HIGH COGNITIVE ABILITY FROM INFANCY

The extant literature on giftedness reflects interest in infancy and early childhood as a means for understanding the origins of HCA (Bock & Ackrill, 1993; Colombo, Shaddy, & Richman, 2000; Dalzell, 1998; Gardner, 1993; Gottfried, Gottfried, Bathurst, & Guerin, 1994; Horowitz & O'Brien, 1985, 1986; Klein & Tannenbaum, 1992; Obler & Fein, 1988; Robinson, 2000; Storfer, 1990; Subotnik & Arnold, 1994; Zigler & Farber, 1985) and as a means for early identification of individuals at promise for high ability (Gottfried et al., 1994; Gross, 1999; Horowitz, 1992; Shaklee, 1992; Sternberg, 1993; Tannenbaum, 1992). However, the empirical prediction of giftedness or HCA is a challenging task. Despite many advances in the field of early cognition (Colombo, 2001; Colombo & Frick, 1999), measures from infancy and early childhood do not readily surrender clues to meaningful long-term prediction. In addition, these issues can be addressed only through the difficult methodological and logistical undertaking of long-term longitudinal follow-up.

We have elsewhere (Colombo et al., 2000) noted that prediction of HCA from infancy can be adequately studied only with prospective longitudinal studies. To date, only a few studies (Gottfried et al., 1994; Shapiro et al., 1989; Willerman & Fiedler, 1974, 1977) meet this criterion, but these have converged on a similar conclusion: High-ability individuals may be reliably identified from the middle of the second year on, but initial differences between high-ability groups and comparison control subjects may be quite subtle or small. To this small literature, we add results from the Kansas Early Cognition Project, in which a large sample of infants were recruited during the first year and prospectively followed until age 4.

THE KANSAS EARLY COGNITION PROJECT: 1998 TO 2003

From 1998 to 2003, we conducted a longitudinal study of the predictive value of measures of early attention for preschool language and cognitive development (see Colombo, Shaddy, Richman, Maikranz, & Blaga, 2004). In this study, 226 infants were recruited at 3 months of age and then followed intensively over the 1st year on measures of attention from habituation protocols augmented with psychophysiological measures. Beginning at 12 months, infants were administered standardized tests of development, language, and mental development on a semiannual basis until 48 months of age. At 12, 18, and 24 months, the Bayley Scales of Infant Development, Second Edition (BSID-II; Bayley, 1994) and the MacArthur-Bates Communicative Development Inventory (MBCDI) were given; at 30, 36, 42, and 48 months, the Stanford-Binet (SB4), and the Peabody Picture Vocabulary Test, Third Edition (PPVT-III) were administered. In addition, the Home Observation for

Measurement of the Environment (HOME) scale (Bradley & Caldwell, 1976) was administered in a home visit at 18 months of age. Table 2.1 describes these measures and their content.

Our intent in conducting this study was to evaluate the predictive validity of the developmental course of attention measures, with the goal of identifying infants at risk for developmental disability and delay. We needed to recruit a sample whose characteristics were at the norm for intelligence, so that variation would be reflected equally above and below average. Although we recruited in a wide variety of residential areas (urban, suburban, and rural) in and around the metropolitan Kansas City area and paid modest stipends to parents for each longitudinal visit, the average IQ score for the sample of 140 infants who persisted through the end of the study (i.e., until 48 months of age) was 115. Although this outcome worked against our original intent, it turned out to be fortuitous for examination of the questions that we address in this chapter. Our strategy in addressing these questions was to identify and classify a high-functioning group from this sample and then to examine the characteristics of this group relative to other infants from this sample.

Classification of High Cognitive Ability in the Early Cognition Project Sample

The first task we faced was to create the high-ability group and the control subjects against which they would be compared. The issue was ultimately resolved by composing three groups based on children's 48-month SB performance. In keeping with Gottfried et al. (1994), the HCA group was formed of children with composite IQ scores of 130 or above.[1] A second group, which we labeled *above-average,* had scores of 100 to 129, and a third, *below-average* group had IQ scores below 100. The 48-month characteristics of these groups are shown in Table 2.2. We chose to compare three groups because we thought that the real task was in discriminating the HCA group from individuals who were above average, and not from a more heterogeneous group that would have resulted from combining participants whose IQs ranged from well above average (e.g., 129) to well below average (e.g., 72).

Stability of Classification

We first asked whether membership in the HCA group was stable across the preschool period. Figure 2.1 presents a "spaghetti plot" of the 23 children

[1]We readily acknowledge the arbitrary nature of cutting this group off at 130. This value was used by Gottfried et al. (1994), so we can make the claim for consistency across the two studies. Nevertheless, any other point we considered seemed no less arbitrary, and this value seemed a good compromise between losing statistical power by raising the cutoff (e.g., to 135 or 140) and losing the integrity and exclusivity of the classification by lowering the cutoff (e.g., to 120 or 125).

TABLE 2.1

Description of Measures Used in the Kansas Early Cognition Project

Name of measure	Acronym used in chapter text	Age and schedule of assessment	Description
Visual habituation	None	Monthly, from 3 to 9 months of age	Laboratory protocol in which infants are shown a visual stimulus in a repetitive series of trials. The duration of the infant's looking to the visual stimulus over the course of the repeated trials is measured. Look duration declines across these trials, indicating that the baby has learned or encoded the stimulus. Look duration also declines over age, suggesting that the speed with which this learning takes place improves. It has been reported that infants who look for shorter durations over age tend to score more highly on IQ assessments in childhood.
MacArthur-Bates Communicative Development Inventory	MBCDI	12, 18, and 24 months	A parent-report questionnaire that measures child communicative behaviors. Includes measures of gestures, receptive and productive vocabulary, and rudimentary use of syntactical rules.
Bayley Scales of Infant Development, Second Edition	BSID-II	12, 18, and 24 months	A widely used standardized test for the developmental status of infants and toddlers. The test is structured, as with most standardized tests, with items of increasing difficulty administered at progressively later ages. This test features the derivation of a Mental and a Motor Index for each child, as well as a measure of the infant's temperament. However, formal assessment of more specific domains are not part of this version of the test. The mental and motor scales yield an overall index score that is standardized for age whose properties are similar to an IQ score ($M = 100$ and $SD = 15$).

Measure	Abbreviation	Age(s)	Description
Home Observation for Measurement of the Environment Inventory	HOME	18 months	A structured interview and observation of the child's environment, including measures of the quality and accessibility of the physical environment and the provision of materials appropriate to the child, and observational indices of the parent's style of interaction with the child.
Stanford-Binet Intelligence Scale, Fourth Edition	SB4	30, 36, 42, and 48 months	A widely used standardized test of intelligence for ages 30 months to adult. This test features subtests that assess verbal reasoning, visual and nonverbal reasoning, quantitative reasoning, and short-term memory. Each subtest has a raw score that can be converted to an age-standardized index, and the raw scores are combined to produce an overall composite score and index. The composite score has the classic IQ-test properties with a mean of 100 and standard deviation of 15.
Peabody Picture Vocabulary Test, Third Edition	PPVT-III	30, 36, 42, and 48 months	A widely used standardized test of receptive vocabulary for ages 30 months to adult. The test yields a raw score and an index score that is standardized within ages. As with an IQ score, the mean for the index is 100.

TABLE 2.2

Characteristics of the Three Groups of Infants (Below Average, Above Average, and High Cognitive Ability) on Measures Taken at 48 Months

	Sample size		Stanford-Binet scores at 48 months Subscales				Composite index	PPVT-III index
Group	n	%	Verbal reasoning	Visual-abstract reasoning	Quantitative reasoning	Short-term memory		
Below-average IQ	13	9.3%	99.42	90.62	100.77	88.54	93.54	101.17
Above-average IQ	112	44.8%	120.06	105.86	115.21	107.19	114.44	114.46
HCA	15	10.7%	130.27	124.93	133.73	125.60	135.00	122.80
Overall	140	100.0%	119.30	106.50	115.86	107.43	114.70	114.21

Note. All group comparisons on all subscales, composite, and Peabody Picture Vocabulary Test, Third Edition (PPVT-III) index are statistically significant at the $p < .01$ level. This table indicates the relative performance of the three groups on the Stanford-Binet and PPVT-III tests at the end of the study. HCA = high cognitive ability.

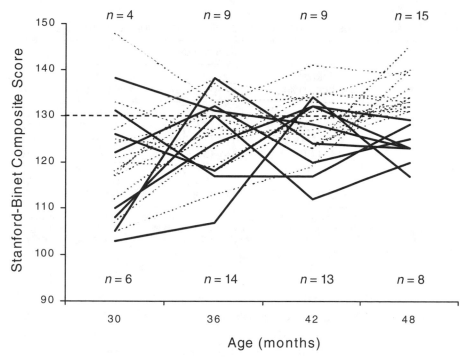

Figure 2.1. Spaghetti plot of 23 preschoolers scoring at or above 130 (dotted line) on the SB4 at any point from 30 to 48 months of age. Sample sizes (denoted by *n*) show number of children scoring above and below the line at any one age. The 8 children from this group who end up not qualifying for the final high cognitive ability (HCA) classification are shown by the solid lines. Note that movement toward the HCA classification is more likely than is movement out or away from it.

whose IQ attained 130 or above at any point from 30 to 48 months. Fifteen of these 23 ended up in the final HCA group, but the figure shows some fluidity in classification across time. Only one participant scored above 130 across all four measurements, but it is evident that the direction of transience can be generally characterized as movement toward the HCA group, rather than away from it. Attaining a score of 130 or above generally becomes more probable with age; only 4 children qualified for HCA membership at 30 months, but 15 qualified 18 months later. Movement out of the HCA range did occasionally occur but was less frequent as participants approached the end of the study.

Table 2.3 illustrates an important point with respect to these classifications. Here, we show a cross-tabulation of attaining a score that would meet the criteria for membership in the three groups on either the BSID-II or SB at any of the seven ages tested. The count and percentage of infants or toddlers in each of the three groups at each of the ages clearly show that although the overall probability of attaining HCA membership across all ages is quite low (only 3.5% of the total overall scores we collected attained HCA status), the proba-

TABLE 2.3
The Age × Group Status Cross-Tabulation of Subjects in the Study

Age (months)	Classification			N
	Below average n (%)	Above average n (%)	High cognitive ability n (%)	
12	96 (50.3)	95 (49.7)	0 (0.0)	191
18	81 (44.8)	99 (54.7)	1 (0.6)	181
24	47 (28.1)	119 (71.3)	1 (0.6)	167
30	18 (11.0)	141 (86.5)	4 (2.5)	163
36	23 (14.7)	124 (79.5)	9 (5.8)	156
42	8 (5.3)	133 (88.1)	10 (6.6)	151
48	13 (9.3)	112 (80.0)	15 (10.7)	140

Note. This table shows the relative distribution of participants across the three status groups at all of the ages measured. Over the ages tested, the data show a strong migration away from the below-average group into the two higher functioning groups. The frequency of individuals characterized as high cognitive ability also increases strongly with age.

bility increased with age; no infants are so classified at 12 months, but a little more than 1 in 10 is classified as such at 48 months. Furthermore, the probability of performing at a level that would fall into the below-average group decreases quite markedly with age; nearly half the sample shows below-average performance at the 12-month assessment, but only 9% are performing at that level at 48 months. It is unlikely that infants in the lower group are moving into the highest group as they age; rather, the whole distribution of performance on these tests is probably moving toward higher scores. This pattern of change may be sample specific, but it may also be a more general characteristic of the development of performance on these scales. This point presages an issue we address later in the chapter concerning the ultimate prediction of HCA status.

Backward Prediction Analyses

We next analyzed measures from the first 2 years in light of the HCA, above-average, and below-average group classifications. Missing data were common at all ages, and so in lieu of traditional within-subject analyses of variance, we used mixed models analysis that allowed us to use all available data. Modeled curves are presented on all graphs.

Infant Attention and Psychophysiological Measures

Detailed measures of visual attention and psychophysiology taken during the first year of life were not sensitive to these groupings. There were no significant differences in look duration from habituation (Figure 2.2), in novelty preference (Figure 2.3), or in various heart-rate-defined phases of attention (see Colombo, Richman, Shaddy, Greenhoot, & Maikranz, 2001, for

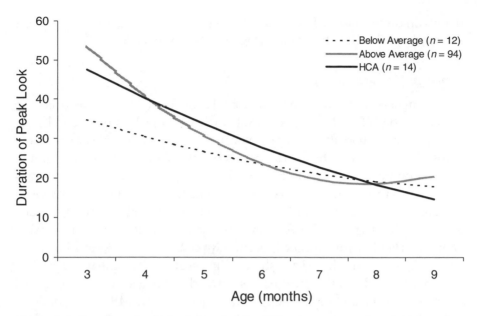

Figure 2.2. Duration of peak look from habituation sequence as a function of group membership. Duration of looking during the 1st year was not different for the three classifications and thus was not a valid predictor of high cognitive ability (HCA).

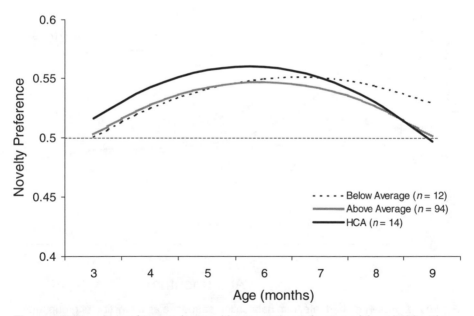

Figure 2.3. Novelty preference (recognition memory performance) from habituation sequence as a function of group membership. Recognition memory performance during the 1st year was not different for the three classifications and thus was not a valid predictor of high cognitive ability (HCA).

details on these phases). There was a trend ($p < .06$) for HCA infants to have slightly lower baseline heart rates (Figure 2.4), however.

Language Measures

Language measures reported from 12 to 24 months were from the MBCDI. The MBCDI changes forms between 12 and 18 months, and aside from parents' report of productive vocabulary, no variables were repeated across these two ages. The data for productive vocabulary on the three groups in question here are shown in Figure 2.5.

Across these ages, the below-average group trails the other two. Although the HCA group was not statistically distinct from the above-average group at 12 months of age, it did diverge from the above-average groups ($p = .03$) at 18 months, and this divergence is essentially preserved ($p = .09$) at 24 months. The HCA group may have been showing an accelerated or enhanced productive "burst" at 18 months, creating a gap that the above-average group closed by the end of the 2nd year. Ancillary variables from the MBCDI reported in Table 2.4 showed a similar pattern: At 12 months, the HCA group was not distinct, but this group was ahead on variables that reflect irregular word use at 18 months and ahead on measures of syntactic marking at 24 months.

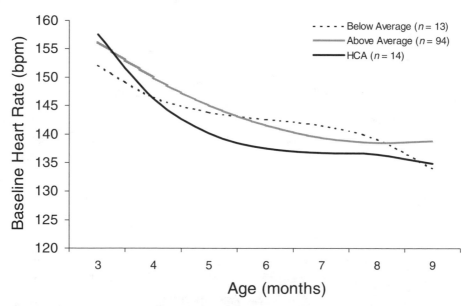

Figure 2.4. Baseline heart rate from habituation sequence as a function of group membership. Children eventually classified as high cognitive ability (HCA) tended to have lower heart rates during looking than did the other two groups, particularly at older ages during the 1st year. This effect approached but did not attain conventional levels of statistical significance, so it remains a suggestive trend. bpm = beats per minute.

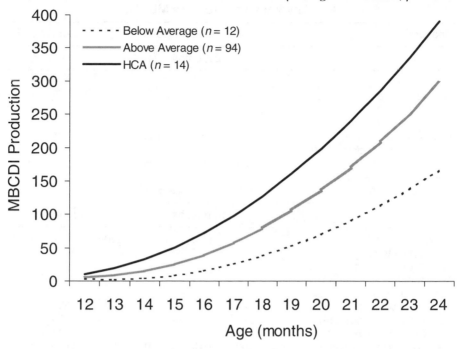

Figure 2.5. Parent-reported productive vocabulary from the MacArthur-Bates Communicative Development Inventory (MBCDI) as a function of group membership. High cognitive ability (HCA) participants started at slightly higher levels of productive vocabulary at 12 months but showed a significantly higher trajectory into the 2nd year, thus producing the significant Group × Age interaction shown here.

Data on PPVT-III performance from 30 months to 48 months are presented in Figure 2.6. All three groups were statistically distinct ($p < .001$) from one another by 30 months. The HCA group performance was already high at 30 months, and scores increased linearly beyond that. The other groups had lower intercepts and showed a tendency for scores to reach asymptotic levels toward 48 months.

Developmental and IQ Measures

The most successful predictors of HCA came from the BSID-II and SB. Because these tests were on the same scale (i.e., standardized $M = 100$, $SD = 15$), we modeled them together to form a continuous developmental function from 12 months to 42 months. The modeled curves shown in Figure 2.7 show the nature of the interaction; the HCA group had the highest intercept and showed a linear increase across these ages. The other two groups had lower intercepts and a quadratic (asymptotic) component as they approached 48 months of age.

TABLE 2.4
Ancillary Variables From the MBCDI

Measure	p	Comparisons	p	Comparisons
		12 months		
Phrases raw	—	—		
Phrases percentile	—	—		
Labeling	—	—		
Words understood raw	—	—		
Words produced raw	.042	HCA = A > B		
Words produced percentile	—	—		
Early gesture raw	.038	HCA = A > B		
Later gestures raw	—	—		
Total gestures raw	.049	HCA = A > B		
		18 months		24 months
Words produced raw	.014	HCA > A = B	.008	HCA = A > B
Use of past tense	—	—	—	—
Use of future tense	—	—	—	—
Absent object production	—	—	.033	A > HCA = B
Use of plural	—	—	—	—
Use of possessive	—	—	.002	HCA = A > B
Use of present progressive	—	—	.019	HCA = A > B
Past tense 18 months	—	—	.013	HCA > A = B
Irregular words raw 18 months	.025	HCA > A = B	.017	HCA = A > B
Overregularized words 18 months	.023	HCA > A = B	—	—
Combining 18 months	—	—	—	—
Complexity raw 18 months	—	—	.001	HCA > A > B

Note. This table shows the results of comparisons of the below-average (B), above-average (A), and high cognitive ability (HCA) groups for measures taken from the MacArthur-Bates Communicative Development Inventory (MBCDI). Entries shown in the table are for comparisons attaining statistical significance. The significance level of the comparison (*p*) is shown, and the nature of the difference among the three groups is shown in the column labeled *Comparisons*. Note that, at 12 and 18 months, only three comparisons are significant, with the B group scoring lower than did the other two groups. However, by 24 months, many additional differences attain significance, and the HCA group begins to pull away from the other two groups.

The composite scores of the SB are derived from eight individual subtests (vocabulary, comprehension, absurdities, pattern analysis, copying, quantitative, bead memory, and sentence memory). The existence of these subtests allowed us to explore the possibility that a limited number of these subcomponents of cognitive function would predict membership in the HCA group. We attempted to make this prediction in several ways, including calculating factor scores to obtain an estimate of ("pure") shared variance on these abilities across ages. In each case, we found no support for the possibility that early signs of exceptionality might be presaged by specific subcomponents. At each assessed age, all of these subtests significantly discriminated membership in the HCA group at 48 months. Thus, by 30 months, these groups had diverged quite strongly on every cognitive skill that we were able to quantify.

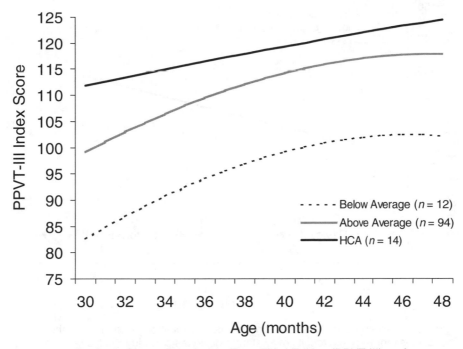

Figure 2.6. Peabody Picture Vocabulary Test, Third Edition (PPVT-III) performance as a function of group membership. Here, the high cognitive ability (HCA) group has attained high levels of achievement by 30 months and shows a linear increase from there; the other groups show growth over time but never attain the levels shown by HCA infants, even at 48 months.

Home Observation for Measurement of the Environment Scale Scores

The last measure analyzed through this backward prediction algorithm was the HOME scale. This scale comprises six subscales that are typically combined to yield a total score. The HCA group was highest on all of the sub-scales (see Figure 2.8), and as such had a significantly different total HOME score. However, this overall difference was driven primarily by the HCA group being statistically significantly different from the other two groups on two subscales: (a) parents' provision of materials for stimulation and (b) the variety of materials seen in the home.

Summary

Overall, the evidence from the backward prediction algorithms suggests two basic conclusions. First, children who will show HCA at 48 months can be discriminated as early as 12 months of age. Second, this group becomes increasingly distinguishable across the 2nd year of life, such that they are easily iden-

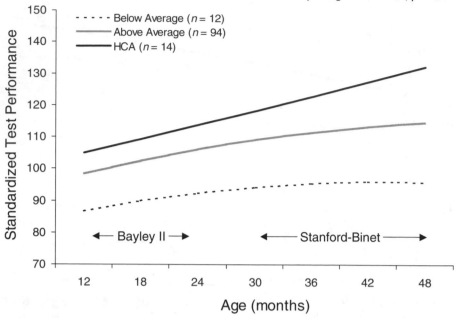

Figure 2.7. Developmental test performance as a function of group membership. These lines represent the results of all standardized tests (Barley Scales of Infant Development, Second Edition mental development index and SB4, which are scored on the same scale) across the entire range of the study. Infants eventually classified as high cognitive ability (HCA) at 48 months are shown as being at an advantage even at 12 months. The other two groups are also distinct from one another. Although there is growth in scores for the other two groups, this growth slows at later ages; the HCA group shows a continued linear trajectory. These differences in trajectory among the three groups produces the significant Group × Age interaction.

tified by 30 months of age. It is important to note that none of the behavioral and psychophysiological measures from the 1st year of life allowed for any level of prediction of HCA. Furthermore, although language measures collected across the 2nd year did differentiate HCA, the pattern of prediction was erratic, with different measures showing prediction at different ages. The developmental tests clearly distinguish this group at 12 months, and this group shows steady linear growth in outstripping norms on both the BSID-II and SB.

Forward Prediction: Discriminant Analyses

To this point, we have sought to explore the issue of prediction to the 48-month classifications by using the classifications and looking backward in time. Gottfried et al. (1994) used this strategy, and it is quite comforting that our results closely conform to theirs. Although backward-prediction algorithms are useful in many ways, their replicability in more prospective approaches is

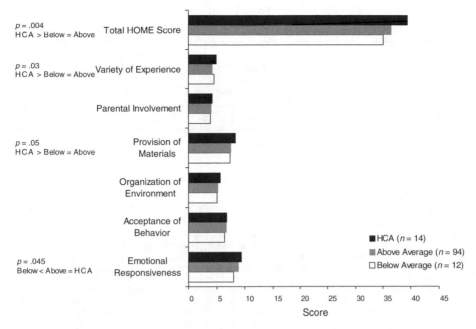

Figure 2.8. Home Observation for Measurement of the Environment Inventory (HOME) scale scores as a function of group membership. The direction and nature of differences in comparisons that attained statistical significance are shown to the left of the y axis. The two higher functioning groups had caregivers who were significantly higher in emotional responsiveness. Children classified as high cognitive ability (HCA) at 48 months had environments with significantly higher levels of materials and a higher variety of experience at 18 months of age; in addition, they had overall HOME scores (top bars) that were statistically significantly higher than those of either of the other two groups.

suspect. Thus, we conducted a set of analyses that sought to conform to the actual prospective sequence that one might follow if working from clinical or prospective data. Here, we asked whether it was possible to use early measures to reproduce the end-state classifications through a discriminant analysis (DA). The DA uses prior measures to predict end-state classifications of all subjects in the different outcome groups, and the distribution of the actual outcomes to predicted outcomes is analyzed in a chi-square test. In some ways, this approach is more conservative than the backward prediction algorithm, but an important limitation of this approach is that the analysis is limited only to subjects with complete data sets. This limitation obviously reduces power and may limit generalizability.

Table 2.5 shows the results of the DA using measures from the 2nd year and then measures from the 3rd. Two aspects of these analyses are worthy of note. First, each DA yielded imperfect but statistically significant levels of prediction of HCA. Indeed, in the final analysis that uses all of the prior data, those few HCA group members remaining in the analysis are all correctly

TABLE 2.5
Results of Discriminant Analyses

Measures	HCA children correctly identified		Non-HCA children correctly identified		p value for χ^2
	No.	%	No.	%	
Bayley MDI and MBCDI raw production at 12, 18, and 24 months	3 of 8	37.5	67 of 68	98.5	.001
Stanford-Binet subscales and PPVT-III at 30 to 42 months	6 of 14	42.8	99 of 102	97.1	.001
All measures listed above (from 12–42 months)	4 of 4	100.0	32 of 32	100.0	.001

Note. This table details the results of the analysis in which a set of continuous measures (listed in the column at far left) are entered into a discriminant analysis. The discriminant algorithm seeks to predict which children end up in the high cognitive ability (HCA) classification at 48 months. The predictions of the discriminant analysis are then analyzed against the actual outcomes of the infants at 48 months. For example, columns 2 and 3 show that the Bayley Mental Development Index (MDI) and MacArthur-Bates Communicative Development Inventory (MBCDI) production correctly identified 3 of the 8 infants (37.5%) who eventually ended up in the HCA classification at 48 months. In addition, prediction of *nonmembership* in the HCA classification is shown in columns 4 and 5. Again, using the Bayley MDI and MBCDI production as an example, 68 infants did not belong in the HCA group at 48 months; the discriminant analysis successfully identified 67 of these (98.5%). The discriminant analysis' prediction is tested against observed outcomes with a chi-square. A significant chi-square emerges when the level of prediction is statistically significant (see far right column). PPVT-III = Peabody Picture Vocabulary Test, Third Edition.

classified. The second point concerns the fact that the measures are remarkably good at avoiding false identification of individuals as potentially gifted. That is, although these measures were fairly good at identifying which toddlers would end up in the HCA group, they were extremely good at identifying which toddlers would not end up in this group.

Questions and Speculations

The current data set adds to and extends the extant literature on the identification of potential giftedness in early development. These data provide support for conclusions from previous prospective and retrospective studies but also tell some new tales.

The Development of High Cognitive Ability?

An assortment of fairly sensitive and sophisticated measures of cognitive function from the 1st year of life did not differentiate children eventually classified as HCA. By 12 months, the below-average group has begun to fall away, but only the BSID-II mental development index score discriminates the HCA group from the above-average group. As with Gottfried et al. (1994), differentiation of the HCA group was increasingly reliable at 18 and 24 months, and by 30 months, the three groups have crystallized on essentially every measure available. It is tempting to speculate that this pattern represents some developmental course, with HCA emerging in the middle of the 2nd year and proceeding forward with all due resolve. Our enthusiasm for this interpretation is curbed somewhat because 30 months—the point at which the HCA group crystallizes—is also the point at which the SB was introduced; scores on the SB are of course the criterion for the group at 48 months. Furthermore, it is worth noting that similar progressions (albeit with lower intercepts) are seen in all of the groups; perhaps it is simply more difficult for them to attain high scores on early forms of these tests. Nevertheless, if we were to use these data for devising a strategy for the early detection of HCA, we would choose to look at measures of endogenous attention in the 2nd year (see Colombo & Cheatham, 2006).

The Determinants of High Cognitive Ability?

The finding that HOME scales taken at 18 months differentially predict HCA is also provocative. Of course, this finding is far from definitive proof of environmental influence as a mediator; it seems intuitively likely that high-IQ parents tend to score well on the HOME scale. Yet although the overall score differentiates HCA, this differentiation is not carried statistically by all the HOME subscales; the best predictors from the HOME scale were scales that assessed the provision of materials and variety of experiences in the home. It is noteworthy that measures of responsiveness, emotion, and involvement were not predictors of HCA, as one might suspect that these too would covary positively with parent IQ. The fact that the HOME scale was administered at about 18 months—exactly when the HCA group begins to diverge—tempts us once again to speculate that the emergence of HCA may be best explained in terms of a developmental systems approach (see Friedman & Shore, 2000, including particularly Colombo et al., 2000). This question will not be resolved until another prospective study of HCA from infancy including statistical control subjects for parental IQ is conducted.

On Not Predicting High Cognitive Ability

To this point, we have characterized the task at hand in terms of our ability to predict giftedness and HCA from infancy. Although the prediction of HCA is imperfect (see Table 2.5), the prediction of non-HCA is fairly close to perfect. We think that the accurate identification for individuals who are not HCA has potential implications for understanding the development of HCA itself; these data suggest that if a child's early performance consistently contraindicates HCA membership, then membership in the HCA classification is highly unlikely. This point is tempered by the general finding that exceptional scores are relatively rare on the BSID-II. Nevertheless, although some children who scored below average at one or more points on the BSID-II did attain HCA status at 48 months, no child scoring below average on the SB beyond 24 months was ever classified as HCA by age 4.

CONCLUSION

The study of infancy and early childhood is critical to the understanding of the origins of giftedness. We have presented data here that show that high ability can be detected early in life, perhaps by the middle of the 2nd year. Although we are disappointed that the identification of high ability could not be accomplished with early measures of attention and psychophysiological function, we have introduced a new paradigm for the consideration of learning and cognition in infancy, and we have sketched out some predictions for its relevance to individual differences, and in particular, to the determination of HCA. It is our hope that in the next decade we will be closer to understanding those factors operating during infancy and early childhood that can contribute to the optimization of individual achievement and abilities. Such progress will be relevant and valuable to the study of giftedness, but it will be relevant and valuable well beyond that discipline as well. Such work will be an important contribution to understanding the nature of the development of intellectual and cognitive function. In turn, this understanding will also help in the identification of individuals at risk as well as those "at promise" in later development. Although the study of infant cognition has long been a discipline concerned with group-based nomothetic laws, it has a clear potential for contributing to the study and promotion of the welfare of the individual. We look forward to the fulfillment of that potential.

REFERENCES

Bayley, N. (1994). *The Bayley scales of infant development* (2nd ed.). San Antonio, TX: Harcourt/Psychological Corporation.

Bock, G. R., & Ackrill, K. (Eds.). (1993). *The origins and development of high ability: Ciba Foundation Symposium 178*. West Sussex, England: Wiley.

Bradley, R. H., & Caldwell, B. M. (1976). Early home environment and changes in mental test performance in children from 6 to 36 months. *Developmental Psychology, 12*, 93–97.

Colombo, J. (2001). Recent advances in the assessment of infant cognition: Implications for LC-PUFA supplementation studies. *Lipids, 36*, 919–926.

Colombo, J., & Cheatham, C. (2006). The emergence of endogenous attention in infancy and early childhood. In R. Kail (Ed.), *Advances in child development and behavior* (pp. 283–322). New York: Ablex Publishing.

Colombo, J., & Frick, J. E. (1999). Recent advances and issues in the study of preverbal intelligence. In M. Anderson (Ed.), *The development of intelligence* (pp. 46–71). East Sussex, England: Psychology Press.

Colombo, J., Richman, W. A., Shaddy, D. J., Greenhoot, A. F., & Maikranz, J. (2001). HR-defined phases of attention, look duration, and infant performance in the paired-comparison paradigm. *Child Development, 72,* 1605–1616.

Colombo, J., Shaddy, D. J., & Richman, W. A. (2000). Cognition, development, and exceptional talent in infancy. In R. C. Friedman & B. Shore (Eds.), *Talents unfolding: Cognition and development* (pp. 123–149). Washington, DC: American Psychological Association.

Colombo, J., Shaddy, D. J., Richman, W. A., Maikranz, J. M., & Blaga, O. M. (2004). The developmental course of attention in infancy and preschool cognitive outcome. *Infancy, 4,* 1–38.

Dalzell, H. (1998). Giftedness: Infancy to adolescence—a developmental perspective. *Roeper Review, 20,* 259–264.

Friedman, R. C., & Shore, B. (Eds.). (2000). *Talents unfolding: Cognition and development.* Washington, DC: American Psychological Association.

Gardner, H. (1993). The relationship between early giftedness and later achievement. In G. R. Bock & K. Ackrill (Eds.), *The origins and development of high ability: Ciba Foundation Symposium 178* (pp. 175–182). West Sussex, England: Wiley.

Gottfried, A. W., Gottfried, A. E., Bathurst, K., & Guerin, D. W. (1994). *Gifted IQ: Early developmental aspects.* New York: Plenum Press.

Gross, M. U. M. (1999). Small poppies: Highly gifted children in the early years. *Roeper Review, 21,* 207–214.

Horowitz, F. D. (1992). A developmental view on the early identification of the gifted. In P. S. Klein & A. J. Tannenbaum (Eds.), *To be young and gifted* (pp. 73–92). Norwood, NJ: Ablex Publishing.

Horowitz, F. D., & O'Brien, M. (Eds.). (1985). *The gifted and talented: Developmental perspectives.* Washington, DC: American Psychological Association.

Horowitz, F. D., & O'Brien, M. (1986). Gifted and talented children: State of knowledge and directions for research. *American Psychologist, 41,* 1147–1152.

Klein, P. S., & Tannenbaum, A. J. (Eds.). (1992). *To be young and gifted.* Norwood, NJ: Ablex Publishing.

Obler, L. K., & Fein, D. (Eds.). (1988). *The exceptional brain: Neuropsychology of talent and special abilities.* New York: Guilford Press.

Robinson, N. (2000). Giftedness in very young children: How seriously should it be taken? In R. C. Friedman & B. Shore (Eds.), *Talents unfolding: Cognition and development* (pp. 123–149). Washington, DC: American Psychological Association.

Shaklee, B. D. (1992). Identification of young gifted students. *Journal for Education of the Gifted, 15,* 134–144.

Shapiro, B. K., Palmer, F. B., Antell, S. E., Bilker, S., Ross, A., & Capute, A. J. (1989). Giftedness: Can it be predicted in infancy? *Clinical Pediatrics, 28,* 205–209.

Sternberg, R. J. (1993). The concept of "giftedness": A pentagonal implicit theory. In G. R. Bock & K. Ackrill (Eds.), *The origins and development of high ability: CIBA Foundation Symposium 178* (pp. 5–16). West Sussex, England: Wiley.

Storfer, M. D. (1990). *Intelligence and giftedness: The contributions of heredity and early environment.* San Francisco: Jossey-Bass.

Subotnik, R. F., & Arnold, K. D. (Eds.). (1994). *Beyond Terman: Contemporary longitudinal studies of giftedness and talent.* Norwood, NJ: Ablex Publishing.

Tannenbaum, A. J. (1992). Early signs of giftedness: Research and commentary. In P. S. Klein & A. J. Tannenbaum (Eds.), *To be young and gifted* (pp. 3–32). Norwood, NJ: Ablex Publishing.

Willerman, L., & Fiedler, M. F. (1974). Infant performance and intellectual precocity. *Child Development, 45,* 438–486.

Willerman, L., & Fiedler, M. F. (1977). Intellectually precocious preschool children: Early development and later intellectual accomplishments. *Journal of Genetic Psychology, 131,* 13–20.

Zigler, E., & Farber, E. A. (1985). Commonalities between the intellectual extremes: Giftedness and mental retardation. In F. D. Horowitz & M. O'Brien (Eds.), *The gifted and talented: Developmental perspectives* (pp. 387–408). Washington, DC: American Psychological Association.

3

ISSUES IN EARLY PREDICTION AND IDENTIFICATION OF INTELLECTUAL GIFTEDNESS

ALLEN W. GOTTFRIED, ADELE ESKELES GOTTFRIED, AND DIANA WRIGHT GUERIN

This chapter comprises three sections: (a) commentary on the Colombo, Shaddy, Blaga, Anderson, and Kannass chapter titled "High Cognitive Ability in Infancy and Early Childhood" (chap. 2, this volume); (b) consideration of issues concerning early prediction of gifted intelligence; and (c) discussion of implications regarding early identification of intellectual giftedness.

COMMENTARY ON "HIGH COGNITIVE ABILITY IN INFANCY AND EARLY CHILDHOOD"

Early prediction and detection of high intellectual ability has long been of interest to developmental psychologists and educators. As early as 1940, Thorndike (1940), in his *Psychological Bulletin* article titled " 'Constancy' of the IQ," reviewed the predictive value of infant and preschool tests and concluded that they are of limited value in predicting school-age intelligence test performance. Subsequent reviews throughout the century have continued to corroborate this general conclusion (e.g., Colombo, 1993; McCall, Hogarty, & Hurlburt, 1972) despite the strong psychometric characteristics of the standardized instruments used.

Regardless of the known difficulty of the task, in their research, the authors of chapter 2, Colombo et al., took on the challenge of identifying in a cohort followed from infancy a subsample of children deemed high in cognitive ability at age 4 years. They did so by incorporating standardized developmental testing as well as measures involving specific cognitive processes.

This research is important for several reasons. First, the researchers attempted to identify early roots and processes that might be involved in the origins and ontogeny of intellectual giftedness. This endeavor is worth further pursuit, particularly in light of new techniques used to assess cognitive development during infancy.

Second, the researchers used both forward and backward analyses (albeit not completely bidirectional across measures). Such analyses are interesting because they are based on different conditional probabilities, as the question addressed by each approach is different. The former is intended to advance predictive hypotheses and models so as to forecast probabilistic events or occurrences. The latter is postdictive, in that differences in the criterion are known or established and then a hypothesized developmental history is tested by determining factors that differentiate (and possibly account for) the designated outcome. These analyses do not necessarily furnish overlapping information about relationships over time. For example, with backward analyses, children designated as intellectually gifted during the school years were found to have performed higher on the Bayley Scales of Infant Development, Second Edition (BSID-II) at approximately 1.5 years of age than did their cohort peer comparison group (A. W. Gottfried, Gottfried, Bathurst, & Guerin, 1994). At the same time, however, high scores on the BSID-II have not been shown to be good predictors of intellectual gifted status. Shapiro et al. (1989) illustrated differences in findings using forward and backward types of analyses in attempting to predict and postdict giftedness using the BSID-II at 13 months and the Wechsler Scale of Intelligence—Revised (WISC–R) at 7.5 years. Children designated as gifted on the WISC–R showed prior differences on the BSID-II; however, advanced development on the BSID-II did not predict gifted performance on the WISC–R.

Third, Colombo et al. used standardized psychometric assessments, infant attention and psychophysiological measures, and appraisals of language and home environment. In this way they attempted to widen the methods used to identify high cognitive ability (HCA) during infancy as well as elucidate the processes that may be involved in the development of HCA.

Fourth, by applying multiple methods the assumption was made that no single measure during infancy may be sufficient in the prediction and understanding of the development of HCA. Bornstein et al. (2006) took a similar approach using sequential developmental measures from 4 months (visual habituation) to 4 years (Wechsler Full Scale IQ). Thus, the strategy Colombo et al. used represents a burgeoning area in terms of understanding not only cross-time relationships between infant and later cognitive functioning but also the multifaceted components involved in the ontogeny of cognitive and advanced intellectual development.

Fifth, prediction necessitates longitudinal methodology. The research reported by Colombo et al. is based on the Kansas Early Cognitive Project. This longitudinal study is impressive because it comprises a considerable number of assessments during the early years using various standardized and contemporaneous developmental measures. Longitudinal designs are extremely difficult to conduct because of expense and time consumption, intense labor required for repeated assessment waves, and the uncertainty of maintaining the study population (for further discussion see A. W. Gottfried, Gottfried, & Guerin, 2006). The Kansas Project began with 227 infants recruited at 3 months of age; 140 children of the original study sample were tested again at 4 years. Furthermore, in longitudinal research, once the measures are in place and the children tested, modifications cannot be made. The investigator is set with the measures that had been selected for that age. If statistically significant and meaningful cross-time results are not obtained, nothing can be done for that sample. Recruiting another cohort and following them up is a daunting endeavor. However, even the finding of no significance is a contribution emerging from longitudinal research to determine important dimensions of prediction or failure to predict and formulate future hypotheses and efforts. Thus, every well-done longitudinal study has something to contribute to our knowledge of development.

We now highlight some of the most relevant findings from the Colombo et al. research regarding the issue of early prediction of HCA. First and foremost, the issue of instability of classification is raised by the cross-time pattern of test scores. Although 15 children ended up in the HCA group at 4 years, all but 1 child revealed instability of classifications across the previous years, clearly indicating that there is no consistent cross-time pattern of scoring above the designated cutoff from infancy through 4 years of age. This result is in accord with the findings of the Fullerton Longitudinal Study, although we did find that virtually all children (90%) who emerged as intellectually gifted at age 8 years evidenced at least one score equal to or greater than 130 during the infant years. This conclusion was based on a backward contingency analysis and not a predictive analysis. Not all infants who showed these elevations became gifted as measured by cognitive assessments, although such scores appear to be part of the developmental process and increases the probability of later giftedness. We interpreted our findings as evidence of early signs of reach, that is, potential for high intellectual performance (A. W. Gottfried et al., 1994). The spaghetti plots provided by Colombo et al. reveal that a number of the children also evidenced early signs of reach as we defined it.

Second, consistent with the findings from the Fullerton Longitudinal Study, emergence of differentiation between the HCA and cohort cognitive groups was evident in the 2nd year of life. Colombo et al. suggested that higher order thinking processes such as self-regulation, attention, and symbolic functions may be responsible for this. It is noteworthy that during this approximate time period socioeconomic status begins to correlate with cognitive functioning (A. W. Gottfried, 1985; A. W. Gottfried, Gottfried, Bathurst, Guerin, & Parramore, 2003), indicating that in the 2nd year of life, family environments and resources associated with social status may be showing up as factors that promote cognitive growth.

Third, the findings reported on home environment variables are also consistent with the Fullerton Longitudinal Study. Home environments of the HCA children were more stimulating as early as infancy. There is concordance regarding the specific role of variety of experience and provision of play materials. We likewise found that these two subscales of the Home Observation for Measurement of the Environment (HOME) Inventory significantly and specifically predicted cognitive outcomes from 1 year to 3.5 years. Furthermore, in the meta-analysis conducted at that time on the relation of early home environment as measured by the HOME and infant and preschool intellectual performance, variety of stimulation and provision of play materials proved to be two of the most pervasive and potent proximal variables related to early cognitive development (A. W. Gottfried, 1984; A. W. Gottfried & Gottfried, 1984). Moreover, only the variety of stimulation scale differentiated the gifted from the cohort comparison group at 1 year of age in the Fullerton Longitudinal Study (A. W. Gottfried et al., 1994). Hence, finding is noteworthy as a reliable and generalizable finding across time and studies.

Fourth, there is the issue of predicting those who did not emerge as HCA. Colombo et al. reported a high success rate in predicting non-HCA individuals. In predicting membership in the non-HCA group, or nongiftedness, a high negative prediction (known as specificity) is almost always likely to occur because of base-rate probabilities (Meehl & Rosen, 1955); that is, the occurrence of nongiftedness is quite high in the population by definition. In the general population, only 2% would be classified as gifted (i.e., at or beyond two standard deviations above the mean), with the remaining 98% being nongifted. Thus, there is a 98% chance of correct classification of nongiftedness without testing by simply labeling all members of the population as nongifted. This is because, by definition, individuals are more likely to be members of the non-HCA, or nongifted, group. To have an efficient test of nongiftedness, one would need to be successful above and beyond the 98% hit rate, which is highly unlikely and cost-ineffective. Thus, we take issue with the view of Colombo et al. that the identification of those who will not likely fall into the category is a tangible step toward the positive identification of individuals who will fall into this classification. Those who are identified as not HCA at one time could be so at a later time, especially given the aforementioned comments about unstable classification in the course of early development. Therefore, consistent contraindications are not necessarily valid in the future because of the instability of performance on various assessment instruments. There is always the chance that an individual not initially classified as gifted would be so at a future point in time. This issue is significant in the identification of giftedness for placement in educational programs.

ISSUES CONCERNING EARLY PREDICTION
OF GIFTED INTELLIGENCE

A fundamental issue in prediction concerns the criterion that is being predicted, in this case IQ at a subsequent and designated point in time. Gifted children are typically identified and classified in the schools during the early to middle elementary school years. Taking this as a reference point, many researchers and educators who study gifted children have asked whether intellectual superiority is stable over time. Does once gifted imply always gifted?

The renowned Terman Study of Genius was based on teachers' nominations followed by intelligence testing. Although it was said that Terman recommended retesting from time to time (Hilgard, 1989, p. 16), repeated systematic IQ testing to determine the stability of IQ on the study population (or even a random sample of them) was not incorporated into the longitudinal design. Burks, Jensen, and Terman (1930) and McNemar (1947) attempted to address this issue by retesting some of the "Termites" (as the study participants came to be labeled) in the course of the investigation, albeit not with a systematic methodology. Other studies conducted in the first half of the 20th century, particularly around the 1930s, also grappled with the issue of stability of intellectual giftedness (e.g., Cattell, 1933; Hollingworth & Kaunitz, 1934; Lincoln, 1935; Nemzek, 1932). The studies by these pioneers are historical and dated and were limited or compromised in terms of methodological design and instrumentation. A tendency for scores to decline over time was most frequently observed, but increases in retest scores among children who were initially tested and classified as gifted were also noticed.

Developmental researchers subsequently conducted long-term longitudinal studies in which children were repeatedly tested on standardized intelligence tests (during the early years sometimes referred to as standardized developmental tests). Examples include the Berkeley Growth Study (Bayley, 1949), Berkeley Guidance Study (Honzik, Macfarlane, & Allen, 1948), Fels Longitudinal Study (Sontag, Baker, & Nelson, 1958), Louisville Twin Study (Wilson, 1983), and Fullerton Longitudinal Study (A. W. Gottfried et al., 1994, 2006).

Because the Fullerton Longitudinal Study is contemporary and conducted by us, we present some data to make a relevant point. Table 3.1 displays the standardized tests used during the course of our investigation. Table 3.2 pre-

TABLE 3.1

Intelligence Tests Administered in the Fullerton Longitudinal Study

Measure	Ages administered (years)
Bayley Scales of Infant Development	1, 1.5, 2
McCarthy Scales of Children's Abilities	2.5, 3, 3.5
Kaufman Assessment Battery for Children	5
Wechsler Intelligence Scale for Children—Revised	6, 7, 8, 12
Wechsler Intelligence Scale for Children—Third Edition	15
Wechsler Adult Intelligence Scale—Revised	17

sents the intercorrelations among the 13 standardized test waves from ages 1 through 17 years. Both the magnitude and, more important, the pattern of correlations are comparable to those obtained in the aforementioned longitudinal studies. Conclusions based on such longitudinal data include the following: (a) the adjacent testing periods typically reveal the highest correlations; (b) correlations decline as the interval between testing waves increase; and (c) with advancement in age, the magnitude of the correlations increases with regard to the final testing wave.

The correlations from preschool (the criterion age used by Colombo et al.) to age 17 years hover in the low moderate range in magnitude. In con-

TABLE 3.2

Correlations Among Standardized Intelligence Test Scores in the Fullerton Longitudinal Study, Ages 1 Through 17 Years

Age (years)	Age (years)												
	1	1.5	2	2.5	3	3.5	5	6	7	8	12	15	17
1[a]	—												
1.5[a]	.41	—											
2[a]	.43	.62	—										
2.5[b]	.33	.63	.64	—									
3[b]	.37	.65	.67	.79	—								
3.5[b]	.37	.54	.68	.74	.76	—							
5[c]	.18	.34	.45	.54	.56	.51	—						
6[d]	.26	.45	.60	.57	.59	.67	.65	—					
7[d]	.22	.41	.55	.56	.59	.63	.62	.79	—				
8[d]	.20	.42	.54	.55	.59	.62	.70	.79	.83	—			
12[d]	.17	.39	.51	.42	.47	.47	.62	.72	.78	.80	—		
15[e]	.15	.35	.48	.40	.45	.45	.56	.64	.70	.77	.80	—	
17[f]	.16	.39	.43	.44	.49	.44	.60	.67	.70	.77	.82	.85	—

Note. All correlations are significant (one-tailed test), $p < .05$, with the exception of those between 1 and 15 years and 1 and 17 years.
[a]Bayley Mental Development Index. [b]McCarthy General Cognitive Index. [c]Kaufman Mental Processing Composite. [d]Wechsler Intelligence Scale for Children—Revised Full Scale IQ. [e]Wechsler Intelligence Scale for Children—Third Edition Full Scale IQ. [f]Wechsler Adult Intelligence Scale Full Scale IQ.

trast, by middle childhood (age 8), correlations with age 17 become moderately strong (.77). Age 8 years is significant for several reasons: (a) as noted earlier, it is the approximate age at which children are often considered for gifted programs; (b) it has been found to predict adult educational and occupational status (McCall, 1977); and (c) it was used in the Fullerton Longitudinal Study to discern intellectually gifted children from their contemporary nongifted cohort peer comparisons. Therefore, a fundamental question is whether there is stability in the gifted classification from middle childhood and thereafter.

The degree of stability or instability of correlations of intelligence test scores across time and the stability of classification of giftedness was addressed by Humphreys (1985, 1989; Humphreys & Davey, 1988). Basing his analysis on longitudinal data from the Louisville Twin Study (Wilson, 1983), Humphreys (1989) pointed out that instability is a monotonic function of the interval between testing periods (i.e., initial and subsequent tests). Assuming test reliability as high as .95, he stated that observed scores over 10 years would be characterized by a correlation between .63 and .70 (notice that the correlation between ages 7 and 17 years in the Fullerton Longitudinal Study is .70, as would be predicted from Humphreys's [1989] analysis). He asserted that a child with an IQ of 140 on the initial test would be expected to have an IQ of 125 a decade later as a result of regression toward the mean. In succinct terms, in the absence of any intervention, IQ scores of gifted children will inevitably regress toward the population mean. Thus, Humphreys (1989) argued that "an educational system should be forgiving of early performance that is less than illustrious and should not give undue weight to early illustrious performance" (p. 203). In addition, Lohman and Korb (2006) have shown that the majority of elementary-age children who score in the top percentiles in cognitive ability and educational achievement in one grade do not necessarily retain as high a level 1 or 2 years later. In other words, children classified as gifted on an initial testing are not likely to be so subsequently. The downward shift in performance is the result of regression effects.

Thus, we return to our original question: What is the stability of the criterion that early measures are intended to predict? At issue is whether researchers interested in early prediction of HCA are compounding the lack of predictability of the early tests with the imperfect stability of subsequent tests. Another issue is the inevitable regression toward the population mean of extreme scores in the absence of intervention and perfect reliability. Therefore, those children with initial scores in the gifted range would not necessarily maintain such scores at a later point in time because of regression toward the mean. By the same token, initial tests may fail to detect children who score below the requisite cutoff for designation of giftedness but who may emerge as gifted on subsequent tests because individuals' scores can fluctuate upward as a result of the lack of perfect reliability. These statistical properties in the context of multiple measures taken across time raise the following question: Is the criterion of intellectual giftedness a moving target? This has significant implications for early identification of intellectual giftedness and educational procedures and policies.

IMPLICATIONS CONCERNING THE EARLY IDENTIFICATION OF INTELLECTUAL GIFTEDNESS

According to Olszewski-Kubilius (2003), there has been little change in educational practice regarding identification of gifted children. Schools typically assess for gifted IQ once, and if the requisite score or gifted classification is not achieved, no future assessment is undertaken (Matthews & Foster, 2005). This perspective roughly corresponds to what Matthews and Foster (2005) termed the "mystery" model, in which IQ is seen as fixed and stable across the life span. Such a conception does not fit with what is now known about the change in IQ performance over the school years as detailed earlier.

The challenges associated with identification of giftedness during the school years raise serious concerns about the potential application of giftedness identification during infancy and early childhood. Matthews and Foster (2005) described early identification as one of the most contentious in the field of giftedness. The problems pertaining to early identification arise because of questions about whether giftedness can be reliably identified during infancy and early childhood. Furthermore, if such identification is undertaken, what is the predictability of the index used with regard to giftedness during childhood and beyond?

In light of the points raised earlier regarding the well-established findings about cross-time instability of intelligence tests scores from infancy through late adolescence, we concur with Perleth, Schatz, and Mönks (2000, p. 303) that "practitioners and researchers should be skeptical of too much optimism about the possibility of predicting high ability and high achievement from early age." Identification of early giftedness could be misleading for children and their families because of the following two types of errors in predictions: (a) false positives, that is, identification of the infant or young child as gifted when that is not the case later or (b) false negatives, that is, designation of infants or young children as not gifted when they would emerge as gifted at a subsequent point in time.

Finally, what is the criterion we are attempting to predict? Is it a changing criterion because of issues of reliability and regression toward the mean? Or perhaps it is not a single index at all (as is IQ) but instead a multifaceted construct. Thus, identification during infancy or early childhood becomes more of a guess as to what it predicts rather than being a known precursor to a specific status. Taking into consideration the converging research evidence regarding change and stability of the IQ, as well as critical issues raised regarding gifted identification in infancy and early childhood, it is of paramount importance to determine the appropriate identification criteria. This involves conceptions of what giftedness is during infancy, early childhood, and beyond. Another question is whether identifying HCA, or giftedness, in infancy reinforces a stability view because it appears to assume that processes regulating giftedness or HCA are present before subsequent environment, parental stimulation, education, motivation, training, and encouragement have come to bear on its unfolding. Contemporary conceptions of giftedness incorporate these latter factors in advancing critical issues facing researchers and educators alike (Borland, 2003). More differentiated views of competence, high ability, giftedness, talent, and expertise are becoming increasingly prominent (see Feldhusen, 2003; Heller, Mönks, Sternberg, & Subotnik, 2000).

When Should Children Be Tested for Intellectual Giftedness?

Because of the questionable predictability of infant and early childhood intellectual measures, as well as the possibility of plasticity in giftedness or nongiftedness across the school years, the issue of classifying young children for selection into programs is of concern. It was previously recommended that "attempts to identify gifted children should be a continuous process to allow for inclusion of children who are not identified as gifted at one point, but who may become identified at a later point" (A. W. Gottfried et al., 1994, p. 178). We further recommended that programs remain open to children who evidence giftedness at a later point, and to use multiple criteria, such as achievement and motivation, to help "provide clues" as to who may emerge as superior and gifted at a subsequent point (A. W. Gottfried et al., 1994, p. 178). Matthews and Foster (2005) are consistent with these recommendations in advancing their "Mastery" approach in which they propose that identification timing should be ongoing as needed and that measures other than IQ are used. The view of ongoing assessment has implications for parent advocacy because parents may need to take the lead on pursuing ongoing assessment for their children.

Although we propose ongoing assessments for those who are not identified as gifted at first testing, we do not advocate retesting children who have already qualified for and been placed in such programs, nor do we advocate removing children from programs on the basis of a later assessment. Because it is known that scores of gifted children are likely to decline just on the basis of regression to the population mean, if they are doing well educationally in their programs, they should remain there. Ongoing assessment for children already identified as gifted and who continue to succeed is unnecessary and valueless.

Prediction Gaps

Aside from statistical regression effects, potential developmental factors may be associated with prediction failures leading to what we term *prediction gaps*. First, individual differences exist in developmental timing of the emergence of giftedness. Second, giftedness exists in aspects of HCA other than IQ. This differentiation encompasses multifactor theories of intelligence (see Borland, 2003; Heller et al., 2000) and special areas such as spatial abilities (see chap. 4, this volume). The third factor pertains to the development of children's academic intrinsic motivation, a topic of research in giftedness included in the potentiality–enrichment theory (A. W. Gottfried et al., 1994) and in the construct of gifted motivation (A. E. Gottfried & Gottfried, 1996, 2004; A. W. Gottfried, Gottfried, Cook, & Morris, 2005). Potentiality–enrichment theory proposed that intrinsic motivation is inherently tied to the emergence of intellectual giftedness as it concerns pleasure inherent in cognitive processing. Hence, those children who enjoy cognitive processing to a greater extent are likely to be more engaged in activities that promote their cognitive excellence. In the conception of gifted motivation, those with superior strivings in academic intrinsic motivation showed superior cognitive and academic performance and are motivationally gifted in their own right independent of intelligence (see A. E. Gottfried, 1985, 1986, 1990, for further elaboration of academic intrinsic motivation). Therefore, motivation itself needs to be included in developmental conceptions of giftedness as well as in identification methods. The last factor proposed herein concerns environment itself and changes in the environment that support and regulate the emergence, continuity, and discontinuity of intellectual giftedness (A. W. Gottfried et al., 1994; Subotnik, Olszewski-Kubilius, & Arnold, 2003).

Implications for Family and Educational Factors

Parents and teachers are on the front line of recognizing gifted potential and signs of reach (A. W. Gottfried et al., 1994). Indeed, Subotnik and Olszewski-Kubilius (1997) pointed out that parents are the first to identify childhood talent and often the first teachers for those who evidence exceptional talent and eminence. Robinson (2000) asserted that parents are better than just test scores in identifying giftedness in young children, and test scores often confirmed parental observation. Parents and educators of infants and young children should be responsive to children's bids for activities and stimulation and provide the requisite exposure, such as variety of stimulation, as well as opportunity to stimulate mastery (A. W. Gottfried et al., 1994; Robinson, 2000). It was found that gifted children were more likely to ask parents for lessons and activities, their parents were more responsive, and the home environments of gifted children were significantly more intellectually and culturally stimulating (A. W. Gottfried et al., 1994). Therefore, it is recommended that one take a developmental approach toward the assessment of superior competence or giftedness. Horowitz and O'Brien (1985, 1986) emphasized the importance of a developmental approach to assessing as well as understanding the processes underlying the emergence of giftedness. Olszewski-Kubilius (2003) asserted that "the fruition of childhood ability and promise is very tenuous, and social, environmental, and psychological variables play a huge role and interact in very complex ways" (p. 499). Feldman (2003) asserted that if the field of gifted education continues to maintain its assumptions that IQ is natural, unchanging, and unchangeable (p. 23), there will be little emphasis on a developmental approach that requires the incorporation of a wider field of talents and abilities.

The study of high ability during infancy and early childhood with an emphasis on early processes and the developmental pathways to giftedness is an important research endeavor. However, extreme caution must be taken in adopting a gifted–nongifted classification for infancy and early childhood because of the aforementioned problems and concerns. Nevertheless, if high ability and potential are to be recognized early, they should not be used to classify children as gifted, but rather their recognition should enable these competencies to be nurtured appropriately. It would be expected that if children are exposed to optimal environments that facilitate the continued development of their potential, their gifts will emerge, albeit possibly at different times across childhood.

REFERENCES

Bayley, N. (1949). Constancy and variability in the growth of intelligence from birth to eighteen years. *Journal of Genetic Psychology*, 75, 165–196.

Borland, J. H. (Ed.). (2003). *Rethinking gifted education*. New York: Teachers College Press.

Bornstein, M. H., Hahn, C.-S., Bell, C., Haynes, O. M., Slater, A., Golding, J., et al. (2006). Stability and cognition across early childhood: A development cascade. *Psychological Science*, 17, 151–158.

Burks, B. S., Jensen, D. W., & Terman, L. M. (1930). *Genetic studies of genius: Vol. III. The promise of youth: Follow-up studies of a thousand gifted children*. Stanford, CA: Stanford University Press.

Cattell, P. (1933). Do the Stanford-Binet IQ's of superior boys and girls tend to decrease or increase with age? *Journal of Educational Research*, 26, 668–673.

Colombo, J. (1993). *Infant cognition: Predicting later intellectual functioning*. Newbury Park, CA: Sage.

Feldhusen, J. F. (2003). Beyond general giftedness: New ways to identify and educate gifted, talented, and precocious youth. In J. H. Borland (Ed.), *Rethinking gifted education* (pp. 34–35). New York: Teachers College Press.

Feldman, D. H. (2003). A developmental evolutionary perspective on giftedness. In J. H. Borland (Ed.), *Rethinking gifted education* (pp. 9–33). New York: Teachers College Press.

Gottfried, A. E. (1985). Academic intrinsic motivation in elementary and junior high school students. *Journal of Educational Psychology, 77,* 631–635.

Gottfried, A. E. (1986). *Children's Academic Intrinsic Motivation Inventory (CAIMI).* Lutz, FL: Psychological Assessment Resources.

Gottfried, A. E. (1990). Academic intrinsic motivation in young elementary school children. *Journal of Educational Psychology, 82,* 525–538.

Gottfried, A. E., & Gottfried, A. W. (1996). A longitudinal study of academic intrinsic motivation in intellectually gifted children: Childhood through early adolescence. *Gifted Child Quarterly, 40,* 179–183.

Gottfried, A. E., & Gottfried, A. W. (2004). Toward the development of a conceptualization of gifted motivation. *Gifted Child Quarterly, 48,* 121–132.

Gottfried, A. W. (1984). Home environment and early cognitive development: Integration, meta-analyses, and conclusions. In A. W. Gottfried (Ed.), *Home environment and early cognitive development: Longitudinal research* (pp. 329–342). New York: Academic Press.

Gottfried, A. W. (1985). Measures of socioeconomic status in child development research: Data and recommendations. *Merrill-Palmer Quarterly, 31,* 85–92.

Gottfried, A. W., & Gottfried, A. E. (1984). Home environment and cognitive development in young children of middle-socioeconomic-status families. In A. W. Gottfried (Ed.), *Home environment and early cognitive development: Longitudinal research* (pp. 57–115). New York: Academic Press.

Gottfried, A. W., Gottfried, A. E., Bathurst, K., & Guerin, D. (1994). *Gifted IQ: Early developmental aspects. The Fullerton Longitudinal Study.* New York: Plenum Press.

Gottfried, A. W., Gottfried, A. E., Bathurst, K., Guerin, D. W., & Parramore, M. M. (2003). Socioeconomic status in children's development and family environment: Infancy through adolescence. In M. H. Bornstein & R. H. Bradley (Eds.), *Socioeconomic status, parenting, and child development* (pp. 189–207). Mahwah, NJ: Erlbaum.

Gottfried, A. W., Gottfried, A. E., Cook, C., & Morris, P. (2005). Educational characteristics of adolescents with gifted academic intrinsic motivation: A longitudinal study from school entry through early adulthood. *Gifted Child Quarterly, 49,* 172–186.

Gottfried, A. W., Gottfried, A. E., & Guerin, D. W. (2006). The Fullerton Longitudinal Study: A long-term investigation of intellectual and motivational giftedness. *Journal for the Education of the Gifted, 29,* 430–450.

Heller, K. A., Mönks, F. J., Sternberg, R. J., & Subotnik, R. F. (Eds.). (2000). *International handbook of giftedness and talent* (2nd ed.). Oxford, England: Elsevier Science.

Hilgard, E. R. (1989). The early years of intelligence measurement. In R. L. Linn (Ed.), *Intelligence: measurement, theory and public policy. Proceedings of a symposium in honor of Lloyd G. Humphreys* (pp. 7–28). Chicago: University of Illinois Press.

Hollingworth, L. S., & Kaunitz, R. M. (1934). The centile status of gifted children at maturity. *Journal of Genetic Psychology, 45*, 106–120.

Honzik, M. P., Macfarlane, J. W., & Allen, L. (1948). The stability of mental test performance between two and eighteen years. *Journal of Experimental Education, 17*, 309–324.

Horowitz, F. D., & O'Brien, M. (1985). Epilogue: Perspectives on research and development. In F. D. Horowitz & M. O'Brien (Eds.), *The gifted and talented: Developmental perspectives* (pp. 437–454). Washington, DC: American Psychological Association.

Horowitz, F. D., & O'Brien, M. (1986). Gifted and talented children: State of knowledge and directions for research. *American Psychologist, 41*, 1147–1152.

Humphreys, L. G. (1985). A conceptualization of intellectual giftedness. In F. D. Horowitz & M. O'Brien (Eds.), *The gifted and talented: Developmental perspectives* (pp. 331–360). Washington, DC: American Psychological Association.

Humphreys, L. G. (1989). Intelligence: Three kinds of instability and their consequences for policy. In R. L. Linn (Ed.), *Intelligence: Measurement, theory and public policy. Proceedings of a symposium in honor of Lloyd G. Humphreys* (pp. 193–230). Chicago: University of Illinois Press.

Humphreys, L. G., & Davey, T. C. (1988). Continuity in intellectual growth from 12 months to 9 years. *Intelligence, 12*, 183–197.

Lincoln, E. A. (1935). A study of changes in the intelligence quotients of superior children. *Journal of Educational Research, 29*, 272–275.

Lohman, D. F., & Korb, K. A. (2006). Gifted today but not tomorrow? Longitudinal changes in ability and achievement during elementary school. *Journal for the Education of the Gifted, 29*, 451–484.

Matthews, D. J., & Foster, J. F. (2005). *Being smart about gifted children: A guidebook for parents and educators.* Scottsdale, AZ: Great Potential Press.

McCall, R. B. (1977, July 29). Childhood IQs as predictors of adult educational and occupational status. *Science, 197*, 482–483.

McCall, R. B., Hogarty, P. S., & Hurlburt, N. (1972). Transitions in infant sensorimotor development and the prediction of childhood IQ. *American Psychologist, 27*, 728–748.

McNemar, Q. (1947). Intellectual status of the gifted subjects as adults. In L. M. Terman (Ed.), *Genetic studies of genius: Vol. IV. The gifted child grows up: Twenty-five years' follow-up of a superior group* (pp. 140–146). Stanford, CA: Stanford University Press.

Meehl, P. E., & Rosen, A. (1955). Antecedent probability and the efficiency of psychometric signs, patterns or cutting scores. *Psychological Bulletin, 52*, 194–216.

Nemzek, C. L. (1932). The constancy of IQ's of gifted children. *Journal of Educational Psychology, 23*, 607–610.

Olszewski-Kubilius, P. (2003). Gifted education programs and procedures. In W. M. Reynolds & G. E. Miller (Eds.), *Handbook of psychology: Vol. 4. Educational psychology* (pp. 487–510). Hoboken, NJ: Wiley.

Perleth, C., Schatz, T., & Mönks, F. J. (2000). Early identification of high ability. In K. A. Heller, F. J. Mönks, R. J. Sternberg, & R. F. Subotnik (Eds.), *International handbook of giftedness and talent* (2nd ed., pp. 283–316). Oxford, England: Elsevier Science.

Robinson, N. M. (2000). Giftedness in very young children: How seriously should it be taken? In R. C. Friedman & B. M. Shore (Eds.), *Talents unfolding: Cognition and development* (pp. 7–26). Washington, DC: American Psychological Association.

Shapiro, B. K., Palmer, F. B., Antell, S. E., Bilder, S., Ross, A., & Capute, A. J. (1989). Giftedness: Can it be predicted in infancy? *Clinical Pediatrics, 28,* 205–209.

Sontag, L. W., Baker, C. T., & Nelson, V. L. (1958). Mental growth and personality development: A longitudinal study. *Monographs of the Society for Research in Child Development, 23* (Whole No. 68).

Subotnik, R. F., & Olszewski-Kubilius, P. (1997). Restructuring special programs to reflect the distinctions between children's and adults' experiences with giftedness. *Peabody Journal of Education, 72*(3 & 4), 101–116.

Subotnik, R. F., Olszewski-Kubilius, P., & Arnold, K. (2003). Beyond Bloom: Revisiting environmental factors that enhance or impede talent development. In J. H. Borland (Ed.), *Rethinking gifted education* (pp. 227–238). New York: Teachers College Press.

Thorndike, R. L. (1940). "Constancy" of the IQ. *Psychological Bulletin, 37,* 167–186.

Wilson, R. S. (1983). The Louisville Twin Study: Developmental synchronies in behavior. *Child Development, 54,* 198–216.

II
CHILDHOOD

4

GIFTEDNESS DURING CHILDHOOD: THE SPATIAL–GRAPHIC DOMAIN

LYNN S. LIBEN

The study of development is often directed toward describing and explaining normative development. But just as one would be misguided if one were to focus on the development of the fractional person in the average-sized American family, so, too, one would be misguided if one were to limit one's study of development to the normative child. Although my own research program was not intentionally designed to study gifted and talented developmental processes or outcomes, it nevertheless offers some relevant data and perhaps insights. The work discussed here concerns children's developing competencies in understanding and producing spatial–graphic representations. These may be defined as stand-for symbols (the representational aspect) that involve marks of some kind (the graphic aspect), whose representational components are distributed over the surface in a way that corresponds to the distribution of components of the referent (the spatial aspect).

I have chosen the area of spatial–graphic representations as the focus of this chapter for several reasons. First, spatial–graphic representations are used in a wide range of academic subjects (e.g., social studies, chemistry, biology,

Portions of the research described here were funded by the National Science Foundation (ESI 01-01758), the National Institute of Education (G-83-0025), and the National Geographic Society, although the opinions expressed here are the author's and no endorsement by these agencies should be inferred.

earth science, economics), in a wide range of occupations (e.g., construction, architecture, engineering, meteorology, epidemiology, geology), and in a wide range of daily tasks (e.g., navigating with a map, assembling toys or furniture, understanding news and weather reports). Second, it is an area in which I have worked for many years, enabling me to draw examples from a diverse group of research projects including those on (a) how children come to understand, produce, and use cartographic maps and other spatial–graphic representations of environmental space; (b) children's participation and success on a related academic competition, the National Geographic Bee; and (c) children's developing appreciation of and ability to control the spatial and aesthetic qualities of photographs. Third, the aesthetic component of the photography research concerns the visual arts, an arena often associated with creativity and giftedness. My hope is that the general acceptance of the idea that there is giftedness in the visual arts will generalize to acceptance of my argument that there is giftedness in spatial thinking more generally. Thus, a final reason for selecting the spatial–graphic domain is that it is an arena commonly accepted as relevant to the volume's focus on gifted and talented students.

The remainder of this chapter is organized as follows. First, I expand on what I mean by spatial–graphic representations (in the section entitled "Defining Spatial–Graphic Representations"). Second, I sample from work that my colleagues and I have conducted to study children's developing spatial–graphic competencies. In doing so, I highlight performance that might well be classified as gifted ("Illustrative Empirical Work"). Finally, I offer some speculations about implications this work has for research, public policy, and education ("Implications for Research and Practice").

DEFINING SPATIAL–GRAPHIC REPRESENTATIONS

There has been considerable discussion of the qualities of spatial–graphic representations and the ways in which there are important developmental progressions in how people understand and produce them (e.g., Gattis, 2001; Liben, 1999; Rochat & Callaghan, 2005; Troseth, Pierroutsakos, & DeLoache, 2004). Particularly central is the argument that spatial–graphic representations are representations, not re-presentations of the referents they symbolize (see also Liben & Downs, 1992). That is, representations do not simply provide some veridical, flattened, scaled-down version of the referent. An excellent discussion of this issue in relation to art is provided by Nelson Goodman in *Languages of Art* (1976), perhaps best summarized by the introductory quote he uses in the book, attributed to Virginia Woolf: "Art is not a copy of the real world. One of the damn things is enough" (p. 3). The same is true for maps, which—contrary to many people's beliefs—are not simply depictions of the world as it is, but rather are creative visions about it (e.g., see Downs, 1981,

1985; Liben & Downs, 1989; MacEachren, 1995). Just as in art there is no one correct way to paint a bowl of fruit, so, too, there is no one correct way to map a city or continent. The cartographic product depends first and foremost on the purpose of the map. The purpose affects what information is depicted, at what scale and orientation, with what symbol and categorization systems, at what level of generalization, and so on (Liben, 2001). The same is true for photography. Again, although many people think that photographs simply capture the world in some raw, veridical way, photographs are symbolic representations, the product of a host of decisions about vantage point, lens, film, exposure time, printing process, paper, and so on (Beilin, 1991; Liben, 2003, 2008). Photographs serve archival functions (as in recording newsworthy or personal events), but they also serve to communicate emotions, to provide aesthetically pleasing images, and to foster psychological insights about self and others (Liben, 2003; Liben & Szechter, 2002).

The recognition that various spatial–graphic representations do more than identify a referent leads to the second major point that understanding spatial–graphic representations involves more than simply identifying the referent of the representation. As explained in more detail elsewhere (see Liben, 1999, 2006a), children must gradually come to (a) understand representations' simultaneous existence as objects in their own right (e.g., as pieces of paper) as well as symbols that stand for something else, (b) differentiate between which qualities of the representational object carry representational meaning and which are simply by-products of the objects' existence (e.g., the placement of the cat's ears, whiskers, body, and tail versus the flatness of the paper), (c) learn what conventions are involved in any particular representational medium (e.g., that a compass rose is a graphic symbol used to indicate north on a map), and (d) appreciate the communicative power achieved by using different representational media or by different qualities within a particular medium.

My empirical work on spatial–graphic representations has focused on two broad areas. One area concerns children's understanding of various kinds of graphic representations of place (e.g., maps, photographs, computer-generated drawings of large environments) and their role in map-intense disciplines (e.g., geography, geology). The second concerns children's appreciation of the way that vantage points may be varied to achieve different photographic outcomes, including variations not only with respect to depicted referential content but also with respect to the expressive value of the photograph.

ILLUSTRATIVE EMPIRICAL WORK

In this section I provide some sense of the diversity of the domain under investigation. What are some illustrations of spatial–graphic representations, and what might one do with them? Three of the research programs mentioned earlier are relevant: mapping, the National Geographic Bee, and photography. Here I focus primarily on the first and touch only briefly on the second and third. I begin by presenting the theoretical foundations of the mapping work and then describe a few sample tasks. In addition to characterizing performance at the group level, I suggest that the performance of particular children might be characterized as *gifted*. I then illustrate the power and contribution of gifted spatial thinking more broadly.

Research on Environmental Representations

The research on children's understanding of environmental representations that I discuss comes primarily from collaborative work with Roger Downs, a geographer at Penn State. We have used a variety of media (including cartographic maps, aerial photographs, scale models, and satellite imagery); here I focus exclusively on line-drawn maps of visible or well-known environments, such as classrooms, college campuses, or small geographic areas such as cities or neighborhoods.

Our work has addressed three components of map understanding: (a) representational or symbolic issues, such as understanding that the color of a symbol does not necessarily specify the color of the referent; (b) spatial issues, such as understanding how to decode paper space to referent space under differing map scales and projections; and (c) logical issues, such as understanding inclusion relations such that being located in a city simultaneously means being located in a county, state, region, country, and continent. Here I focus primarily on spatial issues.

The Spatial Structure of Maps and Map Users

To organize the spatial structure of maps, we have used the "cartographic eye" (Downs, 1981), which specifies three map qualities. One is *viewing distance* or *scale*, which is the ratio between the size of the environmental space and representational space; the second is *viewing azimuth*, which is the direction from which the referent space is depicted (e.g., whether it is north or east at the top of the page); and the third is *viewing angle*, which refers to the slant from which the referent space is seen (e.g., whether it is a 90° overhead angle, creating a *plan view* map, or at a 45° angle, creating an *oblique perspective* map).

To organize the spatial concepts of the map user, we have used the three categories of spatial concepts identified by Piaget and Inhelder (1956). These are *topological concepts*, said to emerge during the preschool years, and *projective* and *Euclidean concepts*, said to emerge together during the early elementary school years and to develop during middle childhood. Topological concepts concern spatial relations that are preserved even with changes in distance and angular metrics (as in the concepts of *next to* or *on*); projective concepts are those that depend on point of view (as in understanding that an object to your right is to my left when we face one another); and Euclidean concepts are those that depend on establishing a stable reference system that thus allows for metric measurement and conservation of distance and angle.

Illustrative Tasks

Many of the tasks we have used are *location* tasks in which children are shown target locations in a space and are asked to indicate the analogous locations on a map, typically by placing stickers on it. The target locations have been defined by objects in a room (Liben & Downs, 1986; Liben & Yekel, 1996), by flags planted on a model landscape or on a college campus (Liben & Downs, 1989), by a person standing at particular spots in a room (Liben & Downs, 1993), or by areas marked on environmental representations such as circled areas of an aerial photograph of a city (Liben & Downs, 1991).

Within a given location task, items may be expected to be more or less difficult insofar as different target locations draw differentially on various spatial concepts. When a target location is, say, *on* or *next to* an easily identified map symbol, the location task requires simply that the child find the correct symbol and understand the topological relation of *on* or *next to*. When the target location is in an undifferentiated area (e.g., a large open area of a floor or college campus), the task requires that the child in some way draw on Euclidean or metric concepts; for example, the child may have to estimate the distances along two axes in the room (the walls) and scale these down proportionately for the map (the two lines depicting those walls).

Spatial concepts may be relevant even for identifying individual symbols. For example, when a round art table is symbolized by an iconic symbol such as paintbrushes, the child may identify the referent without invoking spatial concepts. When, however, the art table is symbolized by a circle (a plan view of the table), the child would need to draw on projective concepts to understand why the symbol is a perfect circle whereas in the real room the child sees an elliptical surface and four legs. Furthermore, if the map has more than one circular symbol, the child needs to draw on spatial concepts to disambiguate which circle stands for which round referent (see Liben & Yekel, 1996).

Also affecting the extent of the spatial challenge is whether the map and space are aligned. When they are not aligned, projective spatial concepts are needed to identify corresponding locations in the space and on the map. For example, in a map of a classroom that is aligned with the space, an object that appears to the child in the upper left corner of the classroom should be marked in the upper left corner on the map. If, however, the map is rotated 180°, that same object should be marked at the lower right corner of the map. In some of the tasks we have used, alignment is explicitly ensured (e.g., maps are placed and held on children's desks in an aligned orientation), whereas in others, alignment is explicitly prevented (maps are fixed at a 180° rotation). In still other cases, alignment is at the discretion of the child, sometimes without any explicit discussion about alignment at all, and sometimes with initial alignment of the map and space but thereafter allowing the child to move the map at will.

We have also used *direction* tasks in which participants are given directional stickers to indicate orientation. For example, in one task discussed later, children were asked to place arrow stickers on a classroom map to show where someone was standing and in which direction he was pointing (Liben & Downs, 1993). We have also used *self-map-space* tasks that ask children to relate what is seen from a particular vantage point in an environment to a map. Illustrative are tasks in which children are shown eye-level views of a space (e.g., an eye-level photograph taken in a room or on a campus) and are asked to place arrow stickers on a map to show where the photographer was standing and in which direction the camera was pointing.

Illustrative Data

To get a more specific sense of the tasks and data, consider an illustration from the classroom location and direction task given to children in kindergarten, first, second, and fifth and sixth grades (Liben & Downs, 1993). In this task, Roger Downs went to various locations in the child's classroom, oriented himself in a particular direction, and pointed straight ahead. Children were asked to place arrows on a classroom map to show each location and pointing direction.

After they completed six items while the map was aligned with the room, children were given a new map and asked to do the same thing, but this time the map on the child's desk had been rotated 180°. The data may be summarized relatively easily: The mean number of correct responses increased with age, and performance peaked sooner in the aligned condition than in the unaligned condition. The particular patterns of item difficulty and age-linked performance were consistent with the theoretical progressions of spatial concepts suggested by Piaget and Inhelder (1956): Items that allow the definition of location by topological concepts elicited better performance; the unaligned condition (that draws on projective concepts) was mastered later.

But what is more important for the present context is the finding that on this task—as well as on any of the others I could have selected—a few children perform dramatically differently from their peers. Consider the percentages of children at each grade who obtain each score on the location task (i.e., zero correct, one correct, etc., up to the maximum of six correct) shown in Figure 4.1. What is remarkable are the few kindergarten children who are performing perfectly or nearly perfectly even in the unaligned condition, a task in which the modal performance for their classmates is zero correct responses.

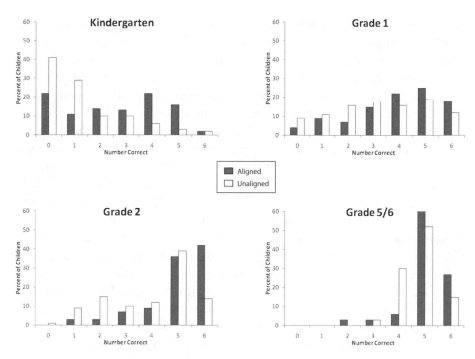

Figure 4.1. Distributions (% of students), within grade, of the number of stickers (six maximum) placed correctly on classroom maps to indicate an adult's location in the room under aligned and unaligned map conditions. Grade 5/6 indicates a mixed fifth- and sixth-grade class.

A second example comes from a model flag-location task (Liben & Downs, 1991). In this task, first- and second-grade children were shown a three-dimensional, desktop model of the local terrain on which had been placed small colored flags at various locations. Children were asked to place colored stickers on a contour map to show the location of the flags. The pattern of data concerning which locations were easier and harder was, in general, consistent with the notion that young children perform better on items that can be solved using topological concepts (i.e., those that can be linked to identifiable landmarks) than on items that draw on Euclidean or metric concepts (i.e., those that are located in some undifferentiated region, thus requiring some kind of measurement in relation to some framework such as coordinate axes). Again, what is really most interesting for the present context are data from individual children. If one looks at the number of correct responses among the first- and second-grade children given this task, apart from predicted item and age differences, what is again remarkable is that even when the modal response for a given age group was zero correct, a few children placed every single sticker correctly.

However, it is not simply the quantitative data on the number of correct responses that argue for giftedness. An even more dramatic demonstration comes from what happened in one first-grade class when we explained the contour maps before the children performed the task. To introduce these maps, I held a three-tiered clay model on the palm of my hand and discussed each of the three layers of the clay mountain with respect to "inches above hand level." I then took the model apart and drew circles on an overhead transparency for each elevation, which resulted in three concentric circles, representing, respectively, the parts of the "mountain" that were 1, 2, and 3 inches above hand level. I then went to a slightly more complex Styrofoam model with additional layers, showing what happened to the contour map when the mountain was steeper or shallower (lines are closer together or farther apart), then to a slightly more complex model of a mountain with two peaks. We then showed an overhead of the contour map that we used in the flag-location task and, almost as a rhetorical question, pointed to an area of the map and asked, "So what is this?" Without hesitation, one first-grade girl raised her hand and correctly answered "Mt. Nittany." We then pointed to another section and asked, "So what is this?" and again, she answered instantly and correctly, "Bald Eagle." We asked if she had seen these maps before, and she said no. Even adults who are experienced with contour maps find it difficult to interpret them so readily.

Throughout our work, we have seen other kinds of outstanding performance. For example, in one task, children were asked to draw a map of their own classroom. Within a single first-grade classroom, children produced maps ranging from those showing a single wall in elevation (straight ahead) view to maps in oblique perspective (e.g., from roughly a 45° angle), to mixed elevation and plan views (i.e., maps containing unsystematic mixtures of elevation and plan components), to plan maps that were almost as accurate as the ones that we had prepared ourselves for other classroom mapping tasks. A sample of the range of drawings is found in Figure 4.2.

Similar variation was evident among first- and second-grade children when they were asked to draw how their school would look to a bird, flying overhead, looking straight down or to draw a map of Chicago based on an aerial photograph of the city (illustrative responses may be found in Liben & Downs, 1991, 1994). What these data reveal is that even as many children are producing only generic place drawings with no apparent understanding of overhead views, others are producing highly specific, scaled, vertical perspective representations.

Before discussing some of the implications of this work, I turn very briefly to the other two lines of research that also demonstrate high levels of performance in related arenas.

The National Geographic Bee

A second line of research concerns children's performance on a geography bee established about 20 years ago by the National Geographic Society

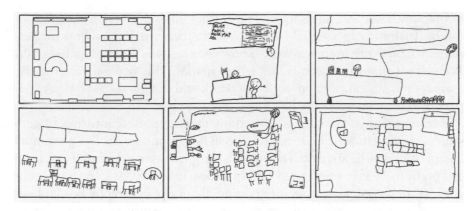

Figure 4.2. Five illustrative classroom maps drawn by first-grade children. One (bottom right) is qualitatively different from his classmates' maps and is remarkably similar to the classroom map drawn by the investigator (top left). From "Fostering Geographic Literacy From Early Childhood: The Contributions of Interdisciplinary Research," by L. S. Liben and R. M. Downs, 1994, *Journal of Applied Developmental Psychology, 15,* pp. 559–562. Copyright 1994 by Elsevier. Reprinted with permission.

(NGS). Each year, millions of fourth- through eighth-grade children compete in their schools, with questions and competition procedures established by NGS. Each school winner takes a written 70-item test supplied and graded by NGS, and up to 100 of the highest-scoring students in each of 55 state-level units (the 50 states, District of Columbia, Department of Defense, and the U.S. territories) are invited to compete in a state-level bee. The winners from each unit are invited to Washington, DC, to compete in preliminary rounds, which yield 10 students for the final round of the bee, moderated by Alex Trebek and broadcast on national television.

My own involvement in the NGS Bee was motivated by the fact that it relates to two of my research interests: one already obvious from the work I have discussed so far—mapping and geography—and the other, gender. The NGS Bee is of interest from the perspective of gender because in any given year, only a few of the state-level winners are girls. Roger Downs and I have conducted research designed to identify correlates of success and to determine whether these differ for boys and girls (see Downs & Liben, 1992; Liben, 2002).

A few key points are relevant here. First, the level of geographic knowledge in some children—even some fourth graders—is simply astounding. Some children answer every written question correctly; the finalists who appear on national television awe their audiences with their seemingly limitless and detailed knowledge. Second, most of the highly successful children pursue this topic with a true passion. Some are passionate about information, in general, and show similarly outstanding performance on other national competitions, but some are passionate about geography in particular. Both self-reports and parent-reports commonly point out these children's early love of maps, atlases, and navigation. Third, from among a very wide range of intellectual and experiential assessments, the best single predictor for performance on the written geography knowledge test was a test of spatial skills. We suspect that the reason is that better spatial skills make it easier to use maps for navigation (e.g., on family car trips), and that map-navigation experience, in turn, increases the likelihood that the child will also consult atlases and other graphic spatial representations that support acquisition of geographic information. Thus, in part, the male advantage on the geography competition can be attributed to a male advantage on spatial skills (e.g., Linn & Petersen, 1985) as well as to other factors (Liben, 2002). In the present context, however, what is most important about the geography bee findings is not the gender difference but rather what participants' performance indicates about gifted geographic thinking. The data from the Bee show that some children master the subject matter of geography very early and very deeply, and that perhaps "geographically gifted children" should be thought about just as, for example, mathematically gifted children are thought about.

Appreciating Spatial and Aesthetic Qualities of Photographs

The third line of research concerns children's developing understanding and control of the spatial and aesthetic qualities of photographs (Liben, 2003, 2006a, 2008; Liben & Szechter, 2002, 2007; Szechter & Liben, 2007). One component of our work explores what kinds of photographs children and adults like, the reasons they have for their preferences, and whether their preferences and explanations change as a function of photography experience. Most relevant here, however, is the work that we have done concerning children's understanding and exploitation of spatial qualities of photographs.

Illustrative is a study in which 8- to 10-year-old children and college students were taken on a walk around campus and asked to take various digital photographs. As participants approached a statue of a mountain lion, they were asked to photograph it so that it would "look kind of scary." One strategy we had anticipated was the use of close-up views. To assess participants' use of this strategy, we printed all photographs at a fixed size (1.50 inches × 2 inches) and then circled and measured the lion's head. In general, these data showed that adults took their photographs far closer to the statue (average head diameters were 0.37 inch and 0.82 inch for children and adults, respectively). These averages, however, again hide some striking variations: A few children used extreme close-up views and, in fact, the single largest lion's head was found in a photograph taken by a child rather than an adult. Examination of the photographs also revealed systematic age-linked variations in viewing angle and viewing azimuth. As a group, adults were more likely to aim directly at the lion's head, but only a few children used noncanonical angles or azimuths for expressive effect. Thus, many adults—but only a few particularly gifted children—appeared to appreciate that even if they had no control of the referent they were photographing, they could nevertheless manipulate the affective tone of their photograph by controlling the vantage point of the camera. Figure 4.3 provides examples of "scary lions" photographs produced by two children, one of whom is prototypical and the other of whom might reasonably be called gifted.

Empirical Evidence of Spatial Giftedness

The three research programs I have sampled from concern substantively diverse domains. Yet, conceptually they share the relevance of spatial thinking; empirically, they share the conclusion that even as there are age-group differences consistent with theories of spatial development, there are individual children who show atypically skilled performance. What should we make of these children? Are they simply precocious? Or are they "off the scale" not simply with respect to rate of development, but perhaps also with respect to the quality of their thought? To address the question of whether there are individuals who are atypically skilled, it may be useful to consider whether there is evidence of spatial giftedness in adults. A National Research Council (NRC; 2006) report titled *Learning to Think Spatially* contains many examples of what might well be called gifted spatial thinking in adults. For example, the executive summary of the report begins by citing Watson and Crick's (1953) well-known double helix model of DNA as an illustration of creative spatial thinking.

Figure 4.3. Photographs taken by 9-year-old children in response to the interviewer's request to make the lion look scary. The one on the left is prototypical of children's photographs; the one on the right is atypical, using a noncanonical viewing distance, angle, and azimuth to influence the affective tone of the photograph. From "Beyond Point and Shoot: Children's Developing Understanding of Photographs as Spatial and Expressive Representations," by L. S. Liben. *In Advances in Child Development and Behavior* (Vol. 31, p. 25), by R. V. Kail, 2004, San Diego, CA: Academic Press. Copyright 2004 by Elsevier. Reprinted with permission.

The three-dimensional structure is complex—two parallel but displaced spiraling chains; simple—the base bonds hold it together and fix angular distances; and beautiful—its elegance and explanatory power. It is the result of a brilliant exercise of imaginative visualization that is constrained by empirical data, expressed by two-dimensional images, and guided by deep scientific knowledge and incisive spatial intuition. (NRC, 2006, p. 3)

A second example from the NRC report linked to the map domain is the classic work of John Snow, a medical health officer who was attempting to understand the etiology of cholera deaths in London during the mid-1800s. By mapping cholera deaths on a map of London that included the locations of water pumps, he inferred that the disease spread through water. His recommendation that the handles be removed from certain water pumps led to a drastic reduction in the number of new cases of cholera. The NRC report documents dozens of other dramatic examples of creative spatial thinking from disciplines as varied as astronomy, chemistry, geology, meteorology, and geography.

IMPLICATIONS FOR RESEARCH AND PRACTICE

The work I have reviewed leads me to the general plea that far more explicit attention be paid to gifted spatial thinking in research, in educational systems, and in society. I am not, of course, unique in suggesting that there are spatial gifts. Spatial abilities have long been a component of intelligence tests (e.g., Guilford, 1967; Thurstone, 1938), spatial intelligence is included among Gardner's (1983) multiple intelligences, and spatial gifts are often recognized in artistically gifted children (Winner, 1996). But spatial thinking is not afforded the level of attention given to other cognitive domains in the American educational system, a conclusion also reached by Gohm, Humphreys, and Yao (1998) and by Shea, Lubinski, and Benbow (2001) from observing the record of achievement among spatially gifted students.

As one index of this difference, consider how rarely spatial skills are used as an admissions criterion in programs for gifted students. It is interesting that even in a noteworthy exception—the Johns Hopkins University Center for Talented Youth (CTY)—the test battery used to identify spatially gifted children is "homegrown." In other words, the spatial admissions test is one developed and administered through CTY and thus differs strikingly from the mechanism CTY uses to judge verbal or mathematical talent, which relies on virtually universally available standardized test scores (see Liben, 2006b).

As might be inferred from the CTY example, there has been no national movement to attempt to identify children with unusual spatial abilities, nor to measure the attainment of spatial concepts and skills comparable to tests of language and mathematical achievement. Although routine assessments undoubtedly have many negative consequences, they can also add value to a domain, a point captured by the well-known adage, "we assess what we value and we value what we assess." My argument is that increased assessment of spatial skills and concepts would be likely to foster increased attention to spatial education for all children (see Liben, 2006b; NRC, 2006) and, even more relevant for the present discussion, would be likely to enhance the rate of identifying spatially gifted children.

Research is needed to find ways to measure gifted spatial thinking in both childhood and adulthood. Such techniques are needed to allow the field to address the important but as yet unexplored question of whether there is developmental continuity in spatial giftedness. For example, are the kindergarten and first-grade children such as those who are so precocious in our mapping tasks poised to develop into Watsons, Cricks, and Snows discussed in the NRC (2006) report? Are they being offered an educational context that fosters these creative outcomes or that stifles spatial creativity and thus deprives society of potentially important, creative, spatial insights in a variety of disciplines? As Ellen Winner (1996) argued in discussions of giftedness in other arenas, "We cannot assume a link between early giftedness, no matter how extreme, and adult eminence. The factors that predict the course of a life are multiple and interacting" (p. 11). What is needed is longitudinal research to study trajectories of spatial giftedness and development, ideally in contexts that would appear to promote spatial thinking as well as in those that do not (e.g., variations in parental spatial scaffolding behaviors; see Szechter & Liben, 2004).

But the goal of increasing attention to spatially gifted children (and to spatial education more generally) will require more than increased attention to the spatial domain within developmental psychology and education. It also requires attention to the domain itself, in two major ways.

First, the spatial domain needs more coherence. Ellen Winner (1996) set the context for this point well in her book *Gifted Children* by suggesting that "the more formal and rule-governed the domain, the more likely it is to yield gifted children. Mathematics and classical music, in which it is clear what needs to be mastered and how excellence can be recognized, are prototypical examples" (p. 5). She continued: "We rarely notice gifted children in diffuse areas like leadership, interpersonal understanding, or self-awareness. But this does not mean they do not exist; we just do not know how to find them" (pp. 5–6). There are, of course, formalisms and rules within specific spatial systems such as Euclidean geometry. What the spatial domain needs, however, is a more comprehensive approach that can integrate the domain more fully. The NRC (2006) report includes efforts in this direction, but it is far from achieving a "grammar of space" or of spatial thinking. Thus, even as developmental psychologists pursue research on spatially gifted children, spatial thinking, and spatial education, it will be important for those who may be called *spatial scientists* to continue to formalize basic building blocks and rules of the domain.

Second, the spatial domain needs more respect. There is a tendency, at least in Western culture, to view image-based representations as somehow less valuable and advanced than other kinds of representations (e.g., linguistic or numerical). Support for this statement may be seen in the absence of required spatial curriculum or achievement levels (i.e., there are neither required courses nor assessments in the spatial domain to parallel those in the verbal and mathematical domains), and in the tendency to respond to tight budgets by cutting art education, one domain that includes at least some explicit education about spatial–graphic representation. Societies need to value domains if they are to support educational programs for all children and if they are to recognize and treasure the resources offered by children who are gifted in that domain (Feldman, 1980; Winner, 1996). Perhaps public awareness of the increasing sophistication and utility of spatial thinking, imagery, and analyses in new technologies (e.g., geographic information systems, satellite imagery, computer-assisted tomography) will indeed lead society to endorse the pronouncement by the late geographer, Peter Gould (1999), that we have arrived at "the Spatial Century" (p. 313).

REFERENCES

Beilin, H. (1991). Developmental aesthetics and the psychology of photography. In R. M. Downs, L. S. Liben, & D. S. Palermo (Eds.), *Visions of aesthetics, the environment, and development: The legacy of Joachim F. Wohlwill* (pp. 45–86). Hillsdale, NJ: Erlbaum.

Downs, R. M. (1981). Maps and mappings as metaphors for spatial representation. In L. S. Liben, A. H. Patterson, & N. Newcombe (Eds.), *Spatial representation and behavior across the life span: Theory and application* (pp. 143–166). New York: Academic Press.

Downs, R. M. (1985). The representation of space: Its development in children and in cartography. In R. Cohen (Ed.), *The development of spatial cognition* (pp. 323–345). Hillsdale, NJ: Erlbaum.

Downs, R. M., & Liben, L. S. (1992). Geography and gender. *Bee Line, 3*.

Feldman, D. H. (1980). *Beyond universals in cognitive development.* Norwood, NJ: Ablex Publishing.

Gardner, H. (1983). *Frames of mind: The theory of multiple intelligences.* New York: Basic Books.

Gattis, M. (Ed.). (2001). *Spatial schemas and abstract thought.* Cambridge, MA: MIT Press.

Gohm, C. L., Humphreys, L. G., & Yao, G. (1998). Underachievement among spatially gifted children. *American Educational Research Journal, 35*, 515–531.

Goodman, N. (1976). *Languages of art*. Indianapolis, IN: Hackett Press.

Gould, P. (1999). *Becoming a geographer*. Syracuse, NY: Syracuse University Press.

Guilford, J. P. (1967). *The nature of human intelligence*. New York: McGraw-Hill.

Liben, L. S. (1999). Developing an understanding of external spatial representations. In I. E. Sigel (Ed.), *Development of mental representation: Theories and applications* (pp. 297–321). Mahwah, NJ: Erlbaum.

Liben, L. S. (2001). Thinking through maps. In M. Gattis (Ed.), *Spatial schemas and abstract thought* (pp. 44–77). Cambridge, MA: MIT Press.

Liben, L. S. (2002). The drama of sex differences in academic achievement: And the show goes on. *Issues in Education, 8*, 65–75.

Liben, L. S. (2003). Beyond point and shoot: Children's developing understanding of photographs as spatial and expressive representations. In R. V. Kail (Ed.), *Advances in child development and behavior* (Vol. 31, pp. 1–42). San Diego, CA: Elsevier.

Liben, L. S. (2006a). Appreciating the meaning and aesthetics of spatial graphic representations during childhood. In L. Balter & C. Tamis-LaMonda (Eds.), *Child psychology: A handbook of contemporary issues* (pp. 263–292). New York: Psychology Press.

Liben, L. S. (2006b). Education for spatial thinking. In W. Damon & R. Lerner (Series Eds.) and K. A. Renninger & I. E. Sigel (Vol. Eds.), *Handbook of child psychology: Vol. 4. Child psychology in practice* (6th ed., pp. 197–247). Hoboken, NJ: Wiley.

Liben, L. S. (2008). Children's developing appreciation of photography as an artistic medium of representation. In C. Milbrath & H. M. Trautner (Eds.), *Children's understanding and production of pictures, drawing, and art: Theoretical and empirical approaches* (pp. 155–184). Cambridge, MA: Hogrefe & Huber.

Liben, L. S., & Downs, R. M. (1986). *Children's production and comprehension of maps: Increasing graphic literacy* (Final report to National Institute of Education No. G-83-0025). University Park: The Pennsylvania State University.

Liben, L. S., & Downs, R. M. (1989). Understanding maps as symbols: The development of map concepts in children. In H. W. Reese (Ed.), *Advances in child development and behavior* (Vol. 22, pp. 145–201). New York: Academic Press.

Liben, L. S., & Downs, R. M. (1991). The role of graphic representations in understanding the world. In R. M. Downs, L. S. Liben, & D. S. Palermo (Eds.), *Visions of aesthetics, the environment, and development: The legacy of Joachim Wohlwill* (pp. 139–180). Hillsdale, NJ: Erlbaum.

Liben, L. S., & Downs, R. M. (1992). Developing an understanding of graphic representations in children and adults: The case of GEO-graphics. *Cognitive Development, 7*, 331–349.

Liben, L. S., & Downs, R. M. (1993). Understanding person-space-map relations: Cartographic and developmental perspectives. *Developmental Psychology, 29*, 739–752.

Liben, L. S., & Downs, R. M. (1994). Fostering geographic literacy from early childhood: The contributions of interdisciplinary research. *Journal of Applied Developmental Psychology, 15,* 549–569.

Liben, L. S., & Szechter, L. S. (2002). A social science of the arts: An emerging organizational initiative and an illustrative investigation of photography. *Qualitative Sociology, 25,* 385–408.

Liben, L. S., & Szechter, L. E. (2007). Children's photographic eyes: A view from developmental psychology. *Visual Arts Research, 33,* 71–83.

Liben, L. S., & Yekel, C. A. (1996). Preschoolers' understanding of plan and oblique maps: The role of geometric and representational correspondence. *Child Development, 67,* 2780–2796.

Linn, M. C., & Petersen, A. C. (1985). Emergence and characterization of sex differences in spatial ability: A meta-analysis. *Child Development, 56,* 1479–1498.

MacEachren, A. M. (1995). *How maps work.* New York: Guilford Press.

National Research Council. (2006). *Learning to think spatially: GIS as a support system in the K-12 curriculum.* Washington, DC: National Academy Press.

Piaget, J., & Inhelder, B. (1956). *The child's conception of space.* New York: Norton.

Rochat, P., & Callaghan, T. (2005). What drives symbolic development? In L. Namy (Ed.), *Symbol use and symbolic representation* (pp. 25–46). Mahwah, NJ: Erlbaum.

Shea, D. L., Lubinski, D., & Benbow, C. P. (2001). Importance of assessing spatial ability in intellectually talented young adolescents: A 20-year longitudinal study. *Journal of Educational Psychology, 93,* 604–614.

Szechter, L. E., & Liben, L. S. (2004). Parental guidance in preschoolers' understanding of spatial-graphic representations. *Child Development, 75,* 869–885.

Szechter, L. E., & Liben, L. S. (2007). Children's aesthetic understanding of photographic art and the quality of art-related parent-child interactions. *Child Development, 78,* 879–894.

Thurstone, L. L. (1938). Primary mental abilities. *Psychometric Monographs, 1.*

Troseth, G. L., Pierroutsakos, S. L., & DeLoache, J. S. (2004). From the innocent to the intelligent eye: The early development of pictorial competence. In R. Kail (Ed.), *Advances in child development and behavior* (Vol. 32, pp. 1–35). San Diego, CA: Elsevier.

Watson, J. D., & Crick, F. H. C. (1953, April 25). Molecular structure of nucleic acids: A structure for deoxyribose nucleic acid. *Nature, 171,* 737–738.

Winner, E. (1996). *Gifted children: Myths and realities.* New York: Basic Books.

5

TOWARD BROADENING OUR UNDERSTANDING OF GIFTEDNESS: THE SPATIAL DOMAIN

ELLEN WINNER

Lynn Liben raises three broad, thought-provoking issues in her chapter on giftedness in the spatial–graphic domain (see chap. 4, this volume). First is the role of the study of giftedness in developmental psychology and the question of why giftedness is such a neglected area of study within psychology. Second, she prods readers to consider just how one should undertake the study of spatial giftedness, which is itself a much neglected domain of study within the area of giftedness relative to the study of mathematical and verbal giftedness. And finally, she leads readers to recognize what can be learned from the study of spatial–graphic giftedness.

WHY STUDY SPATIAL GIFTEDNESS ANYWAY?

There is no major arena of human ability, whether cognitive or social, in which there is not a wide range of capacities, spanning both a high and a low end. However, the age at which signs of giftedness emerge, the forms they take, and what they predict vary by area of ability (Winner, 1996). Children who are verbally gifted often learn to read near-effortlessly by the age of 3 years; those gifted mathematically are fascinated by patterns and numbers from the age of 2 and spend their childhoods tinkering with gadgets; those gifted in music have an intense emotional reaction to music, a strong musical memory, are able to sing in accurate intervals at an early age, and can pick out tunes on a piano, if one is available; and those gifted in drawing have strong visual memories and are able to draw fairly realistically beginning at age 2 or 3, a feat typical children do not begin to achieve until middle childhood, if at all (Bloom, 1985; Winner, 1996). Liben has written about the domain of spatial thinking and has noted how here too one finds striking gradations of ability, with some children and adults clearly at the high end.

Any theory of development must be able to account for individual differences, and thus it must be able to account for giftedness, because giftedness is by definition an extreme individual difference. By the same argument, any theory of development must be able to account for deficiencies in development—areas in which abilities develop in deviant and suboptimal ways. The study of both giftedness and deficits in the spatial arena can inform an understanding of spatial ability. A full understanding of spatial ability would include an understanding of its typical manifestations, its atypical manifestations on either end of the spectrum, and the conditions (whether biological or environmental) that lead to its atypical manifestations.

Although theories of development ought to be able to account for giftedness, the study of giftedness has never formed part of mainstream psychology. There are several plausible explanations for this. Psychology has typically focused more on universals than on individual differences and the atypical. Because giftedness is an atypical state, its study has not become mainstream. In addition, until the emergence of "positive psychology" (Seligman, 2003), there has been a bias in psychology toward the study of deficiencies rather than strengths. Because of society's strong interest in remediation, there has been more emphasis on the study of retardation and learning disabilities than on the study of giftedness and high achievement. The interest that the educational system shows in remediation is not balanced by a parallel interest in fostering giftedness.

Of course, one need not be a developmentalist to study giftedness. One can study high ability at its end state, without examining its development. After all, much of cognitive psychology looks at end states and does not venture into development. But most studies of giftedness have been developmental, probably because signs of giftedness typically appear in childhood (although some gifted individuals do not discover their gifts until adulthood). Cognitive psychologists are fascinated with the question of prediction and explanation. They want to know what early signs of giftedness predict: Will this child become an expert in the area in which she shows giftedness, will she become an adult creator in this area, or will she lose interest and turn to other pursuits? And are those early signs that might predict adult giftedness accurate? Psychology attempts to explain adult giftedness by searching back to childhood to find its origins and its predictor variables in terms of both the individual (what early forms this giftedness took) and the environment (what factors stimulated these early forms to develop).

Much can be learned from taking a developmental approach to the study of giftedness. Consider the following three examples.

Domain Specificity?

One can test whether development is domain specific or general. To the extent that one finds high abilities developing in domain X but not Y, the conclusion is that development is domain specific. There is in fact some evidence for domain-specific development that comes from the study of gifted people. Subtest scores of adults with high IQs correlated less strongly than did the scores of those with ordinary IQs (Detterman & Daniel, 1989). The cognitive profiles of academically gifted children are often uneven with respect to levels of mathematical and verbal ability (Benbow & Minor, 1990). Research is needed to determine how common such uneven profiles among gifted individuals are, and how common it is to have gifts accompanied by absolute rather than relative weaknesses.

Uneven profiles also are characteristic of individuals gifted in music or art. Although impossible to verify, it is intriguing that Simonton (1999) noted that Beethoven had almost no mathematical ability and was not particularly strong verbally either; Csikszentmihalyi, Rathunde, and Whalen (1993) found that artistically gifted adolescents had poor academic skills. Savants are in my mind the single best piece of evidence for the unevenness and domain specificity of abilities in gifted people. Savants are retarded or autistic yet exhibit a striking gift in a particular domain (typically music, visual art, or numerical calculation). They cannot be dismissed as mere imitators whose abilities are irrelevant to an understanding of giftedness in nonsavants. Research has now shown that savants show understanding of the rules of their domain (even if this understanding is tacit), revealing that they are not rote imitators. Their drawings and musical compositions are expressive and have artistic merit (e.g., see Hermelin, O'Connor, & Lee, 1987). Because savant gifts are similar in important respects to nonsavant gifts, savants provide strong evidence that general intelligence is unrelated to high levels of achievement in some domains.

Perhaps there are pure spatial savants to be discovered, ones who reveal their spatial ability not by drawing but by finding their way around or by reading maps. Such a discovery would underscore the domain specificity of spatial talent.

Multiple Trajectories?

Here is a second example of what can be learned from a developmental approach to giftedness: One can test whether there is more than one prototypical developmental trajectory for the ability in question (cf. Fisher & Bidell, 2006). Piaget staked out the position of one general developmental trajectory for each ability, with some children passing through this trajectory more quickly or more slowly than others—although he paid little attention to individual differences in the rate at which children developed, and neo-Piagetians have minimized individual differences in developmental rate (Case & Okamoto, 2000). Certainly neither Piaget nor neo-Piagetians theorized that gifted children follow a developmental trajectory different from that of typical children. If one can demonstrate that a gifted child develops not only more rapidly but also in a qualitatively different manner from the typical child, one will have demonstrated that there is not just one trajectory for the ability in question.

The issue of qualitatively different modes of thinking in gifted children has not been systematically investigated, although strong claims have been made about this for high IQ children. According to clinical observations, high IQ children pose deep philosophical questions, come up with multiple interpretations to questions, and can get at the essential element of a complex problem (Lovecky, 1994). Controlled studies testing whether these observations are true of gifted children in general, only those with high IQs, or perhaps only a subset of IQ-gifted children (e.g., only those above a certain level of IQ; verbally but not mathematically gifted) are needed. These studies must compare gifted children with mental-age-matched peers to disentangle effects of ability level from giftedness.

Gifted children also appear qualitatively different from ordinary children in motivation, but again the evidence remains anecdotal. The gifted children who come to the attention of educators and researchers display an intense drive, or "rage to master." They work for hours with no parental prodding or external reinforcement. As they work, they pose challenges for themselves. Such children also differ from ordinary children in the way they learn. They make discoveries on their own, and much of the time they appear to teach themselves.

I have described a child driven to teach himself to read at age 3; a child who at age 3 begged his father every day to do math games with him; and a child so obsessed with drawing at age 2 that he insisted on drawing before he got out of bed in the morning, while he was getting dressed, during breakfast, during school when he was in kindergarten, and when he invited friends over after school (all he wanted them to do was pose for him; Winner, 1996). Of course it is not known how many children have high ability but low motivation (or high motivation in an area in which they do not have high ability) and who thus do not come to the attention of educators and researchers and who thus are not identified as gifted.

The strong drive that accompanies giftedness, the posing of challenges, the mastery orientation, and the ability to make discoveries independently together suggest that gifted children do not just develop more rapidly than others, but also develop and think differently from others. But systematic research is greatly needed to move beyond anecdotal evidence and determine whether high ability is always accompanied by such qualitative cognitive or motivational differences. Needed are controlled studies comparing gifted children and older children with similar levels of ability that for them are age-typical. Perhaps researchers in behavioral genetics will be able to demonstrate a heritability coefficient for domain-specific passions.

Sufficiency of Training?

I offer one final example of an issue that can be clarified by the developmental study of giftedness: One can test whether giftedness arises only from the effects of intensive practice (suggesting that all of us could become Picassos if we started early enough and worked hard enough and had parents who made sure we sweated it out) or also to biologically based, innate cognitive, perceptual, and motivational characteristics.

In the layperson's view, talents are innate and reveal themselves at a very early age. This view is also heard from researchers whose focus is giftedness and who publish in journals devoted to the study of gifted children (typically IQ gifted children). For example, Gagné (1991) proposed a distinction between the terms *giftedness* and *talent,* with *giftedness* referring to untrained and inborn abilities and *talent* referring to the skills that emerge as these natural aptitudes are trained. A contrasting environmentalist view is now increasingly heard among psychologists who identify their focus as the study of talent or exceptional performance. The evidence for the environmentalist position comes from retrospective studies of eminent individuals. Roe (1952) uncovered the importance of drive as separate from ability: The highest achieving scientists in this study differed from the lesser achieving ones not in intellectual ability but in the capacity for concentration and hard work. However, there was so little variability in ability among the scientists that the possibility of a certain level of necessary innate ability could hardly be ruled out.

The importance of the environment in the development of talent was also demonstrated by Bloom (1985) in a retrospective study. Adults of world-class status in the arts, math, science, or athletics all reported strong family support and years of training in childhood. However, such a finding hardly rules out innate talent: Bloom's subjects also recalled signs of high ability at a very young age, before or at the start of formal training. These memories of early signs of high ability are consistent with parental accounts of child prodigies whose extraordinary abilities seem to emerge from nowhere.

Ericsson, Krampe, and Tesch-Romer (1993) conducted quantitative (but still retrospective) studies claiming to show the necessity of "deliberate practice"—effortful work designed to improve performance. These researchers showed that achievement in piano, violin, ballet, chess, bridge, and athletics is predicted by number of hours of deliberate practice. Thus, the best musicians had engaged in twice as many hours of deliberate practice over their lives as had the least successful ones. However, because children who work the earliest and hardest may well be those with the highest levels of talent, again any contribution of innate talent cannot be ruled out. Most children cannot be persuaded to play music or do math for hours on end, but highly gifted children often cannot be lured away from such activity. The amount of deliberate practice pursued by individuals thus seems to be a function of drive and interest, temperamental factors associated with talent. That is, children with high ability in a given area are likely to have a high drive to master that area.

As pointed out by Schneider (2000), Ericsson did not assess ability levels and thus the possibility of innate ability differences among those who achieved unequal levels of eminence cannot be ruled out. Simonton (1991) has shown that the most eminent classical composers began to compose and made lasting contributions after fewer years of formal training than did their less eminent peers. The fact that they achieved greater heights with less practice suggests another ingredient besides practice—and a likely candidate is a higher level of musical talent.

And so, despite attempts to account for giftedness in terms of nurture, no evidence allows the necessity of an innate component to be ruled out. To the extent that randomly selected children, matched in achievement in a particular area at baseline and then put through the same rigorous spatial training program, attain very different levels of spatial competence, the conclusion is that spatial giftedness has a biological basis and that attained level cannot be explained entirely as a function of training. It seems that environmental stimulation, personality, and temperament variables can promote or strangle giftedness but cannot create giftedness out of normality. Although I believe that the many reports of high performance with only minimal instruction in very young children (see Winner, 1996, for a review) should be sufficient to refute Ericsson's radical nurture view, the best test would be the training study mentioned earlier, and such a study has not been conducted.

HOW SHOULD SPATIAL–GRAPHIC GIFTEDNESS BE STUDIED?

If one is to undertake a study of developing of giftedness in the spatial domain, one must first distinguish between the core abilities involved in spatial reasoning on the one hand and, on the other hand, the socially constructed domains in which spatial reasoning manifests itself.

Candidate core abilities would likely include memory for two-dimensional patterns, memory for three-dimensional forms and arrays, the ability to manipulate (e.g., move around, fold, unfold) and rotate mental images in three-dimensional space, and the ability to draw realistically.

Candidate domains in which spatially gifted individuals are found (some of which are mentioned by Liben) include architecture, geology, mathematics, physics, biology, chemistry, visual arts, and dance. I would add certain activities that do not seem to fall into a formal domain: activities such as assembling toys or furniture, using maps, playing chess, and inventing things.

Once the core abilities as well as the socially constructed domains have been identified, one can ask whether the same core abilities are required for high ability in each domain. It is most likely that the answer to this question is no. For example, mental rotation ability may be more important in physics than in drawing, and some domains may call on spatial as well as nonspatial abilities. For instance, chess is likely to require spatial core abilities as well as logical ones; sculpture and drawing may call on spatial core abilities as well as motoric ones.

Consider the following puzzle that highlights the distinction between core abilities and the socially constructed domain of the visual arts. Is the ability to draw realistically a core ability that predicts that an individual will be considered gifted in the visual arts? Researchers agree that one of the clear signs of artistic giftedness is the ability to draw realistically at a very early age (Milbrath, 1998). It is striking that all visual arts prodigies have been noted for their abilities to draw realistically at a young age (Winner, 1996). But it is not known whether painters who as adults work in an abstract style begin by drawing realistically as young children. There has been a recent rash of claims that the ability to paint in an abstract expressionist style at the age of 2 or 3 is a sign of artistic giftedness. The most well-publicized "abstract expressionist prodigy" was 4-year-old Marla Olmstead (Barron, 2004). This child was reputed to paint like an abstract expressionist, although a home video of her actually painting revealed a child painting no differently than a typical 3- or 4-year-old would. Parents of a number of other young children have created Web sites on which they advertise and sell the "abstract expressionist" works of their preschoolers. And indeed these works are lovely. But they are all age-typical. Preschool children do paint in a way that on the surface resembles abstract expressionism. But this does not make them prodigies, nor does it predict that they will go on to paint like Jackson Pollock or Willem de Kooning. Perhaps the core ability that unites future artists, whether they go on to work abstractly or in a three-dimensional medium, is the ability to represent the world realistically on paper. Such representation requires a sophisticated translation from three-dimensional, infinite space to a relatively tiny two-dimensional space (i.e., the page).

But why is it that there are no *true* abstract expressionist prodigies, child painters whose skill at abstract expressionism rivals and predicts the adult ability to paint in an abstract expressionist style? To date, all known prodigies have manifested themselves in domains that are fairly formal and rule governed, such as the domain of realistic drawing. Spatial giftedness may show itself to be similar to other forms of giftedness in that early manifestations emerge in formal, rule-governed subdomains (e.g., chess, math, classical music) but not in messier subdomains in which one makes one's own rules (e.g., fiction, improvisational jazz). This is just one example of the many interesting puzzles that remain to be investigated about which core abilities predict which domain an individual will choose later on.

The study of spatial giftedness can be carried out retrospectively or prospectively. A retrospective study would first identify adults who excel in a spatial domain and then look backward for evidence of the time and form of emergence of core spatial abilities. This approach was taken by Benjamin Bloom (1985) in his landmark book, *Developing Talent in Young People*. Such a study can demonstrate what core spatial abilities were present early on in those individuals who go on to perform exceptionally as adults in a spatial domain. A prospective study must first identify children who show signs of high core spatial abilities and then follow these children as they grow up. Such a study can reveal what having these high core abilities predicts and how likely it is that the presence of such abilities means that the child will grow up to be a high performer in a spatial domain.

WHAT CAN BE LEARNED FROM THE STUDY OF SPATIAL GIFTEDNESS?

The study of spatial giftedness can illuminate many things about spatial ability that might not be learned if spatial ability is studied only as it manifests itself at the typical level. I venture a few speculations.

First, a better understanding of the components of spatial ability—whether they are "of a piece" or consist of core abilities that develop independently of one another—is needed. For example, if a high ability in mental rotation fails to correlate with high performance in visual memory, then these two skills, although both components of spatial ability, are not tied to one another. I predict that such studies would demonstrate that the core ability of mental rotation is associated with giftedness in most spatial domains (e.g., mathematics, engineering, architecture, map reading, chess, invention) but not with giftedness in the graphic arts. Research has found that college students specializing in the visual arts (and most were studying drawing and painting, and therefore working two-dimensionally) do not excel at mental rotation, whereas science majors do (Casey, Winner, Brabeck, & Sullivan, 1990). Sculptors may well differ, with a core ability in mental rotation, because they must work three-dimensionally. It is difficult to guess where photographers fit in. I also predict that visual pattern recognition is associated with all of these domains, including the visual arts. Anecdotal data show that individuals gifted in mathematics, as well as those gifted in drawing, showed high pattern-recognition skills as children (Winner, 1996).

Research can also probe the question of the origin of spatial ability. As mentioned earlier, some have suggested that high ability is simply a product of many hours of intensive practice and that there is no biological basis to talent (Ericsson et al., 1993; Howe, 1990). If this is true, then subjecting a group of children to the same kind of intensive training in spatial thinking should result in all children reaching the same high level. This is, I believe, a highly unlikely outcome. Few children will accept rigorous training regimens. Without high ability and ease of learning, the motivation to persist is lacking. Gifted children in all domains display a rage to master in their area of high ability. This kind of passion and motivation is not something that can be learned and, without it, children are not willing to put in the kinds of hours that high achievement requires. A rage to master is likely a correlate of high ability. And I predict that both have a biological basis, although this hypothesis is very difficult to prove. The strongest evidence for a biological basis for the intense motivation shown by gifted individuals is the very early age at which the motivation manifests itself and the anecdotal reports by parents that they are baffled as to the origin of the child's passion (Winner, 1996).

Another way to probe the question of whether there is a biological basis to spatial talent is through brain imaging. Imaging the brains of those individuals known to excel in spatial reasoning may reveal atypicalities. Indeed, this claim was made for the brain of Einstein (Diamond, Scheibel, Murphy, & Harvey, 1985; Witelson, 1999). However, there is no way to determine whether Einstein's brain was atypical from the start or was a result of all the years spent thinking about spatial problems. Brains are malleable even in adulthood: For example, adults who learn to juggle increase their brain volume (Draganski et al., 2004). Thus, to discover brain markers of gifted potential (rather than gifted achievement), one must do a prospective study. To uncover the brain markers of spatial giftedness, one would have to image the brains of children prior to spatial training, provide intensive training, and then look back at the pretrained brains of those children who turn out to excel. This is the logic of the study I am currently carrying out with Gottfried Schlaug and Andrea Norton; we are studying the neurological effects of music training and hope to find brain markers of musical talent before training (Norton et al., 2005).

Researchers can also discover something about the relationship between core spatial abilities and socially constructed spatial domains (cf. Carey & Spelke, 1994). A study could follow children with the same profile of core spatial abilities and find out what spatial domains (if any) they choose to go into. Such a study can reveal characteristics in addition to the profile of core spatial abilities that help to determine the domains children go into as adults. The question of what propels children with the same profile into very different domains—for example, mathematics versus sculpture—is a fascinating and yet unresolved question. Is the determining factor personality? Is it the presence of particular role models? Or some other social factors? The fact is, the answer is unknown. This area is ripe for investigation.

I have argued that there are few areas of study in human psychology in which individual differences are not found. And once variation in performance is acknowledged, one must confront the problem of performance at the low end and performance at the high end. The study of giftedness has been relatively ignored until recently in psychology, with far greater attention paid to abilities at the low end. Making matters more challenging for those who would understand spatial giftedness is the fact that the domain of spatial ability has also been ignored by researchers who study giftedness, when compared with the domain of academic ability. One of the most interesting puzzles, in my view, is the identity of the "core" ability (or abilities) that predict(s) later spatial giftedness. Whether the capacity to rotate images mentally, to notice and remember patterns, or to represent realistically are core abilities is simply not known. Another intriguing and unresolved issue is whether individuals with the same core abilities tend to go into the same kinds of spatial professions. And if not, what factors push one child to become an engineer and another a sculptor? Are these factors purely environmental and hence arbitrary (a function of the environment into which one is born), or are they innate?

Chapter 4 of this volume has raised many of these intriguing issues. By focusing on a little-studied area of giftedness, Lynn Liben has shed much light on what it means to be gifted.

REFERENCES

Barron, J. (2004, October 4). Little Jackson Pollocks exploring in oil paint. *New York Times*, p. E1.

Benbow, C. P., & Minor, L. L. (1990). Cognitive profiles of verbally and mathematically precocious students: Implications for identification of the gifted. *Gifted Child Quarterly, 34*, 21–26.

Bloom, B. (Ed.). (1985). *Developing talent in young people*. New York: Ballantine Books.

Carey, S., & Spelke, E. S. (1994). Domain-specific knowledge and conceptual change. In L. Hirschfeld & S. Gelman (Eds.), *Mapping the mind: Domain specificity in cognition and culture* (pp. 169–200). Cambridge, England: Cambridge University Press.

Case, R., & Okamoto, Y. (2000). *The role of central conceptual structures in the development of children's thought*. New York: Wiley.

Casey, M., Winner, E., Brabeck, M., & Sullivan, K. (1990). Visual-spatial abilities in art, maths, and science majors: Effects of sex, handedness, and spatial experience. In K. Gilhooly, M. Keane, R. Logie, & G. Erdos (Eds.), *Lines of thinking: Reflections on the psychology of thought* (Vol. 2, pp. 275–294). New York: Wiley.

Csikszentmihalyi, M., Rathunde, K., & Whalen, S. (1993). *Talented teenagers: The roots of success and failure*. New York: Cambridge University Press.

Diamond, M. C., Scheibel, A. B., Murphy, G. M., Jr., & Harvey, T. (1985). On the brain of a scientist: Albert Einstein. *Experimental Neurology, 88,* 198–206.

Detterman, D. K., & Daniel, M. H. (1989). Correlations of mental tests with each other and with cognitive variables are highest for low IQ groups. *Intelligence, 15,* 349–359.

Draganski, B., Gaser, C., Busch, V., Schuierer, G., Bogdahn, U., & May A. (2004, January 22). Neuroplasticity: Changes in grey matter induced by training. *Nature, 427,* 311–312.

Ericsson, K. A., Krampe, R. T., & Tesch-Romer, C. (1993). The role of deliberate practice in the acquisition of expert performance. *Psychological Review, 100,* 363–406.

Fisher, K., & Bidell, T. R. (2006). Dynamic development of psychological structures in action and thought. In R. Lerner (Ed.), *Handbook of child psychology: Vol. 1. Theoretical models of human development* (pp. 313–339). New York: Wiley.

Gagné, F. (1991). Toward a differentiated model of giftedness and talent. In N. Colangelo & G. A. Davis (Eds.), *Handbook of gifted education* (pp. 65–80). Boston: Allyn & Bacon.

Hermelin, B., O'Connor, N., & Lee, S. (1987). Musical inventiveness of five idiots-savants. *Psychological Medicine, 17,* 685–694.

Howe, M. J. A. (1990). *The origins of exceptional abilities*. Oxford, England: Blackwell.

Lovecky, D. V. (1994). Exceptionally gifted children: Different minds. *Roeper Review, 17,* 116–120.

Milbrath, C. (1998). *Patterns of artistic development in children: Comparative studies of talent*. Cambridge, England: Cambridge University Press.

Norton, A., Winner, E., Cronin, K., Overy, K., Lee, D. J., & Schlaug, G. (2005). Are there pre-existing neural, cognitive, or motoric markers for musical ability? *Brain and Cognition, 59,* 124–134.

Roe, A. (1952). *The making of a scientist*. New York: Dodd, Mead.

Schneider, W. (2000). Giftedness, expertise, and (exceptional) performance: A developmental perspective. In K. A. Heller, F. J. Monks, R. F. Subotnik, & R. J. Sternberg (Eds.), *International handbook of research and development of giftedness and talent* (2nd ed.). London: Elsevier.

Seligman, M. E. P. (2003). Positive psychology: Fundamental assumptions. *American Psychologist, 16,* 126–127.

Simonton, D. K. (1991). Emergence and realization of genius: The lives and works of 120 classical composers. *Journal of Personality and Social Psychology, 61,* 829–840.

Simonton, D. K. (1999). Talent and its development: An emergenic and epigenetic model. *Psychological Review, 106,* 435–457.

Winner, E. (1996). *Gifted children: Myths and realities*. New York: Basic Books.

Witelson, S. (1999). The exceptional brain of Albert Einstein. *The Lancet, 353,* 2149–2153.

III

ADOLESCENCE

6

DEVELOPMENTAL TRANSITIONS IN GIFTEDNESS AND TALENT: CHILDHOOD INTO ADOLESCENCE

DONA J. MATTHEWS

Early adolescence is a period of rapid and dramatic developmental change in every dimension of a person's being: physical, cognitive, social, emotional, and sexual. Parents' and teachers' expectations and demands are increasing; opportunities and possibilities are expanding but still significantly constrained; self-awareness and abstract thought are becoming possible; and issues of identity are paramount.

In a discussion of adolescent cognitive and brain development, Keating (2004) argued that early adolescence, much like early childhood, is a sensitive or critical period in its ability to shape future developmental trajectories. He offered many lines of evidence for this position:

> the interdependence and developmental coordination of numerous cognitive elements, and of cognition with emotion and behavior; the role of puberty in a fundamental restructuring of many body systems; the apparent concentration of changes in the adolescent brain in the prefrontal cortex (which serves as a governor of cognition and action) together with the enhanced inter-regional communication between the prefrontal cortex and other brain regions; and the evidence for substantial synaptic pruning and for non-trivial physiological reversibility of

behavioral and neuroendocrine patterns arising from early developmental experiences. (p. 49)

The challenging and potentially volatile transition from childhood to adolescence becomes further complicated for those who are categorized as academically exceptional or as somehow different than others, including those who are advanced relative to their age peers (Colangelo & Assouline, 2000; Moon, 2006). At an age when healthy self-concept development involves being liked by others, which in turn depends on being both similar to others and unique (Harter, 1999), those who stand out in early adolescence as obviously different can have a harder task of navigating this period. At the same time, the enormous cognitive plasticity of this stage means that "the adolescent period provides the ideal time within life to study the bases of positive human development" (Lerner & Steinberg, 2004, p. 9). School and society therefore have an opportunity—and a responsibility—to foster gifted adolescents' strengths and resiliencies in ways that will optimize their developmental outcomes.

In this chapter, I consider some of the specific challenges experienced by high-ability learners as they grow out of childhood and into adolescence. I also address evolving perspectives on giftedness that can work to obviate some of the added complications, with a focus on talent development and other theoretically grounded evidence-based approaches that incorporate individual and developmental diversity, including the domain specificity and fluidity of cognitive development, and the importance of mindsets in regulating young adults' responses to the challenges and opportunities in their lives.

PREDICTING AND IDENTIFYING GIFTEDNESS

Prediction, identification, and labeling are thorny issues for those interested in the development of giftedness and talent across the life span. Current findings across a number of fields suggest changing perspectives on these concerns, with particular implications at early adolescence.

Predicting Adolescent Giftedness

Does giftedness that is identified in childhood last through adolescence? Conversely, can evidence of childhood advancement be retrospectively found in gifted adolescents? A growing body of evidence illustrates that false positives and false negatives are commonly generated by attempts to predict later giftedness from assessments conducted in early childhood (see chap. 2, this volume). Contrary to popular belief, those who achieve above a given criterion score on a given test at a given age do not necessarily test above a similar cutoff on a subsequent test administration. Conversely, many who have not met the gifted criterion on a first test administration would (if retested) achieve above the same cutoff later, thus becoming eligible for the "gifted" label later in their development (see chap. 3, this volume; Lohman, 2005a).

The younger a child when assessed, the less likely he or she will remain in either the gifted or the not-gifted category (see chap. 3, this volume). And because of the regression to the mean factor, the higher the identification criterion is set, the truer this is (Lohman, 2005a). Referring to analyses based on their longitudinal work, Gottfried, Gottfried, and Guerin pointed out that a child with an IQ of 140 at age 7 would have a predicted IQ of 125 at age 17, as a result of regression toward the mean (chap. 3, this volume). It must also be remembered that—because standard scores such as IQs mark an individual's place on the population normal curve—for every child who moves from above to below the gifted cutoff, someone else moves into the gifted category, whether or not actually tested.

This fluidity calls into question a static categorical approach to identification and has obvious implications for policymaking, including emphasizing the importance of ongoing assessment and flexible noncategorical educational programming for high-ability learners. The longer the gap between identification and programming, the more important this principle is: A test score at age 5 provides little information for curriculum planning at early adolescence. Developmental variability over time is true not only for intelligence test scores but also for exceptional subject-specific academic advancement (Lohman & Korb, 2006).

Many of those who are identified as having a high cognitive ability in childhood will go on to have gifted learning needs as adolescents, but some will not. More important, perhaps, in illustrating why one should avoid attempts at prediction is the fact that most of those who have gifted learning needs during adolescence would not have met categorical criteria when they were younger.

The findings about variability over time support Horowitz's (1987, 2000) dynamic systems approach to child development. Current findings in a number of fields (neuroscience, genetic biology, epidemiology, and cognitive psychology, to name a few) are beginning to provide some of the details of the dynamic and almost infinite complexity of what Horowitz (2000) described as organismic–experiential interactions. There are enormous differences in individuals' internal resources such as temperament and motivation, and in their life experiences—in their "cultural, economic, social, and constitutional" circumstances (Horowitz, 2000, p. 4)—and as these differences multiply exponentially in combination over time, it is little wonder that it is so difficult to predict a given child's likelihood of exhibiting future giftedness.

Keating (chap. 11, this volume) comes to a similar conclusion, noting that extraordinarily high achievers come from varied backgrounds and that currently no formula is available to predict future extraordinary achievement. In short, standardized tools for measuring human potential are far too limited, and the opportunities for developmental influence are far too complex and numerous, to allow a prediction that one individual might achieve more than another at some point in the future. The younger the child, then, or the more distant the future target, the poorer the capacity to predict gifted-level outcomes.

The fact that future giftedness cannot be predicted with a reasonable degree of certainty does not mean there is no role for research and education that focus on gifted development. Instead, it suggests that the focus ought to be on the children and adolescents in school who are so advanced relative to their age peers that they require differentiated academic programming at a certain point in time. In Vygotskyan terms, some students have constantly shifting zones of proximal development that can be matched only when the age-normal curriculum is adapted to meet their exceptional learning needs. By investigating how to identify and address exceptional needs, one learns not only how to meet students' gifted learning needs but also about optimal developmental pathways, heightening one's capacity for teaching and learning with all students.

Identifying Adolescent Giftedness

Graham (chap. 7, this volume) makes a compelling case for going beyond traditional conceptions when looking for giftedness in adolescence and for attending to social and emotional factors as well as intellectual. She documents the underrepresentation of African American and Hispanic students in gifted programs and their overrepresentation in suspensions and expulsions from school. She describes the ways that motivational, social, and individual developmental variables are intertwined at adolescence, creating diverse pathways to engagement in learning and to academic achievement. To understand a student's motivation to achieve, she notes, one must also understand their relationships with others, including what the student thinks and feels about others, and how others think and feel about the student.

Worrell (chap. 8, this volume) concurs with Graham's recommendation that the notion of giftedness be expanded to make it more inclusive. He discusses the key role played by identity at adolescence and its relationship with academic achievement, considering the differential effect of social context, group membership, ethnic identity attitudes, personal identity variables (e.g., intelligence, academic self-efficacy), and social identity or reference group orientation (e.g., racial and ethnic group membership). He points out that a student's academic achievement is not solely individual but rather occurs in a social context that is affected by one's also perceived position within that social context.

These calls to broaden conceptions of giftedness are also made by Liben (chap. 4, this volume) and Winner (chap. 5, this volume). Many lines of research illustrate the importance of a broadly expansive notion of human potential, including the retrospective studies of those who have achieved eminence in a variety of fields (Bloom, 1985; Gardner, 1993; Simonton, 1994; Sosniak, 2006).

If giftedness is not what it has traditionally been conceived as, then, what does it look like or, more particularly for present purposes, what does it look like at adolescence? In their research on talent development, Subotnik and her colleagues (Subotnik, 2004; Subotnik & Calderon, 2008; Subotnik & Jarvin, 2005; see chap. 9, this volume) have provided some useful specifics. They have identified three stages that are common across domains and have observed that within and across domains the developmental timing of stage transitions varies. For example, talent development begins earlier in violin than in wind instruments or voice and earlier in math than in the social sciences or humanities.

According to emerging findings in this line of research, necessary core competencies, appropriate instructional activities, and facilitative mediating factors all vary across stages of talent development. In the beginning, wide exposure and playful exploration are appropriate, but as a child develops competence in a domain, he or she needs more challenge, instruction, and disciplined practice. As students move from competency to expertise, speed of learning becomes less focal, with technical proficiency assumed, although requiring ongoing attention. Important mediating variables at this middle stage include awareness of one's strengths and weaknesses, self-promotion, learning how to play the game, social skills, and a restoration of self-confidence (Subotnik & Jarvin, 2005). This stage in talent development is particularly vulnerable when it coincides with adolescence, and it requires a skillful teacher to make the transition a successful one. Subotnik and Calderon (2008) discussed the importance of encouraging psychosocial strength in developing adolescents, noting that increased competition and advanced-level work can lower their self-confidence. A simple categorical approach to understanding giftedness at adolescence is too limited; gifted identification has to include more than students' intelligence test scores.

Across the age spectrum, educators should be looking for ways that students' learning needs are and are not being matched by the curriculum usually provided. Basic principles of best practice include using multiple measures to diagnose a student's current need for differentiated educational programming, collecting authentic performance samples, and administering domain-specific tests of reasoning, interest, and persistence as well as achievement (Lohman, 2005a, 2005b), all of which become more important as children define their individual identities and move into adolescence.

Labeling

In light of the plasticity of development through adolescence and some of the problematic consequences of labeling, it may be better to label learning opportunities rather than students, offering, for example, more challenging math or language programs to students who appear to be ready for them (Borland, 2003, 2005; Keating, 1991; see also chap. 11, this volume).

GIFTEDNESS AND DIVERSITY

Although "diversity" is often used as shorthand for differences between races—in particular the underrepresentation of certain minorities in gifted programming—there are many kinds of diversity that influence people's understanding of giftedness and talent development. These include both those differences within a given individual (i.e., intraindividual diversity), such as that observed where learning disabilities coexist with giftedness and those differences that occur between individuals (i.e., interindividual diversity), such as differences across race, socioeconomic status, and sex.

Intraindividual Diversity

One commonly held misconception about gifted development is that it applies to all aspects of an individual; that is, that if a person demonstrates gifted learning needs, then he or she will be gifted in all areas of achievement. Although some people do demonstrate gifted-level abilities across many or all areas, they are the exception and not the rule.

Domain Specificity

One of the best understood dimensions of intraindividual diversity is domain specificity: Those who are mathematically gifted, for example, may or may not be linguistically, musically, or scientifically gifted. I address this point in more detail later in the section on domain specificity.

Asynchronous Development

When cognitive skills are maturing more quickly than are physical, emotional, or social abilities, children can experience problems of developmental asynchrony (Coleman & Cross, 2000). The 12-year-old who can express himself like an 18-year-old might be expected to have the emotional maturity of an 18-year-old, and of course he usually does not. Neurologists Eide and Eide (2006) observed, "Often gifted children will have critical and analytical skills that exceed their judgment and restraint" (p. 447). The uneven changes that occur so rapidly across so many domains in early adolescence can be experienced as particularly disconcerting by those whose development is already uneven.

Dual Exceptionality

Some children are exceptionally competent in one or more academic domains and have significant learning problems such as learning disabilities, attention deficit disorder, Asperger's syndrome, or conduct disorders. Such students are twice-exceptional relative to their age-peers. As twice-exceptional children approach adolescence, when fitting into a peer group becomes more important to self-esteem, the likelihood of feelings of alienation and marginalization increases: "As these students continue their educational journey through middle and high school, the challenges of being twice-exceptional become more complicated and may have dire social, academic, and emotional implications if not addressed" (Baum, Rizza, & Renzulli, 2006, p. 145).

Twice-exceptional students cope with the challenges of being twice-exceptional in a number of different ways, often intentionally hiding one or both of their exceptionalities, which of course can cause other problems (Assouline & Colangelo, 2006; Baum & Owen, 2003). Many troubling responses to dual exceptionality have been documented at early adolescence, including acting out at school or becoming the class clown, bullying other students, disengaging altogether from academic and career ambitions, withdrawing from peer interactions, sinking into depression, and using or abusing drugs and alcohol (Baum et al., 2006).

Interindividual Diversity Within the Gifted Population

Another commonly held misconception about gifted development is that it appears more or less the same across all members of society, that mathematical development, for example, will occur in similar ways and at similar developmental stages regardless of a child's race, social class, cultural experience, or sex. Although this is not entirely false, a child's interests and supports for learning—and therefore his or her likelihood of gifted-level development and pathways to its development—can be significantly influenced by cultural experiences and stereotype-based expectations.

Race, Ethnicity, and Socioeconomic Status

Some argue that gifted education is inherently racist or elitist, and should be abandoned altogether (e.g., Fruchter & Siegel, 2004). Some gifted education experts are seriously concerned about racial and socioeconomic underrepresentation but also recognize the need to provide differentiated curriculum for exceptionally advanced learners and advocate ways to provide appropriate learning matches for a more diverse range of gifted learners (e.g., Borland, 2003; Callahan, 2003; Ford, 2003; Renzulli, 2002; Rogers, 2003).

Graham (chap. 7, this volume) documents the research on giftedness at adolescence as it intersects with issues of race: Across the United States, African American students are about half as likely as White students to be in gifted programs. On the basis of her own research on motivation and achievement, and on the findings of Dweck (1999, 2006), Graham concludes that attribution theory can be a powerful tool in addressing these motivational concerns and in improving academic success among minority students. She makes several recommendations for teacher education and professional development, including rectifying the stereotypes that influence teachers' gifted referrals, facilitating their learning about diverse cultural styles, and helping them avoid communicating low-ability messages to certain students.

In his consideration of giftedness at adolescence, Worrell (chap. 8, this volume) concurs with Graham regarding the importance of attribution theory and teacher education, and suggests that one must also attend to the broader societal inequities in students' opportunities to learn. He emphasizes that academic achievement is not just an individual matter, but happens within a social context, influenced by one's perceived social position. He suggests that rather than focus on increasing the numbers of minority adolescents in gifted programs, schools should work to support high-level learning in all children, beginning at preschool, and also broaden conceptions of giftedness.

Rothstein (2004), an economic and educational policy analyst, suggested that closing the achievement gap requires addressing underlying issues of poverty, access to health and dental care, early learning experiences, family structure, educational resources, and cultural attitudes. For this gap to be closed, Rothstein argued, all children must experience early opportunities to thrive and to be engaged by learning. Looked at from this angle, the underrepresentation of Blacks and Hispanics in gifted education may be less a reflection of racism in gifted education than a troubling symptom of much larger economic and cultural disparities.

Lohman (2005a, 2005b, 2006) provided evidence about identification practices that supports this emphasis on providing rich opportunities for learning for all young children. Across ages, a key to culture-fair gifted identification is casting the assessment net widely, that is, using multiple measures in flexible and inclusive ways. This approach encourages more representative inclusion in gifted programming and also enhances educators' understanding about how to foster the development of giftedness in diverse kinds of learners.

Gender

Considering issues of gender in adolescence, Galambos (2004) concluded that "Adolescent boys and girls differ dramatically. It is important to remember, though, that gender differences in characteristics and behavior do not mean that all males are one way and all females are another" (p. 255). Emphasizing the prevalence of within-sex variability and the small size of between-sex differences, she suggested conceptualizing adolescent gender development within a developmental systems approach as part of a dynamic and complex interrelationship of biology, cognition, and socialization.

In general, however, gifted boys are more likely than gifted girls to attribute their successes to their ability and effort, and their failures to lack of effort (Hébert, 2001), which is consistent with what Dweck (2006) called the *growth mindset*. Gifted girls, by contrast, are more likely to exhibit signs of a fixed mindset, attributing their successes to luck or effort and their failures to lack of ability (Reis & Park, 2001). This pattern of gender differences undermines girls' ultimate career success because it depresses the likelihood of them engaging in the most challenging courses and programs. Single-sex math and science classes within coeducational schools can reduce the decline of girls' participation and interest in mathematics as they move into adolescence, allowing gifted adolescent girls to reap the socialization benefits of mixed-sex schools while avoiding stereotypical biases that discourage them from excelling in math and science, with implications for keeping high-level career options available (A. Robinson, Shore, & Enersen, 2007; Shapka & Keating, 2003).

Research that focuses specifically on the interaction of gender, adolescence, and giftedness is sparse and equivocal (Reis, 2006; A. Robinson et al., 2007). On the one hand, sex differences in academic engagement and achievement appear small or nonexistent (Olszewski-Kubilius & Turner, 2002). On the other hand, there are persistent indications of real sex differences in factors such as self-efficacy (A. Robinson et al., 2007). An additional complication is the emerging data on gender as it interacts with other factors, including race. Studies that take race into account indicate that African American girls and White boys demonstrate more confidence in their own ability and show superior learning gains in response to learning opportunities, compared with African American boys and White girls (A. Robinson et al., 2007).

Gifted Education, Diversity, and Global Concerns

In summarizing recent advances in adolescent psychology as a branch of developmental psychology, Hamburg and Hamburg (2004) wrote,

> We live together with billions of people, mostly strangers; we need them and they need us—to make a living, to travel, to cope with widespread problems like infectious diseases and terrorism, and to assure our safe

supplies of food and water, a clean environment, and physical protection. (p. 819)

Global survival may depend on our finding ways to welcome diversity into the power and status elites. Psychologists, researchers, and educators have a dual and profound responsibility, both to support giftedness and talent development in diverse kinds of students and to ensure that the most capable students learn how to respect and collaborate with others with different life experiences.

PSYCHOSOCIAL VARIABLES IN THE DEVELOPMENT OF GIFTEDNESS AND TALENT

From a number of perspectives, educators and psychologists are recognizing that gifted children and adolescents are far more heterogeneous in their psychosocial development and developmental trajectories than they are alike (Moon, 2006). In a review of findings on the social and emotional development of gifted learners, Cross (2005) observed that checklists of characteristics or social and emotional needs of gifted learners are neither reflective of the research nor useful. This emphasis on giftedness as a reflection of individual developmental differences has real practical implications for educators and psychologists: We must pay attention to cultural, economic, social, and constitutional circumstances, and to the complexities of context and experience, taking into account as well as possible the myriad factors affecting each child and adolescent as an individual, and resisting the temptation to categorize students on the basis of any one variable, certainly including giftedness. Simply put, gifted individuals are not alike, except in their need for differentiated instruction.

Engagement, Motivation, and Mind-Sets

Academic giftedness cannot be understood separately from psychosocial factors such as engagement and motivation, and this may be truer at early adolescence than at any other time. The pleasure that children and adolescents take in the learning process is critical to their eventual learning outcomes. As Gottfried, Gottfried, and Guerin note (chap. 3, this volume), the more children take pleasure in cognitive processing, the more likely they are to take part in activities that develop their cognitive abilities. Winner (1996) discussed the "rage to master"—an intense desire to take one's learning as far as possible—as an essential component of extraordinary accomplishment. Analyzing retrospective studies of expertise, Sosniak (2006) concluded that the most obvious common finding relates to the importance of motivational factors applied over time, leading her to "hypothesize that the central challenge of helping people develop exceptional abilities is that of creating and maintaining the motivation necessary to stay with a field for the many years it takes to develop expertise" (p. 297).

Motivation, engagement, and effort may be more important to gifted-level achievement than intelligence. Butterworth (2006) found that mathematical prodigies' cognitive capacity as measured by intelligence tests was highly variable and concluded that their distinguishing factor was zeal:

> Zeal seems to be a characteristic common to all the prodigies described here. They are obsessed with numbers, treat them as familiar friends, and actively seek closer acquaintanceship with them. They also seem to spend a great deal of time thinking and learning about numbers . . . all seem to have a capacity for very hard work. (p. 564)

Dweck (2006) brought together 3 decades of research on attribution theory into a powerful model of attitudes as these can shape a life course. She distinguished between a fixed mind-set, analogous to the entity theory of intelligence and associated with lower achievement and self-esteem, and a growth mind-set, analogous to the incremental theory and associated with greater confidence, risk taking, and academic and career success over time. The definition of giftedness shifts dramatically when educators, psychologists, and others move from a fixed mind-set perspective, in which some students are categorized as inherently smart and some are not, to a growth mind-set, in which intelligence is conceptualized as dynamic, as developing over time with appropriately scaffolded opportunities to learn.

Children's and adolescents' mind-sets are critically important in the development of giftedness and talent. Those who hold a fixed mind-set tend to feel judged and evaluated in everything they produce. If they do not do well on a test, they conclude that they are not smart in that subject area and become less likely to attempt challenging problems, preferring tasks and course work in which they can demonstrate their competence. Those who have a growth mind-set, by contrast, perceive their failures as learning opportunities, providing information about what needs more work. Quite predictably, then, over time a fixed mind-set leads to a fear of failure and therefore of challenge, whereas a growth mind-set encourages intellectual risk taking and is associated with much higher academic and career achievement levels. Teachers, psychologists, and parents undermine children's and adolescents' achievement, self-confidence, and sense of well-being when they model or inculcate a fixed mind-set, whether intentionally or not. However, they can have a highly beneficial effect when they model and nurture a growth mind-set. As Graham (chap. 7, this volume) discusses, this is particularly important for African Americans and other students who are vulnerable to stereotype threat.

Encouraging a growth mind-set (and reducing a fixed mind-set) includes (a) defining intelligence as developing over time with appropriately scaffolded opportunities to learn (and not as innate superior cognitive abilities, or high IQ); (b) praising students for what they accomplish through practice, study, persistence, and good strategies (and not for their intelligence); (c) emphasizing that all meaningful achievement is built on hard work over time (rather than being quick and easy for smart people); (d) welcoming failure and setbacks as opportunities for learning (and not as signs of lack of ability); and (e) recognizing that potential is invisible and unmeasurable (and not something that some children have more of than others; Dweck, 2006).

Academically advanced students are at more risk than others for disengaging from school in the adolescent years, and the greater the degree of advancement, the truer this is (Keating, 1991, 2004). And because authenticity and relevance are essential to intellectual engagement at adolescence (Bransford, Brown, & Cocking, 2000), one of the most effective ways to prevent this is to provide students with scaffolded opportunities to engage at challenging levels in their areas of interest.

Effort, Practice, and Perseverance

High achievement comes from hard work over time: "The personality characteristics associated with success in any field are drive, tenacity, and the willingness to overcome obstacles" (Winner & Martino, 2000, p. 108). Studies of gifted-level achievement across many different domains emphasize the importance of effort and perseverance over time, in a context of appropriate opportunities to learn (Bloom, 1985; Lubinski & Benbow, 2006; Simonton, 1994; Subotnik & Jarvin, 2005; chap. 3, this volume).

Personal Agency

Along with developmental plasticity and diversity, personal agency is gaining considerable attention in the field of adolescent development (Lerner & Steinberg, 2004). It is during early adolescence that the prefrontal cortex becomes essential to behavioral decision making. This is the period in which children can begin to identify their own goals and values independently of the adults in their lives and learn the decision-making skills they will require to make good decisions as adults. As Keating notes (chap. 11, this volume), more attention must be paid to discovering ways to assist early adolescents in creating a structured self that incorporates the mastery, desire, and persistence that are needed to sustain a high level of achievement.

Those who wish to support the development of giftedness and talent in children as they become adolescents will do well to encourage young peoples' emergent sense of personal agency.

Peer Relationships

At a stage in their lives when peer relationships are growing more complex and layered (Brown, 2004), gifted students have at least one strike against them in the popularity game, just by virtue of their intellectual differentness from others (Baum et al., 2006). Gifted learners at early adolescence tend to manage their identity in one of three ways: becoming highly visible by taking on active roles as school leaders, contest winners, or enthusiastic participants in activities; becoming invisible by camouflaging their exceptional abilities so they appear "normal"; or disidentifying with their gifted peers by adopting the behaviors of a more desirable peer group (Coleman & Cross, 2000). The transition from childhood to adolescence is even more challenging when giftedness is further complicated by membership in cultural and linguistic minorities that require a choice of conflicting identities, as discussed by Graham (chap. 7, this volume) and Worrell (chap. 8, this volume).

Social Milieu

Keating's discussion (see chap. 11, this volume) of the importance of the social milieu in fostering the remarkably creative output that became Silicon Valley and led to the innovations that have changed many dimensions of the contemporary life experience illustrates the power of the social environment in adulthood. The findings reported by Colombo et al. (chap. 2, this volume) and by Gottfried et al. (chap. 3, this volume), and the analyses provided by each other author in this volume, show the importance of social and environmental factors in the development of giftedness in those years leading up to adulthood. This may be most true at the sensitive period that is early adolescence, when the power of the social milieu to shape future developmental trajectories is at its height. This area offers promise for future research attention.

DOMAIN SPECIFICITY AND GIFTED DEVELOPMENT

Although not so long ago giftedness was defined as intelligence across most or all cognitive domains, educators and others are increasingly understanding it as domain-specific exceptional ability (Gardner, 1993; Keating, 1991; Matthews & Foster, 2005, 2006; VanTassel-Baska, 2005). The field of gifted education is moving away from a general intelligence model and toward an expertise model of exceptional ability in which it is understood that ability and achievement are specific to a particular knowledge domain.

There have been many approaches to understanding intelligence as multifactored or domain specific (e.g., Cattell, 1971; Gardner, 1983; Guilford,

1967; Thurstone, 1938), but with its focus on domain-specific abilities, the Marland Report (Marland, 1972) laid the educational groundwork for conceptualizing giftedness as a domain-specific phenomenon. About the same time, Stanley and his colleagues at Johns Hopkins University initiated what has become the landmark longitudinal study of giftedness in a single domain, the Study of Mathematically Precocious Youth (SMPY; Lubinski & Benbow, 2006; Stanley, Keating, & Fox, 1974). Proposing the concept of "optimal match," N. M. Robinson and Robinson (1982) suggested that educators should provide a range of options for gifted learners, matching programming to individual subject-specific learning needs and attending to possible learning options within the classroom, the school, the local community, and beyond, including but not limited to full-time gifted programs and university early-entrance programs.

There are often indications in childhood of an individual's future interests, but at early adolescence the areas of exceptional strength become more obvious and important: "During adolescence, the interests of high ability youth become increasingly well-defined, their talents more and more specialized, and their levels of expertise increasingly differentiated" (Moon, 2006, p. 2). Starting in early adolescence, domain specificity has increasing relevance to educational programming, as the higher an achievement criterion is set, the less likely it is that any one student will meet that criterion across domains (see chap. 11, this volume; Matthews & Keating, 1995).

Which Domains?

When giftedness is understood within a special education framework as advanced learning needs relative to one's age peers, the domains of primary concern are the domains of primary focus in the schools, which means in most schools the core subjects of English language arts, mathematics, science, and social studies. This does not mean there is not a role for enriched and expanded learning opportunities in a number of other domains, but it is not the role of gifted education (at least when defined this way) to provide advanced learning opportunities across all possible domains. Simply put, if musical remediation is not usually provided for a child who has trouble learning musical notation, then it is probably beyond the school's responsibility to provide advanced music lessons for musically gifted learners.

Liben (chap. 4, this volume) makes a compelling case for including the spatial domain in gifted education and, by backward extension, in academic curricula more generally. Findings from the ongoing SMPY affirm the importance of the spatial domain and Liben's position that educational policy should attend to this domain as a specific domain of interest (Lubinski & Benbow, 2006).

Domain-Specific and Cross-Domain Developmental Trajectories

Some of the most interesting research in gifted education today is aimed at exploring domain-specific developmental trajectories as they connect with optimal development more broadly, addressing questions such as, What do we know about how giftedness develops in different domains? What is needed at different developmental stages to support gifted development more broadly? Findings from the SMPY, for example, which now includes data for adults well into their careers, emphasize the importance of identifying high-level domain-specific talent at early adolescence and then providing individually targeted optional educational opportunities (see chap. 11, this volume).

Some researchers are considering connections between domain-general and domain-specific development. For example, Subotnik and her colleagues (Subotnik, 2004; Subotnik & Calderon, 2008; Subotnik & Jarvin, 2005) have proposed a stage model that crosses domains conceptually but that incorporates domain-specific and intradomain timing differences. Similarly, Porath and colleagues (McKeough, Okamoto, & Porath, 2002; Porath, 2006) are investigating a "design for development" of gifted students' thinking: "A model of giftedness that specifies universal, or general, characteristics of development and unique specific abilities associated with outstanding performance in a domain can help us understand the developmental trajectory of a variety of forms of giftedness" (Porath, 2006).

Many of the emerging questions in the field include attributes, attitudes, and social–emotional factors that cross domains. Folsom (2006) developed a model for teachers that helps them teach domain-specific content and higher order thinking skills integrated with social–emotional knowledge and skills, empowering students to become more responsible for their own learning. Although this model is in the early stages of research validation, it is highly promising for gifted early adolescents in its inclusive approach to diversity and its focus on authentic engagement in the learning process, supporting the autonomy and exploration of possibility that are so critical at this developmental stage.

CONCLUSION

The developmental trajectories that lead to gifted levels of achievement are highly complex and individual and so are the implications for those who would support gifted development. Learning needs and interests vary across domains and change over time, and supporting optimal outcomes requires attention to be paid to many dimensions of diversity. This is perhaps most true at the sensitive period that is early adolescence, with its rapid simultaneous changes in neural, cognitive, physical, sexual, social, and emotional maturation. We should work toward providing social milieus that foster a growth mind-set and lead to authentic engagement in diverse kinds of meaningful domain-specific learning. This means taking into account the importance to high-level achievement of psychosocial factors such as motivation, effort, personal agency, and persistence over time, and of contexts that reward both individual and collective creativity.

REFERENCES

Assouline, S. G., & Colangelo, N. (2006). Social-emotional development of gifted adolescents. In F. A. Dixon & S. M. Moon (Eds.), *The handbook of secondary gifted education* (pp. 65–86). Waco, TX: Prufrock Press.

Baum, S. M., & Owen, S. (2003). *To be gifted and learning disabled: Strategies for helping bright students with LD, ADHD, and more.* Mansfield Center, CT: Creative Learning Press.

Baum, S. M., Rizza, M. G., & Renzulli, S. (2006). Twice exceptional adolescents: Who are they? What do they need? In F. A. Dixon & S. M. Moon (Eds.), *The handbook of secondary gifted education* (pp. 137–164). Waco, TX: Prufrock Press.

Bloom, B. S. (1985). *Developing talent in young people.* New York: Ballantine Books.

Borland, J. H. (2003). *Rethinking gifted education.* New York: Teachers College Press.

Borland, J. H. (2005). Gifted education without gifted children: The case for no conception of giftedness. In R. J. Sternberg & J. E. Davidson (Eds.), *Conceptions of giftedness* (pp. 1–19). Cambridge, England: Cambridge University Press.

Bransford, J. D., Brown, A. L., & Cocking, R. R. (2000). *How people learn: Brain, mind, experience, and school.* Washington, DC: National Academy Press.

Brown, B. B. (2004). Adolescents' relationships with peers. In R. M. Lerner & L. Steinberg (Eds.), *Handbook of adolescent psychology* (2nd ed., pp. 363–394). Hoboken, NJ: Wiley.

Butterworth, B. (2006). Mathematical expertise. In K. A. Ericsson, N. Charness, P. J. Feltovich, & R. R. Hoffman (Eds.), *The Cambridge handbook of expertise and expert performance* (pp. 553–568). Cambridge, England: Cambridge University Press.

Callahan, C. M. (2003). Searching for answers or creating more questions? A response to Robinson. *Journal for the Education of the Gifted, 26,* 274–282.

Cattell, R. B. (1971). *Abilities: Their structure, growth and action.* Boston: Houghton Mifflin.

Colangelo, N., & Assouline, S. G. (2000). Counseling gifted students. In K. A. Heller, F. J. Mönks, R. J. Sternberg, & R. F. Subotnik (Eds.), *International handbook of giftedness and talent* (2nd ed., pp. 595–607). Amsterdam: Elsevier.

Coleman, L. J., & Cross, T. L. (2000). Social-emotional development and the personal experience of giftedness. In K. A. Heller, F. J. Mönks, R. J. Sternberg, & R. F. Subotnik (Eds.), *International handbook of giftedness and talent* (2nd ed., pp. 203–212). Amsterdam: Elsevier.

Cross, T. L. (2005). *The social and emotional lives of gifted kids: Understanding and guiding their development*. Waco, TX: Prufrock Press.

Dweck, C. S. (1999). *Self-theories: Their role in motivation, personality, and development*. Philadelphia: Psychology Press.

Dweck, C. S. (2006). *Mindset: The new psychology of success*. New York: Random House.

Eide, B., & Eide, F. (2006). *The mislabeled child*. New York: Hyperion.

Folsom, C. (2006). Making conceptual connections between gifted and general education: Teaching for intellectual and emotional learning. *Roeper Review, 28*, 79–87.

Ford, D. Y. (2003). Desegregating gifted education: Seeking equity for culturally diverse students. In J. H. Borland (Ed.), *Rethinking gifted education* (pp. 143–158). New York: Teachers College Press.

Fruchter, N., & Siegel, D. (2004, November 28). Point/counterpoint: Are gifted programs good? No. *The New York Daily News*, 46.

Galambos, N. L. (2004). Gender and gender role development in adolescence. In R. M. Lerner & L. Steinberg (Eds.), *Handbook of adolescent psychology* (2nd ed., pp. 233–262). Hoboken, NJ: Wiley.

Gardner, H. (1983). *Frames of mind: The theory of multiple intelligences*. New York: Basic Books.

Gardner, H. (1993). *Creating minds: An anatomy of creativity seen through the lives of Freud, Einstein, Picasso, Stravinsky, Eliot, Graham, and Gandhi*. New York: Basic Books.

Guilford, J. P. (1967). *The nature of human intelligence*. New York: McGraw-Hill.

Hamburg, B., & Hamburg, D. (2004). On the future development of adolescent psychology. In R. M. Lerner & L. Steinberg (Eds.), *Handbook of adolescent psychology* (2nd ed., pp. 815–819). Hoboken, NJ: Wiley.

Harter, S. (1999). *The construction of the self: A developmental perspective*. New York: Guilford Press.

Hébert, T. P. (2001). "If I had a new notebook, I know things would change": Bright underachieving young men in urban classrooms. *Gifted Child Quarterly, 45*, 174–194.

Horowitz, F. D. (1987). A developmental view of giftedness. *Gifted Child Quarterly, 31*, 165–168.

Horowitz, F. D. (2000). Child development and the PITS: Simple questions, complex answers, and developmental theory. *Child Development, 71*, 1–10.

Keating, D. P. (1991). Curriculum options for the developmentally advanced: A developmental alternative for gifted education. *Exceptionality Education Canada, 1*, 53–83.

Keating, D. P. (2004). Cognitive and brain development. In R. M. Lerner & L. Steinberg (Eds.), *Handbook of adolescent psychology* (2nd ed., pp. 45–83). Hoboken, NJ: Wiley.

Lerner, R. M., & Steinberg, L. (2004). The scientific study of adolescent development. In R. M. Lerner & L. Steinberg (Eds.), *Handbook of adolescent psychology* (2nd ed., pp. 1–12). Hoboken, NJ: Wiley.

Lohman, D. F. (2005a). An aptitude perspective on talent: Implications for identification of academically gifted minority students. *Journal for the Education of the Gifted, 28,* 333–360.

Lohman, D. F. (2005b). The role of nonverbal ability tests in the identification of academically gifted students: An aptitude perspective. *Gifted Child Quarterly, 49,* 111–138.

Lohman, D. F. (2006). Beliefs about differences between ability and accomplishment: From folk theories to cognitive science. *Roeper Review, 29,* 32–40.

Lohman, D. F., & Korb, K. A. (2006). Gifted today but not tomorrow? Longitudinal changes in ability and achievement during elementary school. *Journal for the Education of the Gifted, 29,* 451–484.

Lubinski, D., & Benbow, C. P. (2006). Study of mathematically precocious youth after 35 years. *Perspectives on Psychological Science, 1,* 316–345.

Marland, S. P. (1972). *Education of the gifted and talented.* Washington, DC: Government Printing Office.

Matthews, D. J., & Foster, J. F. (2005). *Being smart about gifted children: A guidebook for parents and educators.* Scottsdale, AZ: Great Potential Press.

Matthews, D. J., & Foster, J. F. (2006). Mystery to mastery: Shifting paradigms in gifted education. *Roeper Review, 28,* 64–69.

Matthews, D. J., & Keating, D. P. (1995). Domain specificity and habits of mind: An investigation of patterns of high-level development. *Journal of Early Adolescence, 15,* 319–343.

McKeough, A., Okamoto, Y., & Porath, M. (2002). *A design for development: The legacy of Robbie Case.* New Orleans, LA: American Educational Research Association.

Moon, S. M. (2006). On being gifted and adolescent: An overview. In F. A. Dixon & S. M. Moon (Ed.), *The handbook of secondary gifted education* (pp. 1–5). Waco, TX: Prufrock Press.

Olszewski-Kubilius, P., & Turner, D. (2002). Gender differences among elementary school-aged gifted students in achievement, perceptions of ability, and subject preferences. *Journal for the Education of the Gifted, 25,* 222–268.

Porath, M. (2006). The conceptual underpinnings of giftedness: Developmental and educational implications. *High Ability Studies, 17,* 145–157.

Reis, S. M. (2006). Gender, adolescence, and giftedness. In F. A. Dixon & S. M. Moon (Eds.), *The handbook of secondary gifted education* (pp. 87–112). Waco, TX: Prufrock Press.

Reis, S. M., & Park, S. (2001). Gender differences in high-achieving students in math and science. *Journal for the Education of the Gifted, 25,* 52–73.

Renzulli, J. S. (2002). Expanding the conception of giftedness to include co-cognitive traits and to promote social capital. *Phi Delta Kappan, 84,* 33–58.

Robinson, A., Shore, B. M., & Enersen, D. L. (2007). *Best practices in gifted education: An evidence-based guide.* Waco, TX: Prufrock Press.

Robinson, N. M., & Robinson, H. B. (1982). The optimal match: Devising the best compromise for the highly gifted student. In D. F. Feldman (Ed.), *New directions for child development: Developmental approaches to giftedness and creativity* (pp. 79–94). San Francisco: Jossey-Bass.

Rogers, K. B. (2003). A voice of reason in the wilderness. *Journal for the Education of the Gifted, 26,* 314–320.

Rothstein, R. (2004). *Class and schools: Using social, economic and educational reform to close the Black-White achievement gap.* New York: Teachers College Press.

Shapka, J. D., & Keating, D. P. (2003). Effects of a girls-only curriculum during adolescence: Performance, persistence, and engagement in mathematics and science. *American Education Research Journal, 40,* 929–960.

Simonton, D. K. (1994). *Greatness: Who makes history and why.* New York: Guilford Press.

Sosniak, L. A. (2006). Retrospective interviews in the study of expertise and expert performance. In K. A. Ericsson, N. Charness, P. J. Feltovich, & R. R. Hoffman (Eds.), *The Cambridge handbook of expertise and expert performance* (pp. 287–301). Cambridge, England: Cambridge University Press.

Stanley, J. C., Keating, D. P., & Fox, L. (Eds.). (1974). *Mathematical talent: Discovery, description, and development.* Baltimore: Johns Hopkins University Press.

Subotnik, R. F. (2004). Transforming elite musicians into professional artists: A view of the talent development process at the Juilliard School. In L. Shavinina & M. Ferrari (Eds.), *Beyond knowledge: Extracognitive aspects of developing high ability* (pp. 137–166). Hillsdale, NJ: Erlbaum.

Subotnik, R. F., & Calderon, J. (2008). Developing giftedness and talent. In F. A. Karnes & K. P. Stephens (Eds.), *Achieving excellence: Educating the gifted and talented* (pp. 49–61). Columbus, OH: Pearson Education.

Subotnik, R. F., & Jarvin, L. (2005). Beyond expertise: Conceptions of giftedness as great performance. In R. J. Sternberg & J. E. Davidson (Eds.), *Conceptions of giftedness* (2nd ed., pp. 343–357). Cambridge, England: Cambridge University Press.

Thurstone, L. L. (1938). *Primary mental abilities.* Chicago: University of Chicago Press.

VanTassel-Baska, J. (2005). Domain-specific giftedness. In R. J. Sternberg & J. E. Davidson (Eds.), *Conceptions of giftedness* (2nd ed.). Cambridge, England: Cambridge University Press.

Winner, E. (1996). *Gifted children: Myths and realities.* New York: Basic Books.

Winner, E., & Martino, G. (2000). Giftedness in non-academic domains: The case of the visual arts and music. In K. A. Heller, F. J. Mönks, R. J. Sternberg, & R. F. Subotnik (Eds.), *International handbook of giftedness and talent* (2nd ed., pp. 95–110). Amsterdam: Elsevier.

7

GIFTEDNESS IN ADOLESCENCE: AFRICAN AMERICAN GIFTED YOUTH AND THEIR CHALLENGES FROM A MOTIVATIONAL PERSPECTIVE

SANDRA GRAHAM

When I was asked to write about giftedness during adolescence, a vivid image immediately came to my mind. I began to hum the first verse of one of my favorite songs from the 1970s: "To be young, gifted, and Black; Oh, what a lovely precious dream." That song was composed in 1969 by singer Nina Simone in memory of her close friend Lorraine Hansberry, an award-winning African American playwright whose brilliant career was cut short when she died in 1965 at the age of 34. Simone's rendition of "To Be Young, Gifted and Black" became enormously popular during the 1970s because of its uplifting message of encouragement and empowerment at the height of the Civil Rights movement. To this day, the song continues to be a kind of national anthem at graduation ceremonies of historically Black colleges and at a variety of special gatherings honoring stellar achievements of African American youth.

What does it mean to be young, gifted, and Black in contemporary America? Or, stated differently, what does it mean to be identified as young, gifted, and Black? Table 7.1 contains data compiled by the Applied Research Center, as reported by Gordon, Piana, and Keleher (2001), showing percentages of students from each of four major racial–ethnic groups in six large school districts in the United States, with a breakdown by race or ethnicity of the percentage of students in gifted programs and expelled or suspended.

TABLE 7.1
Representation in Gifted Programs and Disciplinary Programs Leading to Suspension and Expulsion, by Ethnic Group in Six School Districts

School district	Race/ethnicity of student			
	African American	Latino	Asian/Pacific Islander	White
Boston, MA				
% of students in district	55	23	8	13
% in gifted programs	27	26	9	38
% suspended/expelled	70	19	2	9
Durham, NC				
% of students in district	58	4	2	36
% in gifted programs	26	1	5	67
% suspended/expelled	79	2	0	18
Miami-Dade, FL				
% of students in district	33	53	1	12
% in gifted programs	23	52	1	24
% suspended/expelled	48	43	0	8
Denver, CO				
% of students in district	21	50	3	24
% in gifted programs	18	30	5	46
% suspended/expelled	36	45	2	16
Austin, TX				
% of students in district	18	43	2	37
% in gifted programs	11	24	4	62
% suspended/expelled	36	45	0	18
Los Angeles, CA				
% of students in district	14	69	7	11
% in gifted programs	8	44	25	23
% suspended/expelled	30	58	3	8
San Francisco, CA				
% of students in district	18	24	43	14
% in gifted programs	5	9	60	25
% suspended/expelled	56	19	13	11

Note. Data from Gordon, Piana, and Keleher (2001).

Included are school districts across all regions of the country, with varying representations of race or ethnicity. The data tell the same story in each school district: African American students are significantly underrepresented in programs for the gifted and talented relative to their representation in the district's student population. In Boston, for example, African American students comprise 55% of the district's K–12 population but only 27% of students in gifted programs. Across the country in the city of San Francisco, Black students comprise 18% of the student population but only 5% of those classified as gifted. Other data sources that examine ethnic minority representation in academic programs for the intellectually talented reveal similar patterns. For example, a National Research Council (2002; NRC) report revealed that African American students are about half as likely as White students to be in gifted programs. The NRC report concluded that

> The overall underrepresentation of several racial/ethnic minority groups among top students relative to the white majority is very extensive and long-standing. This limited minority presence among top students is found using virtually all traditional measures of academic achievement, including school grades, standardized test scores, and class rank. (p. 81)

Studies on enrollment in college preparatory math or in accelerated classes, such as Advanced Placement (AP) courses, round out the picture of racial–ethnic disparities in access. For example, African American and Latino students assigned to gifted programs in elementary school are less likely than Asians and Whites to be placed in algebra in eighth grade (an important entrée to college preparatory high school math; NRC, 2002). Similarly, gifted African American students who attend multiethnic high schools with the greatest number of AP courses are least likely to be enrolled in those courses (Solorzano & Ornelas, 2004).

If African American students are underrepresented in gifted programs and related courses for talented college-bound students, then where are they most likely to be found? The third row of data for each school district depicted in Table 7.1 provides a disturbing answer to this question. Here is shown the representation of African American students in school disciplinary policies such as zero tolerance that lead to suspension and expulsion. In every school district depicted in Table 7.1, Black students are proportionately at greater risk than their other-race peers for being removed from school. National data from multiple school districts confirm that African American students are two to three times more likely than White students to be suspended or expelled from school as a result of zero-tolerance policies (Skiba et al., 2006). Also, those ethnic minority students who remain in school will be more likely to be identified as mentally retarded rather than gifted by school officials and to be overrepresented in special education programs (NRC, 2002).

In this chapter, I want to capture what it is like to be young, gifted, and Black in light of the educational realities depicted in Table 7.1. My theoretical perspective is that of a motivational psychologist, so I focus on how contemporary approaches to motivation research can shed light on giftedness in African American adolescents. Motivation is the study of why people think and behave as they do. In an achievement setting, someone would be concerned with motivation if he or she were to ask, for example, why do some gifted students persist to task completion despite enormous difficulty whereas others give up at the slightest provocation? Or why do some talented students set such unrealistically high goals for themselves that failure is bound to occur? Note that this focus on the "why" or the "why not" of achievement is quite different from the study of achievement itself. Educators sometimes confuse the topics of motivation research with the topics of achievement and learning research.

Most contemporary approaches to motivation can be conceptualized within an expectancy–value framework (see Graham & Weiner, 1996). From this perspective, motivation is thought to be determined by both the likelihood of goal attainment, which is the expectancy component, and how much that goal is desired, which is the value component. The study of expectancy addresses beliefs about ability (*"Can I do it?"*), whereas the study of values addresses preferences and desires (*"Do I want it?"*). The notions of "can" versus "want" closely correspond to the distinctions between aptitude and effort expenditure, which are two of the most important constructs in motivation theory and research. In the following sections, I organize my discussion of African American gifted adolescents around overarching questions about "can" and "want." In framing my discussion, I focus on both the normative challenges of adolescence relevant to giftedness as well as the unique challenges that gifted Black adolescents are likely to encounter. To do this, I must cast a broad net and begin with factors that are unique to the everyday lives of people of color. Everything that I write in this chapter is shaped by the recognition that many racial and ethnic minority groups in contemporary America are positioned at the bottom of a status hierarchy wherein barriers to opportunity often override personal strivings for achievement.

Before proceeding further, I want to acknowledge a few of my biases. First, although giftedness and talent can be manifested in many different domains, in this chapter I focus on intellectually and academically talented students. Most psychological research on giftedness concentrates on the intellectual domain (Robinson & Clinkenbeard, 1998), and among adults in this society, intellectual giftedness continues to be the most coveted cultural capital. Second, in framing the discussion around adolescents of color and giftedness, I focus on African American youth. As with almost all psychological constructs that have been examined in populations other than Whites, more is known about African American youth than about other ethnic groups. It is also difficult to generalize to all youth of color because, as illustrated in Table 7.1, African American and Asians as groups reside at opposite ends of the achievement spectrum and may experience being labeled as gifted quite differently.

The third bias is that I tend to focus on the ways in which motivation research sheds light on challenges to achievement strivings rather than on ways in which it promotes optimal outcomes. I hope this preference will not be interpreted as oriented too much toward deficits rather than strengths. It is certainly true that many (and perhaps most) youth who are identified as gifted display high levels of intrinsic motivation to do well in school (e.g., Gottfried & Gottfried, 1996). However, it is also true that a growing literature suggests that many academically talented adolescents are underachieving in school, and some of the explanations for that underachievement enlist motivational constructs (e.g., Neihart, Reis, Robinson, & Moon, 2002). I draw on that literature as I discuss some of the unique motivational challenges of African American gifted adolescents. Finally, my fourth bias is that I approach the study of motivation from a social–psychological perspective. That is, I believe that students' social lives and their academic lives are interrelated and that one cannot fully understand an individual student's motivation to achieve ("can" and "want") without also understanding their relationships with other people— in particular, what they think and feel about others and how others think and feel about them. The social nature of motivation is particularly important during adolescence when peer approval takes on heightened significance.

BELIEFS ABOUT ABILITY: CAN I DO IT?

Most adolescents make two major school transitions during their preteen and teenage years, from elementary to middle school and from middle to high school. At each transition, schools typically become larger, more bureaucratic, more impersonal, more competitive, and more focused on social comparison and public displays of ability. Although there are some exceptions with the growth of small learning communities, the characteristics of secondary schools often are at odds with the developmental requirements and tasks of adolescence, which include the need for close peer relationships, support from adults other than one's parents, identity negotiation, and a heightened self-focus. Eccles and her colleagues have written extensively about how stage–environment mismatch during secondary school transitions can undermine students' self-confidence and motivation to do well in school (see review in Eccles, 2004). A growing literature on the motivational challenges of gifted adolescents is compatible with analyses from the school transition literature; that is, motivational variables related to perceived competence, such as fear of failure, avoiding challenge, self-handicapping, and lack of confidence, appear to differentiate achieving from underachieving gifted students (e.g., Dai, Moon, & Feldhusen, 1998; Neihart et al., 2002; Robinson & Clinkenbeard, 1998).

Racial Stereotypes About Ability

Over and above the normative challenges of adolescence, what are the particular barriers to perceptions of "I can" that African American gifted students might encounter? One of the major challenges involves dealing with racial stereotypes about their group. Stereotypes are culturally shared beliefs, both positive and negative, about the characteristics and behaviors of particular groups. For example, the notions that adolescents are victims of "raging hormones" and that the intellectually gifted are "nerds" are culturally endorsed beliefs about the attributes of those social groups. An important distinction has been made in the stereotype literature between one's own privately held beliefs about members of social groups (personal stereotypes) and the consensual or shared understanding of those groups (cultural stereotypes); the latter is of interest in this chapter.

A great deal of research from social psychology indicates that the cultural stereotypes about African Americans remain largely negative. Even though privately held beliefs have become more positive over the past 50 years (e.g., Schuman, Steeh, Bobo, & Krysan, 1997), studies of cultural stereotypes continue to show that respondents associate being Black (and male) with low intelligence, hostility, aggressiveness, and violence (e.g., Devine & Elliot, 1995). The much smaller stereotype literature on other ethnic groups in the United States also portrays the more marginalized groups in a negative light. For example, cultural stereotypes of Latino youth also depict them as unintelligent and with little personal ambition (e.g., Niemann, Pollack, Rogers, & O'Connor, 1998). So pervasive are these linkages that they are sometimes endorsed even by members of the target ethnic groups (see Kao, 2000). In our own research, for example, we found that African American and Latino adolescents were just as likely as their White classmates to associate being male and Black or Latino with academic disengagement and socially deviant behavior (Graham, Taylor, & Hudley, 1998; Hudley & Graham, 2001).

African Americans and Stereotype Threat

Social scientists have been writing for a long time about the negative consequences of racial stereotypes about intelligence. One particularly provocative program of research relevant to gifted adolescents has been carried out by Claude Steele, Joshua Aronson, and their colleagues on a phenomenon that they label *stereotype threat* (Aronson & Steele, 2005; Steele, 1997). Stereotype threat is the awareness that individuals have about negative stereotypes associated with their group. Although considered to be a general psychological state applicable to any negative group stereotype, the construct originated in the achievement domain and it has been applied to African American students' awareness of the cultural stereotype associating their race with intellectual inferiority. That awareness can be quite debilitating, especially for those African American students who are talented and invested in doing well in school. For example, in a series of studies with Black and White students attending Stanford University, Steele and Aronson (1995) found that Black students performed more poorly than did White students on standardized test items when they were told that the test was diagnostic of their abilities. When told that the test was a problem-solving activity unrelated to ability, there was no difference in the performance of the two racial groups. In ability-related contexts, therefore, what became threatening for African American students was the fear that they might confirm the stereotype or be treated and judged by others on the basis of that stereotype. Steele and Aronson (1995) suggested that stereotype-threatened students often are dividing their attention between the task itself (e.g., taking an SAT exam) and ruminating about the meaning of their performance (e.g., what does this say about me or about members of my racial group?). Furthermore, it is not necessary that the individual student endorse the stereotype; mere awareness of its existence is sufficient to activate threat.

Stereotype threat researchers have documented two motivational consequences of the anxiety associated with thinking about race and intelligence in highly evaluative achievement contexts (Steele, 1997). Some African American students may choose to work especially hard as a way of disconfirming the stereotype. Of course, high effort in the face of increasing academic challenge may be difficult to sustain and may even lead a student to question his or her abilities. Stereotype threat can also have the opposite effect, causing students to minimize effort and downplay the importance of doing well in school. Steele coined the term *disidentification* to describe students who no longer view academic achievement as a domain that is relevant to their personal identity. Disidentification has been operationalized as the absence of a relationship between academic performance and self-esteem, and it has been associated with declining achievement from middle school to high school, particularly among African American boys (Osborne, 1997). A similar process, labeled *disengagement*, occurs when students begin to ignore the feedback from teachers about their performance or to devalue achievement altogether (e.g., Major & Schmader, 2001). Thus, although disidentification and disengagement may be self-protecting mechanisms for coping with negative racial stereotypes, in the long run their detrimental effects on achievement strivings will probably outweigh any short-term self-enhancing effects.

It is important to note that high-achieving African American students appear to be most vulnerable to stereotype threat and the processes of disidentification and disengagement, which makes this body of research particularly relevant to understanding the motivational challenges of gifted Black students (Ford, Grantham, & Whiting, 2008). Also, youth become keenly aware of the racial stereotypes about their group and the reality of discrimination on the basis of those stereotypes by the early adolescent years (see review in C. Brown & Bigler, 2005), which suggests that Black students are vulnerable to stereotype threat during the middle school and high school years. Because African American children are aware as early as preschool that their group may be perceived in a negative light (e.g., Clark & Clark, 1947), the developmental course of stereotype threat is a fascinating topic in need of more research (McKown & Weinstein, 2003).

Asian Americans and the Model Minority Stereotype

Let me digress briefly here to comment on racial stereotypes about intelligence at the other end of the ability spectrum. Unlike African Americans, the cultural stereotype about Asians is that they are hardworking and intellectually gifted high achievers who are especially competent in math and science (Kao, 2000). The term *model minority* was coined in the 1960s to capture those characteristics and to account for the seemingly unprecedented successful entry of East Asian immigrants into mainstream American society. Many studies have now documented that Asians and non-Asians alike are aware of the culturally shared association between high academic achievement strivings and being an Asian American (e.g., Kao, 2000). Asked to describe the stereotypes about their group, over 80% of Asian American college students in one study listed terms such as *smart, nerdy,* and *overachiever* (Oyserman & Sakamoto, 1997).

Although it may be more tolerable to know that one's ethnic group is viewed as smart and hardworking rather than as lazy and dumb, that stereotype also has its own unique set of challenges. Ethnographic, survey, and experimental research all point to psychological and emotional costs associated with living up to the model minority stereotype. Ethnographic studies, for example, detail the anxiety that many Asian American students feel when forced to cope with the perception of their group as academic superstars (e.g., Lee, 1994). Many report feeling frustrated and pressured to attain or maintain high academic achievement because of the expectations placed on them. As one Asian American student poignantly disclosed,

> they (Whites) will have stereotypes, like we're smart. . . . They are so wrong, not everyone is smart. . . . When you get bad grades, people look at you really strangely because you are sort of distorting the way they see an Asian. It makes you feel really awkward if you don't fit the stereotype. (Lee, 1994, p. 419)

Thus, although some African American gifted students worry that their performance might confirm a negative stereotype, some gifted Asian American students worry that their performance might not confirm a positive stereotype. I suspect that coping with ability-related stereotypes in the academic domain, either negative or positive, can lead to performance-avoidant goals that have well-established negative consequences (Elliot, 2005).

Entity Versus Incremental Theories About Ability

Whether individuals are vulnerable to racial stereotypes or to other challenges to "I can" is in part determined by their beliefs about the meaning of intellectual giftedness. For example, if people are labeled as gifted, do they view their abilities as stable and essentially beyond their control ("either you have it or you don't") or as changeable and largely determined by how much effort they exert? To address this question, Carol Dweck and her colleagues proposed a distinction between individuals who hold entity versus incremental theories of intelligence (see reviews in Dweck, 1999, 2006). According to this analysis, children and adults, including gifted youth, hold one of two implicit theories about intelligence. Some individuals are what Dweck (1999) labels *entity theorists:* They believe that intelligence is basically fixed, each person has his or her allotted share, and that person can do little to increase his or her allotment. Entity theorists endorse statements such as "You can learn new things but you can't really change your intelligence." In contrast, other individuals appear to be *incremental theorists:* They believe that intelligence is modifiable through increased effort. Incremental theorists are more likely to agree with statements such as "Smartness is something you can increase as much as you want to." These implicit theories have been related to a variety of achievement-related cognitions and behaviors. For example, students who subscribe to an incremental theory of intelligence prefer challenging tasks so that they can both increase their ability and achieve greater mastery. Entity theorists, in contrast, often avoid challenge because their primary concern is with the adequacy of their presumably fixed ability and what failure might convey about that ability. Younger children tend to be incremental theorists; they believe that effort and ability go hand-in-hand. But by adolescence the perception of ability as a fixed trait becomes more engrained, along with the culturally shared belief that high effort implies less ability (see Barker & Graham, 1987; Stipek & MacIver, 1988).

Adolescents' lay understanding of the "gifted" label is therefore likely to emphasize an entity theory of intelligence, suggesting that academically talented youth are vulnerable to the motivational challenges of holding such beliefs (see Dweck, 1999). As a particularly select (i.e., numerically underrepresented) group, and in light of the possible threats to self-confidence noted earlier, African American gifted students may be especially challenged by worries that they do not have enough (fixed) ability to live up to their academic reputation. Interventions that focus on enhancing the belief that intelligence is malleable rather than fixed have been shown to lead to improved performance by African American students who were vulnerable to stereotype threat (Aronson, Fried, & Good, 2002).

Coping With Discrimination

Similar to people who hold entity theories of intelligence, individuals of color who perceive themselves to be treated unfairly because of their race can lose confidence in themselves and in their ability to be self-efficacious. Perceived discrimination can occur in almost any arena. It can be blatant, intended, and obvious, or subtle, unintended, and not easy to detect. Some researchers have used the term *microaggressions* to capture a particularly subtle but pernicious kind of degradation that many people of color encounter on an almost daily basis (Solorzano, 2000). Examples of microaggressions include being ignored or overlooked while waiting in line, being suspected of cheating because one received a good grade on a test, being followed or observed while in public places, or being mistaken for someone who serves others (Solorzano, 2000). I am reminded of a particularly painful example of microaggression that my husband (a gifted African American man) encountered during his first year of medical school. Beginning his first clinical rotation, the aspiring young physician entered the university hospital, dressed in a white medical coat, shirt, and tie, with a stethoscope around his neck. As he rushed down the corridor on the way to grand rounds, a patient raised her hand, caught his attention, and signaled him to come to her room, by calling, "Oh, waiter, I'm ready for my tray." On the face of it, one such experience may seem fairly benign. But cumulative microaggressions can surely take their toll on mental health.

A growing empirical literature on the correlates of perceived racial–ethnic discrimination among adolescents of color is relevant to gifted adolescents. Among the most prevalent kinds of unfair treatment reported by ethnic minority youth is that which takes place in school. In their study with high-achieving students attending a magnet school, Fisher, Wallace, and Fenton (2000) created an educational discrimination index that included such items as "you were discouraged from joining an advanced level class," "you were given a lower grade than you deserved," and "you were wrongly disciplined or given after-school detention." African American and Latino achieving students were significantly more likely to endorse these items than were their White classmates. Such experiences have been linked to decreased perceptions of mastery among early adolescents of color (Phinney, Madden, & Santos, 1998) and increased negative attitudes about school (Brand, Felner, Shim, Seitsinger, & Dumas, 2003). Perceived discrimination can lead to mistrust of teachers and to the general belief that the school rules and policies are unfair. A number of studies now document that personal experiences with discrimination in combination with racial mistrust can contribute to academic disengagement and other problem behaviors at school for students of all achievement levels (e.g., R. Taylor, Casten, Flickinger, Roberts, & Fulmore, 1994).

In summary, in this section I focused on how beliefs about ability can be challenged for African American gifted adolescents. Black youth must cope with stereotypes linking race to low intelligence and with the widely shared perception that intelligence is a fixed entity that cannot be changed. These youth also confront discrimination, both overt and subtle, that can undermine perceptions of competence.

BELIEFS ABOUT EFFORT: "I CAN, BUT DO I WANT TO?"

This section focuses on the second big construct in motivation research: achievement values. Unlike expectancy, which is largely centered around beliefs about ability, values are rooted in moral constructs such as *ought* or *should,* as illustrated by the belief that one should feel morally obligated to work hard in school, especially if one has high ability. Trying hard in school is often compromised during adolescence because of the tension between the need to achieve and the need to belong, both of which are fundamental human motives in American society (Baumeister & Leary, 1995). A long time ago Coleman (1961) offered a reminder that adolescents care more about being popular than being perceived as smart. It has been reported more recently that adolescents more than younger children report that they downplay effort so they will be liked by popular peers (Juvonen & Murdock, 1995) and few admit to wanting to be among the "brainy" crowd (B. Brown & Steinberg, 1990). After surveying about 20,000 teenagers from many different ethnic groups, Steinberg (1996) lamented that "the adolescent peer culture in contemporary America demeans academic success and scorns students who try to do well in school" (p. 19). Aware of the social costs of high achievement, some gifted adolescents have been shown to sacrifice their talent by denying their giftedness, hiding it, avoiding programs for the gifted, and underachieving (see Swiatek, 2001).

Oppositional Identity

The tension between having friends and being a high achiever plays out in particular ways for African American gifted adolescents, ways that take into account the historical circumstances and cultural forces that have shaped the experiences of African Americans in this country. African Americans are what anthropologist John Ogbu called an involuntary minority—that is, a group that has become part of the American fabric not by choice but as a result of slavery, conquest, or colonization (Fordham & Ogbu, 1986). One consequence of this history is that acceptance of mainstream values about working hard and school success may be perceived as threatening to one's social identity. Particularly during adolescence, African American youngsters may adopt oppositional identities, defined as resistance, whereby they show relative indifference, or even disdain, toward achievement behaviors that are valued by the larger society. On the basis of their interviews with gifted high school students, Fordham and Ogbu (1986) coined the term *acting White* to describe African American high school students' perceptions of their same-race peers who work hard to do well in school. Although scholars disagree about the level of empirical support for the acting-White construct (e.g., Ainsworth-Darnell & Downey, 1998; Cook & Ludwig, 1997), there is more consensus among researchers that many ethnic minority high-achieving adolescents experience a particular kind of conflict between achievement strivings and their desire to be accepted by the general peer group. This conflict is well captured in an ethnographic study by Hemmings (1996), who quoted the lament of one academically successful African American male in an inner-city high school: "You're a nerd if you're sittin' up and doing homework all the time and don't help out other people. You don't want to be a nerd in this school because other kids will ruin your life" (p. 42).

The discourse surrounding oppositional identity during adolescence has become lively among public intellectuals as well as researchers, at least partly because it provides a motivational explanation for the achievement gap between Black and White students. One would be hard pressed to find an article on academic motivation in African American adolescents in the past 10 years that does not explicitly or implicitly make reference to oppositional identity. That construct also has been linked to other motivational phenomena discussed earlier in this chapter, such as stereotype threat and disidentification, as a way to fully capture the academic challenges that African American students face (Steele, 1997). Note that the argument is not that talented Black students who have strong racial identity will devalue doing well in school. By every indication strong racial identity is a buffer that promotes academic engagement (e.g., Spencer, Noll, Stoltzfus, & Harpalani, 2001). Rather, the question is whether some gifted African American adolescents experience more tension as they negotiate their identities as both students and members of their racial group (Ford et al., 2008). The evidence suggests that, indeed, some do.

Whom Do Adolescents Say They Admire?

In my own studies on peer relations during early adolescence, my colleagues and I gather data on social reputations that are relevant to achievement values. Using peer nomination procedures, in one set of studies we asked students of different ethnic groups and grade levels to write the names of their classmates whom they admire, respect, and want to be like (Graham et al., 1998; A. Taylor & Graham, 2007). Our rationale for these questions was that if we can identify the characteristics of classmates whom a student admires, respects, and wants to be like, we can know something about the characteristics that the student values. We were particularly interested in how nominations vary as a function of nominees' achievement level.

In one of the studies (A. Taylor & Graham, 2007) the nominators were African American and Latino students in second, fourth, and seventh grades. The left panel of Figure 7.1 shows the nominations that African American girls in the three grades made of other same-ethnicity girls who were high, average, or low achievers; the right panel shows the same nomi-

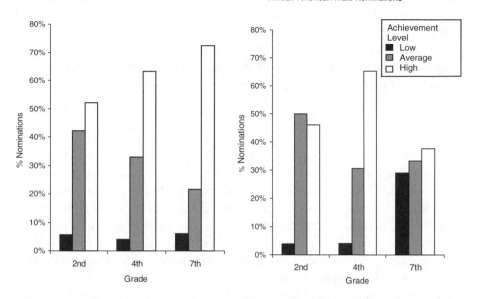

Figure 7.1. Student nominations separated by sex, of who they "admire, respect, and want to be like," considered by academic achievement and grade levels. The left panel illustrates the data for African American girls nominating other same-race same-grade girls, and the right panel shows African American boys' nominations of same-race same-grade boys. From "An Examination of the Relationship Between Achievement Values and Perceptions of Barriers Among Low-SES African American and Latino Students," by A. Z. Taylor and S. Graham, 2007, *Journal of Educational Psychology, 99,* pp. 57–58. Copyright 2007 by the American Psychological Association.

nation data for African American boys nominating other same-ethnicity boys. (I display the data this way because over 80% of the nominations at all three grade levels went to same-ethnicity/same-gender classmates.) The left panel of Figure 7.1 shows that at each grade level, African American girls were much more likely to nominate high achievers as those they admire, respect, and want to be like than they were to nominate low achievers. This difference increased across grade level with 52%, 63%, and 72% of African American girls' nominations going to high achievers at second, fourth, and seventh grade, respectively.

The pattern for African American boys nominating other boys was quite different and showed a clear developmental trend. As with the girls' data, second- and fourth-grade African American boys chose high achievers or average achievers over low achievers as those they admired, respected, and wanted to be like. Seventh-grade African American boys, however, showed no preference for any single achievement group over another. Low achievers were just as likely to be nominated as were average and high achievers. With regard to the data across grade level, the critical comparison is the increasing preference for low achievers to be admired and respected. These data suggest that by the time African American boys reach middle school, they look more admiringly on their less academically inclined peers. We have some data to suggest that these low-achieving male peers are admired for their athletic prowess and popularity among classmates.

The Importance of Gender

I report these data in part to underscore the particular challenges associated with being young, gifted, Black, and male. These gender-linked challenges have not adequately been acknowledged. In mainstream gender research on motivation, a dominant theme is the heightened vulnerability of girls to motivational deficits. Some argue that gender role socialization and cultural stereotypes about women and achievement lead many gifted girls to question their academic competence more, particularly in math; to display more maladaptive reactions to failure; to perceive more barriers to success; and to experience more conflict between individual achievement strivings and social conformity (see reviews in Eccles, Wigfield, & Schiefele, 1998; Ruble & Martin, 1998). Even research on stereotype threat underscores that developmental gender literature, for it draws many parallels between the academic plight of African Americans and that of women in math and science (Steele, 1997).

I believe that gender analyses in motivation research may need to be reframed. In research on motivation and achievement that examines ethnic as well as gender differences, including research on gifted populations, it is evident that ethnic minority males (i.e., African American and Latino) are faring more poorly than are females (e.g., Ford, Harris, Tyson, & Trotman, 2000; Osborne, 1997; R. Taylor et al., 1994). The Ethnicity × Gender differences increase across the school years and are particularly apparent when the measures are so-called markers of adolescent success (i.e., high school graduation) and young adult mobility (i.e., enrollment in and completion of college; see review in Sidanius & Pratto, 1999). The harsh disciplinary practices such as school suspension that were depicted in Table 7.1 also fall disproportionately on African American males (e.g., Skiba, 2001). I suggest that ethnic minority adolescent males, more than other groups, must cope in unique ways with the challenges to "can" and "want" that I discuss in this chapter.

WHAT CAN BE DONE?

I conclude with a few recommendations for educational reforms that are needed to both increase the number of gifted African American adolescents in today's schools and enhance the quality of their experiences. None of the recommendations are discussed in detail, and they surely reflect my biases. They are offered as food for thought.

First, among the most obvious needed reforms are alternative ways to identify gifted students that go beyond traditional methods of testing. As revealed in research on stereotype threat, the anxiety elicited by fear of confirming negative stereotypes about race and intelligence can deplete the cognitive resources needed to do well on standardized tests. These same concerns can be raised about high-stakes testing in general, which has had deleterious effects on children of color (e.g., Jacob, 2001; Ryan & Brown, 2005).

Second, because teacher referrals are the main vehicle by which students get the opportunity to be tested as gifted (e.g., Ford et al., 2000), it is essential that teachers be aware that referrals are subjective judgments about the behavior of other people and therefore are vulnerable to all of the known biases that can be present when inferences are made about other people. Some of those biases emerge from cultural stereotypes linking race to low intelligence and antisocial behavior that I mentioned earlier in this chapter. Moreover, as research in social psychology has documented, racial stereotypes often are activated and used outside of conscious awareness (e.g., Bargh & Chartrand, 1999). Unconscious stereotypes are unintentional because they are not planned responses; involuntary, because they occur automatically in the presence of an environmental cue; and effortless, in that they do not deplete an individual's limited information-processing resources. By automatically categorizing people according to cultural stereotypes, perceivers can manage information overload and make social decisions more efficiently. Particularly among perceivers at the front end of a system, such as teachers dealing with classroom disorder, decisions often must be made quickly, under conditions of cognitive and emotional overload, and in situations in which much ambiguity exists. These are the very conditions that are known to activate unconscious beliefs (Fiske, 1998). Most important, even nonprejudiced, well-intentioned perceivers are vulnerable to using stereotypes outside of conscious awareness (Graham & Lowery, 2004).

Third, and related to unconscious biases, teachers, counselors, and other decision makers need to be particularly sensitive to the cultural orientations of the students they teach and evaluate. For example, cultural styles preferred by African American learners that emphasize oral modes of communication, physical movement, affective expressiveness, and group orientation should not be misinterpreted as disrespect, disengagement, or disobedience (see Ford et al., 2000). The term *culturally relevant pedagogy* (e.g., Hale, 2001; Ladson-Billings, 1994) has become part of the contemporary educational discourse to capture teachers' needed sensitivity. Although the construct emerged as a pedagogical lens through which to think about improving the performance of low-achieving ethnic youth, its principles of acknowledging the connection between culture and learning and incorporating a wider range of teaching practices are equally applicable to the instruction of talented youth. Ford and her colleagues have persuasively argued that the goals of education for the gifted and goals of culturally relevant pedagogy are closely intertwined (Ford & Harris, 1999).

Fourth, in light of challenges to perceptions of "I can" during adolescence, teachers need to be especially vigilant about not using instructional practices that can indirectly and unintentionally communicate low-ability messages. For example, it has been documented that undifferentiated praise for success at easy tasks, unsolicited offers of help, and too much sympathy following failure can lead students to attribute their academic setbacks to low ability (Graham, 1991). Furthermore, altering pedagogical practices to be more effort- rather than ability-oriented can have immediate impact on students' motivation, even among those who are highly identified with the achievement domain. Cohen, Steele, and Ross (1999) found that African American college students displayed more subsequent task motivation when feedback about poor performance was accompanied by criticism and communicated high expectations than when the same feedback was accompanied by general praise as a buffer. Such feedback, labeled *wise* by Cohen et al. (1999), can shift the attribution for failure away from low ability and toward those factors such as lack of effort that are under volitional control.

Fifth, a more complete understanding of gender differences in outcomes for African American students has implications for the role that parents play in the achievement strivings of their sons and daughters. There is reason to believe that the parental socialization experiences of African American adolescent girls may contribute to their apparently greater resiliency in school contexts and to their continued valuing of achievement. For example, the racial socialization literature suggests that some African American parents are more likely to teach their daughters about racial pride which can then enhance achievement strivings, whereas they are more likely to instruct their sons about racial prejudice and discrimination, which might heighten their perception of the school environment as unsupportive (Bowman & Howard, 1985; see review in Hughes et al., 2006). African American parents need to recognize the importance of a balance between preparing their children to cope with the potential barriers to educational opportunity and instilling the expectation that working hard does indeed pay off. I believe that the study of how racial socialization affects gender differences in motivation and achievement among ethnic minority youth is a potentially rich topic for future research.

And finally, educational practices in secondary schools that limit access and opportunity for gifted students of color need to be rethought. For example, a large body of data suggests that academic tracking in secondary school works to the disadvantage of minority youth. As shown in Table 7.1, Black and Latino students are less likely to be in gifted programs than are Whites and Asians. And this pattern is not solely a function of lower test scores, for there is evidence that African American and Latino students are less likely than Asian and White students with the same high test scores to be in accelerated courses (e.g., NRC, 2002; Oakes, 1995). Because tracking in multiethnic schools resegregates youth along racial lines, African American students who are fortunate enough to be in gifted tracks will have limited contact with other African American peers at a time when ethnicity takes on added significance and adolescents are particularly motivated to affiliate with same-race peers (Shrum, Cheek, & Hunter, 1988). Thus, academic tracking undermines both "can" and "want" for gifted students of color, which leads one to question both the wisdom and fairness of such practices.

Reconciling equity and the need to be inclusive in gifted education with exceptionality and the need to meet the needs of remarkably intellectually talented children is a complex problem with no simple solutions. As long as identification and selection procedures for gifted placement rely mainly on established tests of cognitive abilities, there will be racial–ethnic imbalances such as those displayed in Table 7.1. Experts in gifted education need to develop creative ways that meet standards of scientific rigor and objectivity to seek out extraordinarily talented youth in all racial–ethnic groups at all ages. That may be the best way to promote the field of giftedness and ensure its continued vitality.

REFERENCES

Ainsworth-Darnell, J., & Downey, D. (1998). Assessing the oppositional culture explanation for racial/ethnic differences in school performance. *American Sociological Review, 63*, 536–553.

Aronson, J., Fried, C., & Good, C. (2002). Reducing the effects of stereotype threat on African American college students by shaping theories of intelligence. *Journal of Experimental Social Psychology, 38*, 113–125.

Aronson, J., & Steele, C. M. (2005). Stereotypes and the fragility of academic competence, motivation, and self-concept. In A. J. Elliot & C. S. Dweck (Eds.), *Handbook of competence and motivation* (pp. 436–456). New York: Guilford Press.

Bargh, J., & Chartrand, T. (1999). The unbearable automaticity of being. *American Psychologist, 54*, 462–479.

Barker, G., & Graham, S. (1987). A developmental study of praise and blame as attributional cues. *Journal of Educational Psychology, 79*, 62–66.

Baumeister, R., & Leary, M. (1995). The need to belong: Desire for interpersonal attachment as a fundamental human motivation. *Psychological Bulletin, 117*, 497–529.

Bowman, P., & Howard, C. (1985). Race-related socialization, motivation, and academic achievement: A study of Black youth in three-generation families. *Journal of the American Academy of Child Psychiatry, 24*, 134–141.

Brand, S., Felner, R., Shim, M., Seitsinger, A., & Dumas, T. (2003). Middle school improvement and reform: Development and validation of a school-level assessment of climate, cultural pluralism, and school safety. *Journal of Educational Psychology, 95*, 570–588.

Brown, B., & Steinberg, L. (1990). Academic achievement and social acceptance: Skirting the "brain-nerd" connection. *The Education Digest, 55*(7), 57–60.

Brown, C., & Bigler, R. (2005). Children's perceptions of discrimination: A developmental model. *Child Development, 76*, 533–553.

Clark, K., & Clark, M. (1947). Racial identification and preference in Negro children. In T. Newcomb & E. Hartley (Eds.), *Readings in social psychology* (pp. 602–611). New York: Holt.

Cohen, G., Steele, C., & Ross, L. (1999). The mentor's dilemma: Providing critical feedback across the racial divide. *Personality and Social Psychology Bulletin, 25*, 1302–1318.

Coleman, J. (1961). *The adolescent society*. New York: Free Press.

Cook, P., & Ludwig, J. (1997). Weighing the "burden of 'acting White' ": Are there race differences in attitudes toward education? *Journal of Policy Analysis and Management, 16*, 256–278.

Dai, D., Moon, S., & Feldhusen, J. (1998). Achievement motivation and gifted students: A social cognitive perspective. *Educational Psychologist, 33*, 45–63.

Devine, P. G., & Elliot, A. J. (1995). Are racial stereotypes really fading? The Princeton trilogy revisited. *Personality and Social Psychology Bulletin, 21*, 1139–1150.

Dweck, C. S. (1999). *Self-theories: Their role in motivation, personality, and development*. Philadelphia: Psychology Press.

Dweck, C. S. (2006). *Mindset: The new psychology of success*. New York: Random House.

Eccles, J. (2004). Schools, academic motivation, and stage-environment fit. In R. Lerner & L. Steinberg (Eds.), *Handbook of adolescent psychology* (2nd ed., pp. 125–153). New York: Wiley.

Eccles, J., Wigfield, A., & Schiefele, U. (1998). Motivation to succeed. In N. Eisenberg (Ed.), *Handbook of child psychology: Vol. 3. Social, emotional, and personality development* (5th ed., pp. 1017–1095). New York: Wiley.

Elliot, A. J. (2005). A conceptual history of the achievement goal construct. In A. J. Elliot & C. S. Dweck (Eds.), *Handbook of competence and motivation* (pp. 52–72). New York: Guilford Press.

Fisher, C., Wallace, S., & Fenton, R. (2000). Discrimination distress during adolescence. *Journal of Youth and Adolescence, 29*, 679–694.

Fiske, S. (1998). Stereotyping, prejudice, and discrimination. In D. Gilbert, S. Fiske, & G. Lindzey (Eds.), *Handbook of social psychology* (Vol. 2, 4th ed., pp. 357–411). Boston: McGraw-Hill.

Ford, D., Grantham, T., & Whiting, G. (2008). Another look at the achievement gap: Learning from the experiences of gifted Black students. *Urban Education, 43*, 216–239.

Ford, D., & Harris, J. (1999). *Multicultural gifted education*. New York: Teachers College Press.

Ford, D., Harris, J., Tyson, C., & Trotman, M. (2000). Beyond deficit thinking: Providing access for gifted African American students. *Roeper Review, 24,* 52–58.

Fordham, S., & Ogbu, J. (1986). Black students' school success: Coping with the "burden of 'acting White.' " *Urban Review, 18,* 176–206.

Gordon, R., Piana, L., & Keleher, T. (2001). *Facing the consequences: An examination of racial discrimination in the U.S. public schools.* Oakland, CA: Applied Research Center.

Gottfried, A. E., & Gottfried, A. W. (1996). A longitudinal study of academic intrinsic motivation in intellectually gifted children: Childhood through early adolescence. *Gifted Child Quarterly, 40,* 179–183.

Graham, S. (1991). Communicating low ability in the classroom: Bad things good teachers sometimes do. In S. Graham & V. Folkes (Eds.), *Attribution theory: Applications to achievement, mental health, and interpersonal conflict* (pp. 17–36). Hillsdale, NJ: Erlbaum.

Graham, S., & Lowery, B. (2004). Priming unconscious racial stereotypes about adolescent offenders. *Law and Human Behavior, 28,* 483–504.

Graham, S., Taylor, A., & Hudley, C. (1998). Exploring achievement values among ethnic minority early adolescents. *Journal of Educational Psychology, 91,* 606–620.

Graham, S., & Weiner, B. (1996). Theories and principles of motivation. In D. Berliner & R. Calfee (Eds.), *Handbook of educational psychology* (pp. 63–84). New York: Macmillan.

Hale, J. (2001). *Learning while Black: Creating educational excellence for African American children.* Baltimore: Johns Hopkins University Press.

Hemmings, A. (1996). Conflicting images? Being Black and model high school students. *Anthropology & Education Quarterly, 27,* 20–50.

Hudley, C., & Graham, S. (2001). Stereotypes of achievement strivings among early adolescents. *Social Psychology of Education, 5,* 201–224.

Hughes, D., Rodriguez, J., Smith, E., Johnson, D., Stevenson, H., & Spicer, P. (2006). Parents' ethnic-racial socialization practices: A review of research and directions for future study. *Developmental Psychology, 42,* 747–770.

Jacob, B. (2001). Getting tough? The impact of high school graduation exams. *Educational Evaluation and Policy Analysis, 23,* 99–121.

Juvonen, J., & Murdock, T. (1995). Grade-level differences in the social value of effort: Implications for self-presentation tactics of early adolescents. *Child Development, 66,* 1694–1705.

Kao, G. (2000). Group images and possible selves among adolescents: Linking stereotypes to expectations by race and ethnicity. *Sociological Forum, 15,* 407–430.

Ladson-Billings, G. (1994). *The dreamkeepers*. San Francisco: Jossey-Bass.

Lee, S. (1994). Behind the model-minority stereotype: Voices of high- and low-achieving Asian American students. *Anthropology & Education Quarterly, 25,* 413–429.

Major, B., & Schmader, T. (2001). Coping with stigma through psychological disengagement. In J. Swim & C. Sangor (Eds.), *Prejudice: The target's perspective* (pp. 219–241). San Diego, CA: Academic Press.

McKown, C., & Weinstein, R. (2003). The development and consequences of stereotype consciousness in middle childhood. *Child Development, 74,* 498–515.

National Research Council. (2002). *Minority students in special and gifted education.* Washington, DC: National Academy Press.

Neihart, M., Reis, S., Robinson, N., & Moon, S. (Eds.). (2002). *The social and emotional development of gifted children: What do we know?* Waco, TX: Prufrock Press.

Niemann, Y., Pollack, K., Rogers, S., & O'Connor, E. (1998). Effects of physical context in stereotyping of Mexican-American males. *Hispanic Journal of Behavioral Sciences, 20,* 349–362.

Oakes, J. (1995). Two cities' tracking and within-school segregation. *Teachers' College Record, 96,* 681–690.

Osborne, J. (1997). Race and academic disengagement. *Journal of Educational Psychology, 89,* 728–735.

Oyserman, D., & Sakamoto, I. (1997). Being Asian American: Identity, cultural constructs, and stereotype perception. *Journal of Applied Behavioral Science, 33,* 435–453.

Phinney, J., Madden, T., & Santos, L. (1998). Psychological variables as predictors of perceived ethnic discrimination among minority and immigrant adolescents. *Journal of Applied Social Psychology, 28,* 937–953.

Robinson, A., & Clinkenbeard, P. (1998). Giftedness: An exceptionality examined. *Annual Review of Psychology, 49,* 117–139.

Ruble, D., & Martin, C. (1998). Gender development. In N. Eisenberg (Ed.), *Handbook of child psychology: Vol. 3. Social, emotional, and personality development* (5th ed., pp. 993–1016). New York: Wiley.

Ryan, R., & Brown, K. (2005). Legislating competence: High stakes testing policies and their relations with psychological theories and research. In A. Elliot & C. S. Dweck (Eds.), *Handbook of competence and motivation* (pp. 354–372). New York: Guilford Press.

Schuman, H., Steeh, C., Bobo, L., & Krysan, M. (1997). *Racial attitudes in America: Trends and interpretations.* Cambridge, MA: Harvard University Press.

Shrum, W., Cheek, N., & Hunter, S. (1988). Friendship in school: Gender and racial homophily. *Sociology of Education, 61,* 227–239.

Sidanius, J., & Pratto, F. (1999). *Social dominance.* New York: Cambridge University Press.

Skiba, R. (2001). When is disproportionality discrimination? The overrepresentation of Black students in school suspension. In W. Ayers, B. Dohrn, & R. Ayers (Eds.), *Zero tolerance: Resisting the drive for punishment in our schools* (pp. 176–187). New York: New Press.

Skiba, R., Reynolds, C. R., Graham, S., Sheras, P., Conoley, J. C., & Garcia-Vazquez, E. (2006). *Are zero tolerance policies effective in the schools? An evidentiary review and recommendations.* Washington, DC: American Psychological Association Zero Tolerance Task Force.

Solorzano, D. (2000). Critical race theory, racial microaggressions, and campus racial climate: The experiences of African American college students. *Journal of Negro Education, 69,* 60–73.

Solorzano, D., & Ornelas, A. (2004). A critical race analysis of Latina/o and African American advanced placement enrollment in public high schools. *The High School Journal, 87*(3), 15–26.

Spencer, M., Noll, E., Stoltzfus, J., & Harpalani, V. (2001). Identity and school adjustment: Revisiting the "acting White" assumption. *Educational Psychologist, 36,* 21–30.

Steele, C. (1997). A threat in the air: How stereotypes shape the intellectual identities of women and African Americans. *American Psychologist, 52,* 613–629.

Steele, C., & Aronson, J. (1995). Stereotype threat and the intellectual performance of African Americans. *Journal of Personality and Social Psychology, 69,* 797–811.

Steinberg, L. (1996). *Beyond the classroom: Why school reform has failed and what parents need to do.* New York: Simon & Schuster.

Stipek, D., & MacIver, D. (1988). Developmental change in children's assessment of intellectual competence. *Child Development, 60,* 521–538.

Swiatek, M. (2001). Social coping among gifted high school students and its relationship to self-concept. *Journal of Youth and Adolescence, 30,* 19–39.

Taylor, A. Z., & Graham, S. (2007). An examination of the relationship between achievement values and perceptions of barriers among low-SES African American and Latino students. *Journal of Educational Psychology, 99,* 52–64.

Taylor, R., Casten, R., Flickinger, S., Roberts, D., & Fulmore, C. (1994). Explaining the school performance of African-American adolescents. *Journal of Research on Adolescence, 4,* 21–44.

8

WHAT DOES *GIFTED* MEAN? PERSONAL AND SOCIAL IDENTITY PERSPECTIVES ON GIFTEDNESS IN ADOLESCENCE

FRANK C. WORRELL

I was honored to be asked to respond to chapter 7 of this volume by Sandra Graham on giftedness in adolescence. When I read the chapter, I found, as expected, that Graham's social–psychological perspective and my psychosocial perspective have much in common, including a focus on the interaction of motivation and social context. Therefore, I have endeavored to expand on some of the issues that Graham addresses in her chapter, in the hope of stimulating discussion among researchers and practitioners concerned with giftedness in adolescence. Graham (chap. 7, this volume) concludes with five general recommendations: (a) find alternative ways to identify gifted and talented students, (b) educate teachers to minimize the role of unconscious and unintentional stereotypes of gifted referrals, (c) educate teachers about the cultural styles preferred by African American learners, (d) educate teachers so that they do not use instructional practices that communicate low-ability messages to students, and (e) rethink the educational practices in secondary schools that work to the disadvantage of minority youth.

In this chapter, I discuss identification practices in some detail, as I believe that there are some fundamental misunderstandings in this area. I highlight some of the more recent research on teachers and the messages that they send. I also address the potential role played by identity variables such as stereotype threat. In addition, I discuss the concept of oppositional identity, which relates to Graham's notion of "I can, but do I *want* to?" Finally, I briefly discuss the idea of cultural learning styles. Although much of what I discuss is applicable to adolescents of all ethnic and racial backgrounds, the implications may be different for youth who are traditionally underrepresented in gifted and talented education (e.g., African Americans, Latinos).

THE ISSUE OF IDENTIFICATION

To understand the issue of minority underrepresentation in gifted and talented education (GATE) that has been the focus of much scholarly commentary and criticism (e.g., Baldwin, 1985; Ford, 1998; Plummer, 1995; A. Robinson, Bradley, & Stanley, 1990; Worrell, 2003), one must appreciate how the identification process works. Several decades of these criticisms have resulted in little change in the underrepresentation problem, in part because finding compelling alternatives to standard identification procedures is a difficult task.

Where Does Identification Generally Occur?

When individuals think about giftedness, they almost inevitably think of the education sector because the identification of and programming for the gifted have been almost exclusively conducted in that arena. The association between giftedness and education was strengthened with the Marland (1972) report, which provided the first federal definition of gifted education. In this report, Marland, who was then the U.S. commissioner of education, argued that children who had exceptional ability and were capable of high performance should be provided with more differentiated instruction than could be provided in the general education classroom. He indicated six domains in which giftedness could occur (intellectual functioning, specific academic abilities, creativity, leadership, visual and performing arts, and psychomotor ability) and noted that specialists were required to identify these exceptional children.

Despite the federal acknowledgment of gifted students in the schools, there is no federal mandate for gifted and talented education and, concomitantly, no federal funding for gifted and talented education. Thus, the decision to provide GATE programs has been and continues to be decided by states and is affected annually by the states' fiscal situation. Even when states have surpluses, states tend to view it as being in their best interest to keep the education budget manageable by limiting the number of students who qualify for GATE programs. In 2002, only 29 states mandated gifted education services (Council of State Directors of Programs for the Gifted and National Association for Gifted Children, 2003).

Who Qualifies for the Gifted Label?

Two decades ago, Sternberg and Davidson (1986a, 1986b) highlighted 17 definitions of giftedness in the research literature, which they classified as either implicit (i.e., they cannot be tested empirically) or explicit. However, almost all definitions of giftedness "indicate or imply that giftedness is manifested in some performance or achievement that is valued in a particular societal context" (Worrell, 2003, p. 425). Thus, it can be argued that anyone who demonstrated superior functioning (e.g., the top 1%–5%) in a domain valued by society has the potential to achieve the descriptor *gifted*. Indeed, in his definition, Marland (1972) included psychomotor ability, leadership, and the visual and performing arts alongside the more traditional gifted domains such as intelligence, academic performance, and creativity.

Marland's (1972) recommendations did not result in a sea change in educational practice, or in how students are identified for GATE programs, and most school districts continue to identify gifted students in intellectual and academic domains. Larger districts (e.g., Houston, Los Angeles, New York, Philadelphia) have at least one school for the visual and performing arts, but these schools usually accommodate a small fraction of the talented students in these domains. Moreover, although individual high schools in some districts are known for the caliber of their sports programs (particularly football and basketball), these programs are not conceived of as GATE programs even though they function like GATE programs in actuality—that is, students are screened and individuals with superior talent are identified and provided with individual instruction in a community of learners who also are strong in that talent domain.

Thus, to earn a place in a GATE program in most school districts in the nation, students need to have high IQ scores or high scores in academic subject areas. There are at least two reasons for the sustained attention on the intellectual and academic domains. First, reading, writing, and arithmetic—supplemented with the social, biological, and physical sciences and the humanities—continue to form the core of K–12 educational programming. The second reason is equally compelling:

> Even our most competent regular education teachers are not prepared to teach music, drama, dance, or painting to individuals who are gifted in these areas. And even if they were, our current school system does not have the time built in for these subjects. If schools are expected to identify and educate potentially talented students in areas other than the academic, society must provide additional resources for schools in these areas. (Worrell, 2003, p. 432)

Without intending to disparage, and in light of the training and preparation of teachers in schools, one can ask the question, Would we and should we leave the education of a potential Mozart or Picasso in their respective areas of giftedness to the public school system? Thus, the students who qualify for the gifted label in schools are those who excel in the core academic domains.

Identification Procedures

As indicated, critics have argued that alternatives to IQ should be used in identifying minority students for GATE programs. However, a basic concern for any gifted identification procedure is predictive validity, or the accuracy with which a test of giftedness predicts actual performance in a GATE program. The best single predictor of achievement in any academic domain is typically previous achievement in that domain (Tickell & Smyrnios, 2005; Troutman, 1978), and IQ is a strong predictor of achievement across all academic domains (Brody, 1997; Ceci & Williams, 1997; Neisser et al., 1996). Thus, the continued use of IQ tests for gifted identification should be expected, the Black–White gap in IQ notwithstanding (Jencks & Phillips, 1998), especially because the weight of the research evidence in this area indicates that the commonly used IQ tests are not biased against minority groups in terms of structural or predictive validity (Frisby & Braden, 1999; Reynolds & Carson, 2005). As I discuss later in this chapter, research over the past decade (e.g., Steele, 1997) suggests that testing situations can have a disproportionately negative impact on the performance of students from stereotyped groups. However, these negative effects are the result of the social context of testing and not of the tests themselves, and performance in both academic and nonacademic domains is affected (e.g., Stone, Lynch, Sjomeling, & Darley, 1999).

If districts were to eliminate the use of IQ tests for identifying gifted students, domain-specific achievement tests would be a good logical alternative because they are the best predictors of future performance in their domains. However, the differences present in IQ are also evident in achievement scores from the early elementary school years (Ferguson, 1998; Lee, 2002; Phillips, Crouse, & Ralph, 1998) and in teacher-made tests in the classroom. These findings indicate that the lack of minority adolescents from certain backgrounds in GATE programs stems in part from the lower overall distribution of scores, whether selection is based on IQ or achievement. The increasing use of gifted rating scales does not solve this problem, as most of these scales require teachers to provide global impressions of students, and the pattern of intercorrelations among the subscales and with achievement calls into question the concurrent validity of the constructs (Worrell & Schaefer, 2004). In sum, although no one would argue against the use of alternative identification measures for GATE programs, there are currently no alternative measures with good evidence of incremental predictive validity beyond IQ and previous achievement.

TEACHER EXPECTATIONS

Since the initial publication of the Pygmalion in the Classroom study (Rosenthal & Jacobsen, 1968), a tremendous amount of research attention has addressed the role of teacher expectations, with an emphasis on the presence and potency of these effects. Jussim and Harber (2005) summarized the literature on this topic. They concluded that although self-fulfilling prophecies occur, they are typically small and not cumulative and that teachers' expectations predict student outcomes because they are accurate, not because they are self-fulfilling. Jussim and Harber also observed, however, that self-fulfilling prophecies are more likely to occur among stigmatized groups, a claim that is in keeping with the findings of Weinstein (2002) and her colleagues (McKown & Weinstein, 2002) over several decades.

Weinstein and her collaborators have found that children in elementary schools—from first grade to fifth grade—can distinguish between teacher treatment of low achievers and teacher treatment of high achievers (Brattesani, Weinstein, & Marshall, 1984; Kuklinski & Weinstein, 2001; Weinstein & Middlestadt, 1979):

> Across these studies, children report on average that high achievers are favored in their interactions with teachers. They are accorded higher expectations . . . more opportunity . . . and more choice in the classroom than low achievers. In contrast, in the eyes of children, low achievers are likely to receive more frequent negative feedback . . . and more teacher-directed treatment . . . than high achievers. (Weinstein, 2002, pp. 95–96)

Weinstein (2002) went on to describe "the sensitivity with which children interpret the implicit meaning underlying teacher behavior" (p. 99), and how teacher beliefs about the malleability of intelligence—that is, whether teachers view ability as fixed or malleable—interact with their behaviors to create classrooms that communicate messages to children about their potential to achieve.

The work on self-fulfilling prophecies and teacher expectation effects is particularly applicable in the case of students from stigmatized groups who have the potential to be successful in GATE programs. First, African American and Hispanic children are more likely to live in poverty than are their Asian and White counterparts, and they are also less likely to have parents with a college education (Hoffman & Llagas, 2003). In other words, these groups often have less educational capital, which can have implications for navigating the school system and gaining access to talent development programs both during the school year (Sosniak, 1999) and in the summer (Sosniak, 2005). Second, the impact of teacher beliefs on Black students is greater than the impact on White students, even when the beliefs are not biased (Ferguson, 1998; McKown & Weinstein, 2002). Thus, when students from stigmatized groups are admitted to GATE programs, they are likely to have a lower sense of efficacy and greater doubts about their ability to succeed (Gabelko & Sosniak, 2002), and they are also especially vulnerable to teacher beliefs. These findings highlight the need for ongoing support mechanisms.

THE ROLE OF IDENTITY

Identity plays a key role in adolescence (Erikson, 1968) and is associated with the question, Who am I? Indeed, personal identity constructs such as academic self-efficacy and intrinsic motivation have been shown to have robust relationships with academic achievement (e.g., Lepper & Henderlong, 2000; Schunk & Pajares, 2002). However, as Erikson (1968) noted, other fundamental questions of identity include, "Who am I in this social context" and "What does my membership in a particular group say about me." More recent research has highlighted relationships between social identity constructs and academic achievement (e.g., Arroyo & Zigler, 1995; Oyserman, Kemmelmeier, Fryberg, Brosh, & Hart-Johnson, 2003). The two most comprehensive explanations of the role of social identity constructs on academic achievement are cultural ecological theory (Ogbu, 1978, 1989, 2004; Ogbu & Simons, 1998) and stereotype threat (Steele, 1997, 2003; Steele & Aronson, 1998).

Cultural Ecological Theory

In cultural ecological theory, Ogbu (1978) asks three major questions: (a) Was a racial or ethnic group's incorporation into American society voluntary or involuntary; (b) Is the racial or ethnic group treated fairly and equitably, or is it discriminated against; and (c) How does the group respond to society's treatment, especially if society treats the group negatively? Ogbu argued that ethnic groups such as African Americans, Chicanos, and Native Americans are involuntary minorities and are on the receiving end of discriminatory and unfair treatment. As a consequence, some members of these groups may develop an identity in opposition to mainstream culture (including schooling) and may associate doing well in school with *acting White* (Fordham & Ogbu, 1986). These group members can develop attitudes and engage in behaviors that are incompatible with educational success.

Although several scholars have argued against the propositions laid out in cultural ecological theory, and some authors have found no evidence that Black students equate doing well in school with acting White (e.g., Cook & Ludwig, 1998), research provides support for some of Ogbu's claims. Oyserman et al. (2003) found that members of involuntary minority groups who adopted an in-group-only racial–ethnic self-schema had lower academic engagement and achievement than did their peers who adopted racial–ethnic self-schemas incorporating their own group as well as the larger society. In another study, Worrell (2007) found that ethnic identity attitudes focused on the ingroup had a negative relationship with grade point average (GPA), whereas attitudes indicating a willingness to engage with other groups had a positive relationship with school GPA. However, these findings applied only to African Americans and not to Latinos, Whites, or Asian Americans. Moreover, the negative relationship between ethnic identity and achievement occurred in school but not in the talent development program, highlighting the interaction of individual and context.

In a dissertation study, Gardner-Kitt (2005) found that anti-White racial identity attitudes were positively related to problem behaviors and negatively related to perceived school climate. Finally, Ford (2005) examined the notion of acting White directly by interviewing over 900 African American students in Grades 4 through 12, 46% of whom were identified as GATE students. More than 75% of the participants had heard the terms *acting Black* and *acting White*. Participants reported that acting White involved behaving intelligently and being achievement-oriented, whereas acting Black involved behaving "ghetto" and acting stupid. These findings suggest that for some students, including gifted and talented students, certain social identity attitudes may result in lower academic engagement and achievement.

Students whose reference group orientation is at odds with academic achievement (Ford, 2005; Gardner-Kitt, 2005; Oyserman et al., 2003; Worrell, 2007) are on the horns of a dilemma that is exacerbated in adolescence: Do they choose to be Black or to be good students; to fit in with their friends or to face accusations of betraying their ethnic heritage; or to belong to a group with which they share an ethnic heritage or to belong to the group of high achievers that includes many individuals who are not like them and who may also not embrace them? Arroyo and Zigler (1995) found that racelessness scores, consisting of items measuring achievement attitudes, impression management, alienation, and stereotypical beliefs, were related to higher academic achievement for both African American and White adolescents but were also related to higher depression scores for the African Americans. In sum, members of stigmatized groups may pay a high price if they choose to achieve.

Stereotype Threat

The stereotype threat phenomenon (Steele, 1997; Steele & Aronson, 1998) provides another cogent explanation for underachievement on the part of stigmatized groups:

> When a negative stereotype about one's group becomes relevant to the situation that one is in, it signals the risk of being judged or treated stereotypically, or of doing something that would inadvertently confirm

the stereotype. Whether this predicament affects behavior depends not on whether one has internalized the stereotype as self-doubt, but on whether one cares about the domain in which the stereotype applies. (Steele & Aronson, 1998, p. 403)

In U.S. society, a widespread stereotype of African Americans is that they are less intelligent than are Whites. Therefore, in competitive academic situations or situations in which one can infer the intelligence of the group on the basis of performance (e.g., diagnostic or ability testing), stereotype threat is likely to occur. Of particular importance in this context is that students with strong academic identities (e.g., potential gifted and talented students) and students who are invested in doing well academically are most likely to be vulnerable to stereotype threat (Aronson, 2002; Steele, 2003; Steele & Aronson, 1998). Aronson (2002) also pointed out that the context alone could invoke a diagnostic testing situation without overt action on the part of examiners.

Much of the initial research on stereotype threat was conducted with college students (e.g., Steele & Aronson, 1998). However, the effect has been demonstrated in school-age populations in more recent research. In a two-part study, McKown and Weinstein (2003) revealed two important findings. First, they found that a majority of students from as young as 8 years old could recognize that an individual belonged to a stigmatized group, and that the percentage of students who could do this increased to over 90% by age 10. Moreover, members of stigmatized groups (i.e., African Americans and Latinos) recognize the stigma more quickly than do members of nonstigmatized groups (i.e., Asian Americans and Whites). Second, McKown and Weinstein (2003) found that "children from stigmatized groups [performed] significantly worse under diagnostic testing conditions" (p. 509) than did their peers from nonstigmatized groups. Thus, the stereotype threat phenomenon can occur across educational levels from elementary school to college. Therefore, although tests are not necessarily biased, testing situations can still yield lower test scores for students from negatively stereotyped groups.

Summary

Although Ogbu (2004) and Steele (1997) have put forward different explanations for the underachievement of minority groups in the United States, cultural ecological theory and stereotype threat have a common foundation. Both perspectives involve the interplay of personal identity (e.g., intelligence, academic self-efficacy) and social identity or reference group orientation (e.g., racial and ethnic group membership). This foundation serves as a reminder that academic achievement is not merely an individual endeavor; rather, it occurs in a social context and is framed by one's perceived position in the social structure of the society. In essence, both theories require an examination of the conflict inherent in being from a stigmatized group and being a high achiever, a conflict that many minority adolescents need to navigate, and one that is still not fully understood. Or as Graham (chap. 7, this volume) indicated, "I can, but do I *want* to?"

CULTURAL LEARNING STYLES

The issue of cultural learning styles has aroused heated debates in the educational literature (Frisby, 1992, 1993a, 1993b; Hale, 1993; Irvine & York, 2001; Richardson, 1993). Hale-Benson (1986) articulated the basic premise of cultural learning styles for African Americans in this way:

> The Black community of educational and psychological scholars must consider seriously the need to articulate a new conceptualization of the development and behavioral styles of Black children . . . our own definitions of aptitude, intelligence, and achievement within the context of African and African-American culture. . . . The hypothesis of this book is that Black children grow up in a distinct culture. . . . The hypothesis is that certain characteristics, peculiar to Black culture, have their roots in West Africa and have implications for the way in which Black children learn and think. (p. 4)

However, the claims of Black cultural learning styles have not held up well under serious research scrutiny (Frisby, 1993a, 1993b; Irvine & York, 2001).

Moreover, the basic premise of the argument raises serious concerns about culture and its relationship to academic achievement (Frisby, 1992). Several questions need to be addressed in this line of research. First, what characteristics of West African culture are being manifested by African American students in the 20th and 21st centuries? Second, how does one explain the relative success of some Black immigrants from West Africa and the Caribbean in the U.S. educational system (Waters, 1999; Worrell, 2005), especially as the education systems in all of the former European colonies are far more Eurocentric than the U.S. system? Third, if separate definitions of intelligence and achievement are created without concern for predictive validity, how can one know that Black students will succeed in the American educational context? Finally, how can one assume that there is a pan-West African culture, especially in light of the now-recognized need to examine data separately for different Asian (Kitano & DiJiosia, 2002; Pang, 2001; Thao, 2005; Yoon & Cheng, 2005), Black (Waters, 1999; Worrell, 2005), and Hispanic subgroups (Lopez, Lopez, Suarez-Morales, & Castro, 2005)?

The idea of cultural learning styles was a rational response to the poor performance of Black students in the education system and the inability to solve this problem after decades of research and commentary. Nonetheless, there is compelling evidence that the behaviors related to academic achievement cut across cultures (McDermott, 1999). More promising approaches include getting rid of the "structural inequalities in access to knowledge and resources" (Darling-Hammond, 2001, p. 465) for students from poor and minority backgrounds, "designing appropriate instruction for culturally diverse students" (Irvine & York, 2001, p. 484), and organizing education to minimize or buffer against the deleterious effects of stereotype threat (see Cohen, Garcia, Apfel, & Master, 2006).

HOW CAN THE NUMBERS OF GIFTED MINORITY ADOLESCENTS BE INCREASED?

If the goal is to merely increase the number of underrepresented students in GATE programs, then the solution is a relatively easy one. One way to accomplish this goal is to simply mandate that GATE programs proportionately reflect the demographic makeup of the student body of the school or district in which they are located. Thus, fewer Asian, White, and wealthy students would be admitted and greater numbers of African American, Latino, Native American, Southeast Asian, and poor students would be admitted. However, if solutions of this type are implemented without considering teacher expectations and stereotype threat concerns, they can result in increases in negative stereotypes of these students and, most important, undermine the self-efficacy and achievement potential of the very students that the policy is supposed to assist.

In light of the major potential negative consequences of a simple demographic solution to the problem of minority underrepresentation in GATE programs, it might be more productive to focus on increasing the number of underrepresented students who qualify for and can be successful in GATE programs. This solution requires more work and much more time. I propose two broad-based strategies to help us achieve this goal: (a) working on increasing achievement in all children from underrepresented groups beginning in the early elementary years and (b) investigating the mechanisms by which social identities affect achievement-related attitudes and behaviors.

Increasing Achievement Across All Groups

As illustrated by data from a variety of sources (e.g., Camara & Schmidt, 1999; Frederick D. Patterson Research Institute, 1997; Jencks & Phillips, 1998; Lee, 2002), there are major gaps in achievement across ethnic and racial groups, and identification for GATE programs provides an indication that a given student's performance or potential performance is in the superior range relative to peers. Thus, increasing the numbers of underrepresented students in GATE programs requires increasing the pool of these students performing at high levels in the school system. In other words, current identification practices preclude increasing the numbers of minorities in GATE programs without raising the distribution of achievement for minority groups relative to other groups.

However, increasing the numbers of ethnically diverse students in GATE programs is difficult because general academic interventions result in all groups gaining and may have no effect on the achievement gap (Ceci & Papierno, 2005). Thus, the initial goal may be misguided. Perhaps rather than focusing on increasing the numbers of ethnically diverse students in GATE, school systems should focus on ensuring that even the lowest achievers have mastered reading and mathematics and are prepared to succeed in adult society. Furthermore, targeted interventions should include increasing the resources given to and the effectiveness of teachers assigned to schools in minority and low-income areas (Darling-Hammond, 2001; Weinstein, 2002).

In addition, targeted interventions need to begin in the preschool and elementary school years. If there are few talented students in the elementary school grades, there will be fewer talented adolescents. GATE identification typically begins around Grade 2, and the majority of students identified for GATE programs are already assigned to these programs before they begin the middle school years. One way to increase identification is to deepen the pool of primary-grade students who are targeted for talent development programs, not by using proportional demographic representation as program criteria but rather by looking for the potential of talent beyond the anticipatory socialization (e.g., Merton, 1957; T. Robinson, 1990) that many students bring with them from their previous environments.

Thus, one of the goals of the selection process for GATE programs is to seek out talent in students in whom that talent has not already been cultivated and is evident. In 2001, Worrell, Szarko, and Gabelko made the following observation:

> Children who grow up in families with a history of success in school have learned many sets of lessons required for academic success [e.g., paying attention to adult speaking, following teachers' instructions, mastery of preliteracy and prenumeracy skills]—even before they enter kindergarten. Not only are such students usually unaware that they have "learned" these lessons, but schools treat these lessons as if they were "natural" to all academically talented pupils. Consequently, those students who have not prelearned these lessons are, almost certainly, not going to be taught them in school. Pupils who attend school without benefit of these prelearned lessons are likely to be told, over and over again, that they do not have the stuff of which school success is made, without ever being told that such "stuff" is learned. (p. 81)

The grail, the goal of equity in gifted and talented education, will remain forever distant if educators do not look for and find the hints of talent in unexpected places. In the Academic Talent Development Program at the University of California, Berkeley, a summer program for academically talented students, the program intentionally encourages participation instead of putting up roadblocks. About 20% of the more than 2,000 students who attend the program each summer are not identified as gifted or talented at their home schools, although they meet the summer program's criteria based on achievement, teacher recommendations, and student interests. Moreover, although GATE-identified students rated themselves significantly higher on ability than did nonidentified students, they did not rate themselves differently on program outcomes, including the level of challenge in the program, amount learned, or enjoyment (Worrell & Gabelko, 2005). Thus, students did not have to be already enrolled in a GATE program to benefit from the program, and being identified before the program started did not result in higher engagement or greater academic success. There is no reason to believe that these outcomes would be different in GATE programs in the schools.

Interventions must also include a focus on educating teachers differently for several reasons. First, even well-meaning teachers can communicate low expectations to students beginning as early as first grade (Weinstein, 2002). Second, teachers need to know that in the cultural context of the United States, students from stigmatized groups are more susceptible to negative messages from teachers (Ferguson, 1998; McKown & Weinstein, 2002). They also need to know that certain classroom practices related to grouping, curriculum, and evaluation can counter teachers' communication of negative stereotypes and convey positive expectations to all students (Weinstein, 1998). Finally, teachers need to understand the important role they play in student achievement. Despite claims about the importance of parent involvement and the belief that many teachers share that they cannot have an impact on students whose parents are not willing to work with them, the biggest contributions to student achievement in the classroom come from effective teaching (Sanders & Horn, 1998).

The retention of students in GATE must also be a key priority (Ford, 1995, 1998). To develop talents to a high level, it is necessary to engage in talent development activities for a sustained period. Sosniak (1999) reported on a group of extremely talented adults who were studied in the Development of Talent Research Project (Bloom, 1985). These individuals had demonstrated outstanding achievement in several different areas, including concert piano, sculpture, swimming, tennis, mathematics, and neurology. Sosniak (1999) identified three phases in the development of talent. In Phase 1, prior to adolescence, the individuals were "exposed regularly to activities connected with their subsequent talent fields . . . and they learned in informal ways about knowledge and skills of the activity in which they would eventually excel" (p. 167). In Phase 2, which began around adolescence, Sosniak reported that these individuals "were spending considerable time engaged with their talent field" (p. 167). Sosniak noted that the lives of these individuals' families were now arranged around the talent development enterprise, and found that the students "began working with more sophisticated teachers in more formal and disciplined ways" (p. 167).

Sosniak (1999) described Phase 3 as "focused and all-encompassing" (p. 168). She pointed out that it was in this phase that these individuals "were most fully introduced to the [talent] community modeling the highest standards of the field. And it was during this period that the students needed to make their own commitments to the pursuit of excellence" (p. 168). Sosniak's description of the long-term commitment required for developing talent to a high level is exemplified in the following anecdote. When I attended the conference at which this paper was first presented, I spent one evening watching a skating competition on television with my sister. At the end of one of the routines, a reporter asked a skater to comment on how he had put on such a wonderful performance. His response was, "25 years of practice." That same evening, another reporter indicated that another skater—the 2006 Winter Olympics gold medalist—had begun skating 16 years previously. The importance of dedicated and appropriate practice in the development of talent is acknowledged in athletics as described earlier and in the visual and performing arts; too often, however, this important aspect of developing talent is ignored in academic domains.

Data from a 2005 study by Ford also speak to this issue. She asked the students to indicate how much time they spend during the week engaged in a variety of activities. As indicated in Figure 8.1, both GATE-identified students and nonidentified students reported spending more time each week in activities such as talking on the phone, playing sports, or playing video games than they spent on studying, assigned reading, or personal reading. It is critical to communicate to students the importance of task commitment (Renzulli, 1986) and incremental views of intelligence (Dweck, 1986) alongside educating teachers about the importance of their roles and the negative effect of low expectations. As Adelman (2006) so cogently put it, "Wishing doesn't do it; preparation does!" (p. 103).

Examine the Contributions of Social Identities to Achievement

Despite the increasing number of position papers and empirical studies on the role of social identities (e.g., Aronson, 2002; McKown & Weinstein, 2003; Ogbu & Simons, 1998; Oyserman et al., 2003; Steele, 2003), very little is known about the mechanisms by which these processes work and, more important, how much variance they account for in student achievement, although there is promising work in the area using student affirmations

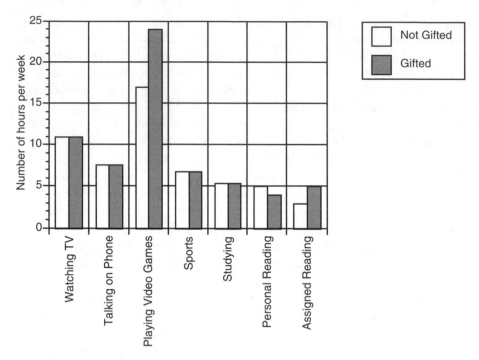

Figure 8.1. Number of hours per week by gifted/nongifted label. Data from Ford (2005).

(Cohen et al., 2006). How pervasive are the attitudes of anti-intellectualism and oppositional identity in minority communities, and why are some students more vulnerable to peer pressure against achievement than are others? How does one counter the influence of stereotype threat and develop achievement-oriented cultures in groups to whom society continues to communicate messages about their inability to achieve?

These questions are important for several reasons. First, the achievement gap still exists (Lee, 2002; Worrell, 2005; see Figure 8.2). As educational researchers, we must pursue all logical explanations for the gap. Second, some still see the achievement gap as resulting solely from the gap in IQ (e.g., Rushton & Jensen, 2005a, 2005b). However, IQ accounts for at most 50% of the variance in achievement, leaving 50% to be accounted for by other factors. In other words, IQ may be the best single predictor of academic achievement, but it is not the only predictor. Moreover, Turkheimer, Haley, Waldron, D'Onofrio, and Gottesman (2003) demonstrated quite compellingly that "the relative importance of environmental differences in causing differences in observed intelligence appears to vary with the SES [socioeconomic status] of the homes in which children are raised," (p. 627) with SES contributing more

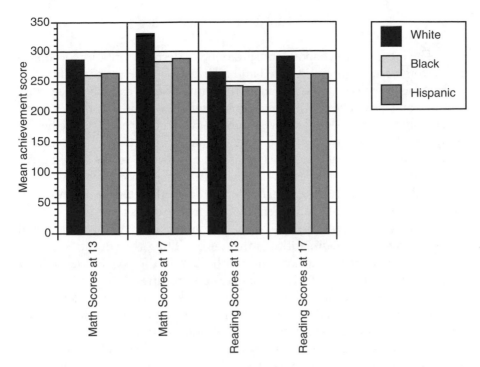

Figure 8.2. Mean achievement scores in reading and mathematics for African American, Latino, and White students from the 2004 National Assessment of Education Progress. Data from http://nces.ed.gov/pubs2007/minoritytrends/ind_3_9.asp

to the variance in IQ in lower SES environments. Turkheimer et al. (2003) concluded that much is unknown about the interaction of intelligence and socioeconomic status.

Third, new instruments such as the Multigroup Ethnic Identity Measure (Phinney, 1992) and the Cross Racial Identity Scale (Vandiver et al., 2000) allow researchers to measure cultural identities from early adolescence through adulthood. Studies using these instruments (e.g., Worrell & Gardner-Kitt, 2006; Worrell, Vandiver, Schaefer, Cross, & Fhagen-Smith, 2006) have replicated findings from qualitative studies, indicating that different identity profiles exist in minority populations, and other studies have indicated that different identity attitudes have different relationships with variables related to achievement (Gardner-Kitt, 2005). Research shows that variables such as self-efficacy and intrinsic motivation have direct relationships with achievement and that gifted and talented students report higher levels on these constructs. What is not yet known is whether different identity profiles have differential relationships with self-efficacy and intrinsic motivation, with concomitantly differential implications for achievement.

CONCLUSION

The focus of this chapter is the profound underrepresentation of adolescents from certain groups in gifted and talented education. It is difficult to understand how a country as affluent as the United States can have such long-standing and pervasive gaps in educational attainment, and why there are still so few solutions after decades of research. I have argued that a public health approach is required to solve this problem—that is, increase the achievement of all members of underachieving groups and not just those who might qualify for GATE programs. Research has highlighted the importance of what lessons students learn at home, what teachers do in the classroom, and what students do in school. If assignment to GATE continues to be based on the prelearning that students bring with them from home, GATE programs will continue to reflect the disparities of the nation. Thus, the education system must look beyond what students bring with them to the possibilities of what students will be able to do with appropriate opportunities for learning. Teachers must be trained to be effective purveyors of knowledge to students from all groups, and teacher education programs must include information on the importance of teacher expectations and cultural identities.

Finally, the education system must acknowledge and promote the importance of engaged time and task commitment in the talent development process. Students' talents will not blossom unless students are given the appropriate guidance and encouragement for sustained periods. Finding an adolescent who is gifted in writing presumes a system that has exposed and encouraged writing in childhood. If the goal is to increase the number of talented adolescents, more children and preteens must be provided with the time, resources, and opportunities to develop their talents. Schools and teachers must highlight the importance of effort and persistence in the development of talents, most particularly in the case of students for whom the school setting is the only one in which their talent is being systematically and intentionally developed. Both teachers and students need to learn that talent is transformed into high performance by way of a willingness to try, investment in time for guided practice, and persistence when tasks become difficult or failure has occurred. Thanks to these understandings about the development of talent, students, irrespective of their backgrounds, will be well prepared to achieve success at the highest levels.

REFERENCES

Adelman, C. (2006). *The toolbox revisited: Paths to degree completion from high school through college*. Washington, DC: U.S. Department of Education.

Aronson, J. (2002). Stereotype threat: Contending and coping with unnerving expectations. In J. Aronson (Ed.), *Improving academic achievement: Impact of psychological factors on education* (pp. 279–301). San Francisco: Elsevier Science.

Arroyo, C. G., & Zigler, E. (1995). Racial identity, academic achievement, and the psychological well-being of economically disadvantaged adolescents. *Journal of Personality and Social Psychology, 69,* 903–914.

Baldwin, A. Y. (1985). Programs for the gifted and talented: Issues concerning minority populations. In F. D. Horowitz & M. O'Brien (Eds.), *The gifted and talented: Developmental perspectives* (pp. 223–249). Washington, DC: American Psychological Association.

Bloom, B. S. (Ed.). (1985). *Developing talent in young people.* New York: Ballantine Books.

Brattesani, K. A., Weinstein, R. S., & Marshall, H. H. (1984). Student perceptions of differential teacher treatment as moderators of teacher expectation effects. *Journal of Educational Psychology, 76,* 236–247.

Brody, N. (1997). Intelligence, schooling, and society. *American Psychologist, 52,* 1046–1050.

Camara, W. J., & Schmidt, A. E. (1999). *Group differences in standardized testing and social stratification* (Report 99-5). New York: The College Entrance Examination Board.

Ceci, S. J., & Papierno, P. B. (2005). The rhetoric and reality of gap closing: When the "have-nots" gain but the "haves" gain even more. *American Psychologist, 60,* 149–160.

Ceci, S. J., & Williams, W. M. (1997). Schooling, intelligence, and income. *American Psychologist, 52,* 1051–1058.

Cohen, G. L., Garcia, J., Apfel, N., & Master, A. (2006, September 1). Reducing the racial achievement gap: A social-psychological intervention. *Science, 313,* 1307–1310.

Cook, P. J., & Ludwig, J. (1998). The burden of "acting White": Do Black adolescents disparage academic achievement? In C. Jencks & M. Phillips (Eds.), *The Black-White test score gap* (pp. 375–400). Washington, DC: Brookings Institution Press.

Council of State Directors of Programs for the Gifted and National Association for Gifted Children. (2003). *State of the states: Gifted and talented education report, 2001–2002.* Washington, DC: National Association for Gifted Children.

Darling-Hammond, L. (2001). Inequality and access to knowledge. In J. A. Banks (Ed.), *Handbook of research on multicultural education* (pp. 465–483). San Francisco: Wiley.

Dweck, C. S. (1986). Motivational processes affecting learning. *American Psychologist, 41,* 1040–1048.

Erikson, E. H. (1968). *Identity: Youth and crisis.* New York: Norton.

Ferguson, R. F. (1998). Teachers' perceptions and expectations and the Black-White test score gap. In C. Jencks & M. Phillips (Eds.), *The Black-White test score gap* (pp. 273–317). Washington, DC: Brookings Institution Press.

Ford, D. Y. (1995). Desegregating gifted education: A need unmet. *Journal of Negro Education, 64,* 52–62.

Ford, D. Y. (1998). The underrepresentation of minority students in gifted education: Problems and promises in recruitment and retention. *The Journal of Special Education, 32,* 4–14.

Ford, D. Y. (2005). *African American students' perceptions of barriers to achievement: A clarion call to gifted education.* Paper presented at the annual meeting of the National Association of Gifted Children, Louisville, KY.

Fordham, S., & Ogbu, J. U. (1986). Black students' school success: Coping with the "burden of acting White." *Urban Review, 18,* 176–206.

Frederick D. Patterson Research Institute. (1997). *The African American education databook: Vol. II. Preschool through high school education.* Fairfax, VA: Author.

Frisby, C. L. (1992). Issues and problems in the influence of culture on the psychoeducational needs of African-American children. *School Psychology Review, 21,* 532–551.

Frisby, C. L. (1993a). "Afrocentric" explanations for school failure: Symptoms of denial, frustration, and despair. *School Psychology Review, 22,* 568–577.

Frisby, C. L. (1993b). One giant step backward: Myths of Black cultural learning styles. *School Psychology Review, 22,* 535–557.

Frisby, C. L., & Braden, J. P. (Eds.). (1999). Bias in mental testing [Special issue]. *School Psychology Quarterly, 14*(4).

Gabelko, N. H., & Sosniak, L. A. (2002). "Someone like me": When academic engagement trumps race, class, and gender. *Phi Delta Kappan, 83,* 400–405.

Gardner-Kitt, D. (2005). Black student achievement: The influence of racial identity, ethnic identity, perception of school climate, and self-reported behavior (Doctoral dissertation, The Pennsylvania State University, 2005). *Dissertation Abstracts International, 66*(4-B), 2292.

Hale, J. E. (1993). Rejoinder to ". . . myths of Black cultural learning styles": In defense of Afrocentric scholarship. *School Psychology Review, 22,* 558–561.

Hale-Benson, J. E. (1986). *Black children: Their roots, culture, and learning styles* (Rev. ed.). Baltimore: Johns Hopkins University Press.

Hoffman, K., & Llagas, C. (2003). *Status and trends in the education of Blacks* (NCES 2003-034). Washington, DC: U.S. Department of Education, National Center for Education Statistics.

Irvine, J. J., & York, D. E. (2001). Learning styles and culturally diverse students: A literature review. In J. A. Banks (Ed.), *Handbook of research on multicultural education* (pp. 484–497). San Francisco: Wiley.

Jencks, C., & Phillips, M. (Eds.). (1998). *The Black-White test score gap.* Washington, DC: Brookings Institution Press.

Jussim, L., & Harber, K. D. (2005). Teacher expectations and self-fulfilling prophecies: Knowns and unknowns, resolved and unresolved controversies. *Personality and Social Psychology Review, 9,* 131–155.

Kitano, M. K., & DiJiosia, M. (2002). Are Asian and Pacific Americans overrepresented in programs for the gifted? *Roeper Review, 24,* 76–80.

Kuklinski, M. R., & Weinstein, R. S. (2001). Classroom and developmental differences in a path model of teacher expectancy effects. *Child Development, 72,* 1554–1578.

Lee, J. (2002). Racial and ethnic achievement gaps trends: Reversing the progress toward equity? *Educational Researcher, 31,* 3–12.

Lepper, M. R., & Henderlong, J. (2000). Turning "play" into "work" and "work" into "play": 25 years of research on intrinsic and extrinsic motivation. In C. Sansone & J. M. Harackiewicz (Eds.), *Intrinsic and extrinsic motivation: The search for optimal motivation and performance* (pp. 257–307). San Francisco: Academic Press.

Lopez, C., Lopez, V., Suarez-Morales, L., & Castro, F. G. (2005). Cultural variation within Hispanic American families. In C. L. Frisby & C. R. Reynolds (Eds.), *Comprehensive handbook of multicultural school psychology* (pp. 234–264). Hoboken, NJ: Wiley.

Marland, S. P., Jr. (1972). *Education of the gifted and talented: Vol. 1. Report to the Congress of the United States by the U.S. Commissioner of Education.* Washington, DC: U.S. Government Printing Office. (ERIC Document Reproduction Service No. ED056243)

McDermott, P. A. (1999). National scales of differential learning behaviors among American children and adolescents. *School Psychology Review, 28,* 280–291.

McKown, C., & Weinstein, R. S. (2002). Modeling the role of child ethnicity and gender in children's differential response to teacher expectations. *Journal of Applied Social Psychology, 32,* 159–184.

McKown, C., & Weinstein, R. S. (2003). The development and consequences of stereotype consciousness in middle childhood. *Child Development, 74,* 498–515.

Merton, R. K. (1957). *Social theory and social structure.* Glencoe, IL: Free Press.

Neisser, U., Boodoo, G., Bouchard, T. J., Jr., Boykin, A. W., Brody, N., Ceci, S. J., et al. (1996). Intelligence: Knowns and unknowns. *American Psychologist, 51,* 77–101.

Ogbu, J. U. (1978). *Minority education and caste: The American education system in cross-cultural perspective.* New York: Academic Press.

Ogbu, J. U. (1989). The individual in collective adaptation: A framework for focusing on academic underperformance and dropping out among involuntary minorities. In L. Weis, E. Farrar, & H. G. Petrie (Eds.), *Dropouts from school: Issues, dilemmas, and solutions* (pp. 181–204). New York: SUNY Press.

Ogbu. J. U. (2004). Collective identity and the burden of "acting White" in Black history, community, and education. *Urban Review, 36,* 1–35.

Ogbu, J. U., & Simons, H. D. (1998). Voluntary and involuntary minorities: A cultural-ecological theory of school performance with some implications for education. *Anthropology and Education Quarterly, 29,* 155–188.

Oyserman, D., Kemmelmeier, M., Fryberg, S., Brosh, H., & Hart-Johnson, T. (2003). Racial-ethnic self-schemas. *Social Psychology Quarterly, 66,* 333–347.

Pang, V. O. (2001). Asian Pacific American students: A diverse and complex population. In J. A. Banks (Ed.), *Handbook of research on multicultural education* (pp. 412–424). San Francisco: Wiley.

Phillips, M., Crouse, J., & Ralph, J. (1998). Does the Black-White test score gap widen after children enter school? In C. Jencks & M. Phillips (Eds.), *The Black-White test score gap* (pp. 229–272). Washington, DC: Brookings Institution Press.

Phinney, J. S. (1992). The Multigroup Ethnic Identity Measure. *Journal of Adolescent Research, 7,* 156–176.

Plummer, D. L. (1995). Serving the needs of gifted children from a multicultural perspective. In J. L. Genshaft, M. Bireley, & C. L. Hollinger (Eds.), *Serving gifted and talented students: A resource for school personnel* (pp. 285–300). Austin, TX: Pro-Ed.

Renzulli, J. S. (1986). The three-ring conception of giftedness: A developmental model for creative productivity. In R. J. Sternberg & J. E. Davidson (Eds.), *Conceptions of giftedness* (pp. 53–92). New York: Cambridge University Press.

Reynolds, C. R., & Carson, A. D. (2005). Methods for assessing cultural bias in tests. In C. L. Frisby & C. R. Reynolds (Eds.), *Comprehensive handbook of multicultural school psychology* (pp. 795–823). Hoboken, NJ: Wiley.

Richardson, T. Q. (1993). Black cultural learning styles: Is it really a myth? *School Psychology Review, 22,* 562–567.

Robinson, A., Bradley, R. H., & Stanley, T. D. (1990). Opportunity to achieve: Identifying mathematically gifted black students. *Contemporary Educational Psychology, 15,* 1–12.

Robinson, T. (1990). Understanding the gap between entry and exit: A cohort analysis of African American students' persistence. *Journal of Negro Education, 59,* 207–218.

Rosenthal, R., & Jacobsen, L. (1968). *Pygmalion in the classroom: Teacher expectation and pupils' intellectual development.* New York: Rinehart & Winston.

Rushton, J. P., & Jensen, A. R. (2005a). Thirty years of research on race differences in cognitive ability. *Psychology, Public Policy, and Law, 11,* 235–294.

Rushton, J. P., & Jensen, A. R. (2005b). Wanted: More race realism, less moralistic fallacy. *Psychology, Public Policy, and Law, 11,* 328–336.

Sanders, W. L., & Horn, S. P. (1998). Research findings from the Tennessee Value-Added Assessment System (TVAAS) database: Implications for educational evaluation and research. *Journal of Personnel Evaluation in Education, 12,* 247–256.

Schunk, D. H., & Pajares, F. (2002). The development of academic self-efficacy. In A. Wigfield & J. S. Eccles (Eds.), *Development of achievement motivation* (pp. 15–31). San Francisco: Elsevier Science.

Sosniak, L. A. (1999). An everyday curriculum for the development of talent. *The Journal of Secondary Gifted Education, 10,* 166–172.

Sosniak, L. A. (2005, June 6). *The summer educational divide.* Retrieved February 22, 2006, from http://www.sfgate.com/cgi-bin/article.cgi?file=/chronicle/archive/2005/06/06/EDG6LD39U91.DTL

Steele, C. M. (1997). A threat in the air: How stereotypes shape intellectual identity and performance. *American Psychologist, 52,* 613–629.

Steele, C. M. (2003). Stereotype threat and African-American student achievement. In T. Perry, C. M. Steele, & A. G. Hilliard, III (Eds.), *Young, gifted, and Black: Promoting high achievement among African-American students* (pp. 109–130). Boston: Beacon Press.

Steele, C. M., & Aronson, J. (1998). Stereotype threat and the test performance of academically successful African Americans. In C. Jencks & M. Phillips (Eds.), *The Black-White test score gap* (pp. 401–427). Washington, DC: Brookings Institution Press.

Sternberg, R. J., & Davidson, J. E. (1986a). (Eds.). *Conceptions of giftedness.* New York: Cambridge University Press.

Sternberg, R. J., & Davidson, J. E. (1986b). Conceptions of giftedness: A map of the terrain. In R. J. Sternberg & J. E. Davidson (Eds.), *Conceptions of giftedness* (pp. 223–243). New York: Cambridge University Press.

Stone, J., Lynch, C. I., Sjomeling, M., & Darley, J. M. (1999). Stereotype threat effects on Black and White athletic performance. *Journal of Personality and Social Psychology, 77,* 1213–1227.

Thao, P. (2005). Cultural variation within Southeast Asian American families. In C. L. Frisby & C. R. Reynolds (Eds.), *Comprehensive handbook of multicultural school psychology* (pp. 173–204). Hoboken, NJ: Wiley.

Tickell, G., & Smyrnios, K. X. (2005). Predictors of tertiary accounting students' academic performance: A comparison of year 12-to-university students with TAFE-to-university students. *Journal of Higher Education Policy and Management, 27,* 239–259.

Troutman, J. G. (1978). Cognitive predictors of final grades in finite mathematics. *Educational and Psychological Measurement, 38,* 401–404.

Turkheimer, E., Haley, A., Waldron, M., D'Onofrio, B., & Gottesman, I. I. (2003). Socioeconomic status modifies heritability of IQ in young children. *Psychological Science, 14,* 623–628.

Vandiver, B. J., Cross, W. E., Jr., Fhagen-Smith, P. E., Worrell, F. C., Swim, J. K., & Caldwell, L. D. (2000). *The Cross Racial Identity Scale.* State College, PA: Author.

Waters, M. C. (1999). *Black identities: West Indian immigrant dreams and American realities.* Cambridge, MA: Harvard University Press.

Weinstein, R. S. (1998). Promoting positive expectations in schooling. In N. M. Lambert & B. L. McCombs (Eds.), *How students learn: Reforming schools through learner-centered education* (pp. 81–111). Washington, DC: American Psychological Association.

Weinstein, R. S. (2002). *Reaching higher: The power of expectations in schooling.* Cambridge, MA: Harvard University Press.

Weinstein, R. S., & Middlestadt, S. E. (1979). Student perceptions of teacher interactions with male high and low achievers. *Journal of Educational Psychology, 71,* 421–431.

Worrell, F. C. (2003). Why are there so few African Americans in gifted programs? In C. C. Yeakey & R. D. Henderson (Eds.), *Surmounting the odds: Education, opportunity, and society in the new millennium* (pp. 423–454). Greenwich, CT: Information Age.

Worrell, F. C. (2005). Cultural variation within American families of African descent. In C. L. Frisby & C. R. Reynolds (Eds.), *Comprehensive handbook of multicultural school psychology* (pp. 137–172). Hoboken, NJ: Wiley.

Worrell, F. C. (2007). Ethnic identity, academic achievement, and global self-concept in four groups of academically talented adolescents. *Gifted Child Quarterly, 51,* 1–15.

Worrell, F. C., & Gabelko, N. H. (2005, April). *Differences in self-reported performance of GATE-identified and non-identified students.* Paper presented at the annual meeting of the American Educational Research Association, Montreal, Quebec, Canada.

Worrell, F. C., & Gardner-Kitt, D. L. (2006). The relationship between racial and ethnic identity in Black adolescents: The Cross Racial Identity Scale (CRIS) and the Multigroup Ethnic Identity Measure (MEIM). *Identity: An International Journal of Theory and Research, 6,* 293–315.

Worrell, F. C., & Schaefer, B. A. (2004). Reliability and validity of Learning Behaviors Scale (LBS) scores with academically talented students: A comparative perspective. *Gifted Child Quarterly, 48,* 287–308.

Worrell, F. C., Szarko, J. E., & Gabelko, N. H. (2001). Multi-year persistence of nontraditional students in an academic talent development program. *The Journal of Secondary Gifted Education, 12,* 80–89.

Worrell, F. C., Vandiver, B. J., Schaefer, B. A., Cross, W. E., Jr., & Fhagen-Smith, P. E. (2006). Generalizing nigrescence profiles: A cluster analysis of Cross Racial Identity Scale (CRIS) scores in three independent samples. *The Counseling Psychologist, 34,* 519–547.

Yoon, J. S., & Cheng, L. L. (2005). Cultural variation within East Asian American families. In C. L. Frisby & C. R. Reynolds (Eds.), *Comprehensive handbook of multicultural school psychology* (pp. 265–300). Hoboken, NJ: Wiley.

IV

ADULTHOOD AND THE LATER YEARS

9
DEVELOPMENTAL TRANSITIONS IN GIFTEDNESS AND TALENT: ADOLESCENCE INTO ADULTHOOD

RENA F. SUBOTNIK

Giftedness, a dynamic construct, develops over time. During the transition from adolescence into adulthood, gifted individuals move first from broad educational experiences to more narrowly focused efforts in universities, colleges, institutes, or conservatories, followed by the pursuit of scholarly productivity, innovation, or artistry. The focus of this chapter is on the catalysts for these transitions. I take the view of talent development as the transformation of abilities into competencies, competencies into expertise, and expertise into outstanding performance or seminal ideas. I build the discussion on four main propositions:

1. Psychologists and educational practitioners who study and serve gifted individuals have two roles: (a) work vigorously to identify a wide range of individuals with potential talents and (b) promote, as vigorously, the development of talents among those who show "they can and they want to" (see chap. 7, this volume). The focus of this chapter is on (b), the latter charge for the field.
2. The conception of giftedness changes over the life span according to shifting standards of outstanding performance. Thus, most prodigies do not grow into adults who generate exceptional

scholarly productivity or artistry. Nor were such gifted adults always identified as gifted children (although they most likely were identified as gifted adolescents or gifted young adults).

3. As argued by Horowitz (chap. 1, this volume), at key nodal points, a number of variables become increasingly important to the manifestation of talent. Although the starting point of talent development varies by domain, talent development in all domains is affected by opportunities available and opportunities taken.

4. During the advanced stages of talent development, psychosocial variables play increasingly significant roles in achieving goals and aspirations.

To address these propositions, I review the scholarship on talent development as a set of transitions during which abilities are transformed into competencies, expertise, and beyond. Finally, I explore the stages of talent development experienced by gifted adolescents as they move into scholarly productivity or artistry in adulthood, focusing on the increasingly important role played by psychosocial variables in the fulfillment of their potential.

TALENT DEVELOPMENT AS A SET OF TRANSITIONS

An important distinction exists between explanations of giftedness based on high intelligence as measured by tests (usually in the form of IQ) and those associated with abilities and achievement in specific domains (Gagné, 2005; Good & Dweck, 2005; Matthews & Foster, 2006). IQ has been shown to be a reliable measure of school achievement over time, beginning in early-middle childhood (see chaps. 2 and 3, this volume). However, exceptional performance on an IQ test does not predict exceptional performance beyond school into adult activities or professions. For example, Subotnik, Kassan, Summers, and Wasser (1993) surveyed Hunter College Elementary School graduates (1948–1959) using a questionnaire modeled after the instrument used by Terman and Oden (1959) in their study of high-IQ adults at midlife. Like the Terman sample, the Hunter graduates were from high socioeconomic status (SES) families. In the Hunter study, the respondents scored a mean IQ of 157 as children (almost four standard deviations above the mean, or truly exceptional) on the Stanford-Binet L-M. Out of a total population of 600 Hunter respondents, 210 completed extensive surveys and 74 participated in follow-up interviews. At ages 40 to 50, the sample reported being relatively happy, mentally stable, and productive middle- and upper middle-class citizens. These accomplishments were no doubt a reflection of their personal values and efforts. Yet, according to the researchers, the value added of an extraordinarily high IQ was not evident, given the high SES and educational levels of their parents. The most notable difference between the Terman and Hunter samples was the higher level of career achievements of the women in the Hunter sample, certainly the result of historical effects (Subotnik, Karp, & Morgan, 1989). Few of Terman's men went on to make path-breaking contributions, and only two respondents from the Hunter study met criteria for national-level influence in their fields, both in the domain of politics.

According to Tannenbaum (1986), the outcomes of both the Terman and Hunter studies support his theory that high IQ may be necessary but is not sufficient for transforming measured potential into the production of important new ideas, material inventions, or performances. He qualified his argument further by indicating that very high IQ is necessary (although not sufficient) only for some domains. Tannenbaum's framework, on the basis of historical analysis, presents four factors in addition to relatively high general intelligence that are key to talent development: (a) "special" or domain-specific abilities, (b) psychosocial variables, (c) support from family or community, and (d) chance.

Special (domain-specific) abilities in Tannenbaum's (1986) model are those associated with acuity in a domain, such as the location and direction abilities required in the spatial domain (see chap. 4, this volume). Psychosocial variables include motivation, persistence and drive, and the will to overcome obstacles to meet a goal. (From the interviews conducted with Hunter College Elementary School graduates, the research group concluded that the drive for eminence or other forms of outstanding success was not central to the life goals of most of the graduates.) Teachers, community or family members, and eminent thinkers or performers provide support in the form of cheerleading or mentoring. Mentors may serve as intellectual sparring partners, emotional supporters, or providers of professional contacts (Jacobi, 1991). Finally, in Tannenbaum's (1986) model, the role of chance includes taking advantage of opportunities that come one's way, or happening to live during a period when one's talent matches a societal need.

The field of giftedness studies and gifted education has historically invested a great deal of creative energy into identification practices and policies. It is time now to match those efforts with educational and clinical provisions, including evidence-based instruction and learning opportunities for those who emerge from their early learning experiences motivated and ready to take on the challenges of the domain.

AGE DIFFERENCES IN DOMAIN TRAJECTORIES

In 1986, Feldman and Goldsmith published a key study on prodigies, which served as the basis for their theory of coincidence. They defined prodigies as individuals who perform at extremely high levels within a specific field at a very early age (before adolescence). According to the theory of coincidence, prodigious behavior results from working with a master teacher or mentor, family recognition and support, and deep passion for a specific domain of interest, in concert with a child's biological proclivities for a certain domain. Similar to Tannenbaum's (1986) tip to chance, Feldman and Goldsmith acknowledged that the environment needs to be receptive to the individual and his or her place in the domain. Although prodigies are defined by extraordinary expertise, they rarely achieve transformational performances or eminence. In other words, the path to expertise is foreshortened in the early lives of prodigies, but they often do not make the transition from expertise to great innovation.

One of the key contributions of this work on prodigies is the observation that some domains are more (or less) accessible to advanced work by young people in different fields: For a domain to yield possible child prodigies, it must be in physical or conceptual reach of children (see chaps. 4 and 5, this volume). For example, Feldman and Goldsmith (1986) were able to find prodigies in mathematics, music, and chess, but not in the physical sciences or philosophy.

VARIABLES ASSOCIATED WITH ACHIEVING ADULT GIFTEDNESS OR EMINENCE

Definitions of giftedness change in the course of development. Always a relative term, exceptional performance on a reading test in second grade can be a gateway to grouping for instruction with other advanced readers. A local science fair winner in eighth grade has the opportunity to compete with others for regional and even national recognition. However, the science fair project would not be expected to break new ground but rather demonstrate advanced understanding and insights in a science field. In adulthood, a gifted musician, scientist, or professional is one who is admired by members of his or her field for exceptional leadership or creativity. In her longitudinal study of secondary school valedictorians from highly diverse communities in Illinois, Arnold (1995) discussed how skills needed for meeting the challenges of a perfect grade point average differ from those needed for handling the curveballs thrown at a person by professional and private challenges in adulthood. Some of the valedictorians had the wherewithal, resources, and personal strength to be exceptional in university and beyond, and most did not. Katchadourian and Boli's (1994) 10-year follow-up of Stanford freshmen, an academically talented cohort, revealed that patterns of values exhibited in college retained their salience through adulthood, leading to different career outcomes and sources of satisfaction in life. In the current chapter, I argue that (a) once a person is old enough to participate in a domain trajectory, his or her level of giftedness is defined by the domain; (b) standards, rules, and stakes change during the transition from adolescence into adulthood; and (c) many highly competent people have the ability and training to be eminent but do not exercise the drive, personal fortitude, and social skills required for creative risk taking.

In a review of the key scholarly literature in the field, Subotnik and Calderon (2008) identified variables associated with developing talent or giftedness in specific domains. Most theories or models of talent development concern themselves with identifying the variables that enhance or inhibit fulfillment of potential, without attention to sequence or changes in importance of variables over time. None of the models in the literature assess the talent development process in terms of age-based stages, reflecting how newer conceptions of development are concerned with sequences related to domain rather than to age. As mentioned earlier, domains in which prodigies have been known to exist (e.g., violin performance) traditionally begin exposure and training at an early age. In contrast, most adolescents in quantitative social sciences (e.g., sociology, psychology, political science) are novices into their postsecondary years.

In addition to the work of Tannenbaum (1986) and Feldman and Goldsmith (1986), Sternberg (2005) and Csikszentmihalyi (1996) have offered theories that delineate the variables associated with talent development. Neither differentiates by age-related factors. Sternberg (2005) agreed that the likelihood of talent fulfillment depends on the contributions of internal psychosocial variables and support from someone in the person's environment, and Csikszentmihalyi's work promotes a more nuanced understanding of Tannenbaum's concept of chance. According to Csikszentmihalyi (1996), creative products result from the interaction of a domain, a field, and the individual; put in other words, it is essential to be in the right place at the right time, with the right set of abilities. Furthermore, Csikszentmihalyi discussed the effects of historic, economic, political, social, and cultural contexts on societal periods of high creativity that may affect the likely convergence of opportunity and fortune for a talented individual.

In general, adolescence is the time during which individuals begin to identify their personal interests and decide whether to pursue those interests or engage in other activities to meet parental or societal expectations. Hence, in general, adolescence can be viewed as the transition period between competence and expertise. It follows that early adulthood is the period during which talented individuals attempt to move from expertise to eminence in those same domains.

VARIABLES ASSOCIATED WITH TALENT AND GIFTEDNESS DEVELOPMENT

Subotnik and Calderon (2008) noted four additional talent development models or frameworks that not only identify variables but also put those variables into a sequential trajectory focused on domain-specific accomplishment.

Renzulli's (2005) model begins with a triad of basic factors—above-average ability, creativity, and task commitment—and includes a three-step, sequential curriculum designed to channel these factors into creative productive giftedness. Gagné (2005) started with a foundation of natural abilities that are catalyzed by external supports and internal forces that lead to outstanding mastery in a field. Simonton (2005) promoted a third model to explain the emergence of giftedness at the level of eminence with a special focus on environmental triggers for genetic factors. Finally, Piirto (2004) began with genes, personality, and cognitive skills that are then affected by internal and external factors leading to recognition by peers for creative productivity.

Of the models described thus far, all but Gagné's (2005) posit some combination of abilities (whether general or special) being transformed by internal psychosocial and external support factors into the building blocks of *eminence* in a specific domain. It is notable that Gagné viewed the acquisition of expertise as the end point of his talent development model. Subotnik and Jarvin (2005) argued that *expertise* reflects mastery over the given knowledge of a discipline or domain but is not equated with innovation. According to Subotnik and Jarvin, the talent development process should explain and support performance beyond expertise. Although the role of chance is not mentioned explicitly in most of the models, the availability of external conditions supporting giftedness can be viewed as a chance factor (i.e., being born into a family, community, or culture that recognizes, values, and invests in one's abilities).

TALENT AND GIFTEDNESS DEVELOPMENT DESCRIBED AS A SET OF STAGES

In 1985, Bloom and his colleagues published a model for developing gifts and talents that not only included variables presented in a sequence from personal proclivities developed by commitment, to instruction and guidance, to eminence but also placed the variables in "stages" somewhat paralleling developmental periods. Bloom et al. emphasized accomplishment in specific domains over generic giftedness as an outcome, and focused on the central role played by parents and teachers in enhancing the abilities of young people. The Bloom three-stage model was based on retrospective studies of very high performing adults in six fields, two each in the arts, academics, and sport.

The first stage of talent development described by Bloom and his colleagues (1985) usually takes place during childhood. Children with high levels of proclivities recognized by parents or teachers—such as physical conditioning, eye–hand coordination, or academic aptitude—are exposed to informal and recreational activities to which they respond with rapid progress. The second stage of the model, which often takes place during adolescence, is characterized by a more formal approach to content, skills, rules, and techniques in the domain. The second-stage experience is also designed to socialize gifted young scholars, artists, or athletes into the values of the domain.

The third stage of the Bloom (1985) model focuses on developing a niche of creative expression that becomes the signature of one's talent. The rules have been mastered, thus allowing for meaningful rule breaking and risk taking. During this stage, details become less important than larger conceptions, and psychosocial skills are key to acquiring an audience for scholarly productivity or artistry.

THE CENTRAL ROLE OF PSYCHOSOCIAL VARIABLES IN TALENT DEVELOPMENT

Jarvin and I (Jarvin & Subotnik, 2005; Subotnik & Jarvin, 2005) spent 3 years at three of the nation's most renowned conservatories of music to study the transformation of college-age adolescent musicians into *artists*, the term used to mark outstanding musicianship. The goal of our work was to explore the changing role of psychosocial variables in domain-specific talent development. This approach mirrors Horowitz's (1987) system theory whereby variables change in their dynamic interactions over time. In the course of the study, the research team conducted interviews and observations with 20 faculty members (who are active performers as well) in the string, brass, and vocal departments, 53 students, and 8 gatekeepers (those who hire soloists or write reviews of performances for major newspapers). The goal of the study was to document the movement of musicians in late adolescence or early adulthood from (a) abilities to competencies, (b) competencies to expertise, and (c) expertise to artistry, with a special focus on psychosocial variables.

Students entering the string department at the conservatories were in the second and third stages of the Subotnik and Jarvin (2005) talent development model, moving from competencies to expertise and even (in some cases) to artistry. Same-aged brass students were engaged in the second stage, moving from competencies to expertise, since they need to be more physically developed than violin students before they can master the breathing techniques associated with brass instruments. And because vocal students' instrument (their voice) continues to develop through adolescence, they are most likely to be admitted to conservatories on the basis of their raw, untrained potential. As their learning curve in conservatory is much steeper than that of their fellow students in strings and brass, we classified the vocal students as being in the first transitional stage of our model, moving from abilities to competencies.

The psychosocial variables important at each stage of the model are presented here. Wherever possible the variable descriptions are accompanied by quotations from studio teachers and gatekeepers who are also successful performers.

Stage 1: Psychosocial Dimensions: Transition From Ability to Competency

Our study participants identified several psychosocial variables from the literature as especially important in the first developmental stage of moving from ability to competency in music performance. They told us that intrinsic motivation, persistence through good and bad times, responsiveness to external rewards, and teachability—all starting in the first stage—are key to the transformation of potential to fulfillment throughout the process of talent development. Intrinsic motivation is only one of two psychosocial variables that study participants argued was not teachable. They expressed a belief that should the other psychosocial skills be initially absent, they could be learned with appropriate instruction or intervention.

Intrinsic Motivation

Without intrinsic motivation and musical ability in the form of musicality, students do not make the necessary sacrifices of time and other opportunities for disciplined practice. A faculty member in the vocal department told us that

> Intrinsic motivation is very important because it's the thing that allows you to walk through the door. It's what allows you to present yourself as a princess or a hunchback on the level of a performer. Once you're on the stage, it's what keeps you singing and your body working; on a day-to-day level, it's what allows you to keep sending your package to this or that person like conductors and young artist programs, applying and sending a check for one hundred dollars to yet another competition.

Persistence Through Good and Bad Times

In all fields there will be setbacks—for example, a concept not quite mastered in spite of great effort, or a competition lost. Students must learn to view setbacks as normal phenomena. Concurrently, good times can distract students from disciplined focus on their preparation. Expert teachers help their students to modulate their responses to both good and bad times (see also Good & Dweck, 2006). As reported by one of our brass faculty respondents:

> Persistence through good and bad times is something every artist or musician should experience because then they'll know their limitations. Once you know your breaking point, then you learn how to deal with things.

Responsiveness to External Rewards

Although intrinsic motivation is key to persistence, other sources of motivation also play important roles in reinforcing students' desire to excel, including proving themselves to significant others and to audiences for whom they perform. One faculty member of the vocal department told us,

> I often think I can tell when someone sings to prove something, not just because they love it, because there's something in the persona of the singer that is challenging. This was sometimes true of Maria Callas, and in a gladiatorial way, it becomes very exciting, that musical chip on the shoulder.

Teachability

In recent years, studio teachers have been especially concerned about students with great potential entering their studios who are not receptive to instruction. Some come in with counterproductive techniques, limited tastes in repertoire, or narrow worldviews that impede understanding of the music to be performed. As one brass faculty member commented,

> Some people just have their own idea about playing, and they do not want to hear from you. Why are they here? Why do they even come to school? This I do not understand. Sometimes it seems that they want my blessing or something.

Stage 2: Psychosocial Dimensions: Transition From Competency to Expertise

As mentioned in connection with Stage 1, our study participants associated intrinsic motivation, persistence through good and bad times, and responsiveness to external rewards with the second stage of talent development as well. In the second stage of the Subotnik–Jarvin model, the variable of teachability takes a different form, and new variables are introduced, including knowing one's strengths and weaknesses, self-promotion and learning to play the game, social skills, and restoring self-confidence.

Teachability

Being open to learning is considered a great virtue at the first stage of talent development. At the second stage, however, students are more often expected to "bite back," to question and to differentiate their views and styles from those of their teachers. A vocal faculty member reported,

It seems to me that later, people become too teachable and therefore overly influenced by coaches and directors and conductors such that they lose themselves because they are too open to everyone else. The individual gets lost.

Knowing Your Strengths and Weaknesses

At the second stage of talent development, students take more responsibility from their teachers for monitoring their strengths and weaknesses:

> Well, you don't want to practice the things that you know because then you're not using your time efficiently. If you're working on your weaknesses, I think it makes practicing more fun. It really develops your analytical skills because you normally practice alone, so you're the only person who really knows what you can and can't do. But, sometimes you need somebody to hear you on the other side of your instrument, someone other than yourself. (brass faculty member)

Self-Promotion and Learning to Play the Game

Like responsiveness to extrinsic rewards, self-promotion and learning to play the game are not always considered attractive pursuits in young people. However, done thoughtfully and with care, these expressions of practical intelligence (Sternberg & Wagner, 1986) are important for garnering opportunities and support for oneself beyond those that can be provided by teachers and mentors:

> Self-promotion is quite important for a singer, especially a young singer who is a very good performer and communicator, but who will not get along on the strength of that alone. This is the functional end of "knowing how to play the game," knowing which competitions are on the up and up and which are a pointless waste of time, which can be said of many of them. It helps you find out who is good to sing to, how to call them up and sing for them, and then who can put you in touch with other people who can be helpful to you. It is important to know how to respond graciously to an invitation to sing and so on. (vocal faculty member)

Social Skills

Talented individuals need to be dependable colleagues because so many activities are group endeavors, from orchestra playing to chamber music. Furthermore, most performing opportunities come through the grapevine of musical friends and colleagues.

Restoring Self-Confidence

As students take more responsibility for their strengths and weaknesses and encounter others with perceived equal or greater developed ability, many lose confidence. Teachers, friends, and parents can help students come to positive and realistic terms with this change in self-image, find niches in which they can specialize, and work harder.

Stage 3: Psychosocial Dimensions: Transition From Expertise to Artistry (or Scholarly Productivity)

During the third stage of the talent development process, gifted individuals become experts in their domains and are poised to make original contributions. As one of our gatekeepers noted, no one wants to attend a concert that sounds like "pushing the play button" (Subotnik, Jarvin, Moga, & Sternberg, 2003). Now that the background skills and knowledge of the field are mastered, personal relationships with the public and with colleagues, as well as intrapersonal strength, help to ensure that performances or ideas have an audience. The importance of intrinsic motivation, persistence through good and bad times, and responsiveness to extrinsic rewards remains constant. Teachability is no longer as relevant as it was in the earlier stages. Additional variables or changes include capitalizing on strengths, promoting oneself through a mentor or agent and mastering the game, social skills, self-confidence, risk taking, and charisma.

Capitalizing on Strengths

At this stage, rather than balancing disciplined practice on strengths and weaknesses, most professional time is focused on strengths and finding opportunities to feature those strengths.

> If you know perfectly well that you're not the world's top technician, but you know that you do have musical responses that go across to other people, you would head not for the concert stage, but for chamber music. (violin faculty member)

Promoting Oneself Through a Mentor or Agent and Mastering the Game

At this stage, talented individuals seek out mentors or agents who will take over the role of promotion and help them maneuver through systems of schedules, taxes, licenses, advertising, contracts, and so on.

Social Skills

Social skills of collegiality and engaging patrons are the bread and butter of a successful musical career.

Self-Confidence

During this final and ongoing stage of the talent development process, whether or not one's confidence is restored from Stage 2, one must exude self-confidence to engage listeners when taking artistic risks:

You have to exude energy for the audience because if they don't feel that you're confident, then they won't be in your corner when you're performing. That's something that every artist should learn because to be an artist you have to enlighten people; it's more than just entertainment. (brass faculty member)

I know one celebrated pianist who takes me aside after every performance, while this person is surrounded by adulation, and says, "Was it okay?" and he means it. It's not a ritual. He, from the core, means it. Having enough self-confidence to perform is essential, but questioning oneself throughout one's career seems to be something that every great artist has [done]. (artistic director, concert hall)

Risk Taking

An exciting performer keeps the audience on the edge of their seats. Risk is slightly off perfection such that the performance is unique and not an exact replica of a recording. A great artist controls this relationship with masterful technique and brilliant insight:

> In performance, there is an absolute interesting knife-edge where you have to go across a very thin place with drops on both sides. What I do with my pupils is say, "One side is control and on the other side is letting go of control and losing it. You have to get the audience to feel on the edge of their seats the way the performer must feel on the edge of control and letting go." (violin faculty member)

Charisma

This was the third variable (in addition to musicality and intrinsic motivation) that a large majority of our respondents said was not teachable. Charismatic performers go beyond risk taking to use their personalities to engage the public with their music.

> The tradition is that you have to be quite serious about your performance because the magnetism that you can emit from being so concentrated and hypnotizing your listener does not come by gyrating and all that. Charisma is important. We can't excite anyone without that charisma which is generated. When one meets a person, you know if that person is interesting or just a wet dishrag. It's there or it's not. (violin faculty member)

The performance world at the highest levels recognizes the role of psychosocial variables and provides coaches and even courses explicitly for this purpose. The research conducted with this model is currently being tested in the domain of mathematics to explore further the implications of our findings about musical development for the academic domain (Subotnik, Pillmeier, & Jarvin, 2008).

PREDICTION IN TALENT DEVELOPMENT

Let us return now to the five variables Tannenbaum (1986) identified as essential to transforming potential into fulfillment, and consider how they relate to the prediction of talent development in the transition stage from late adolescence into adulthood.

General Ability

There is no consistent agreement across scholars about the need for high levels of general intellectual ability (or g) for talent development in all domains. However, because a high level of g is associated with school achievement often necessary for admission into the best colleges and universities, one could argue that those domains that are heavily academic or scholarly might be most affected by general reasoning ability. By itself, g has not been shown to be sufficient to predict eminent performance in any field (see also chaps. 1 and 6, this volume).

Special Ability

There is no consistency among scholars on the source of specialized abilities (whether innate, entirely developed, or a combination; Gagné, 2005; Good & Dweck, 2006; Matthews & Foster, 2006), but experts do agree that some type of proclivity for a domain attracts the attention of teachers and others who support talent development. The time when such abilities "appear" varies by domain; for example, one might predict better the potential for a brilliant career for an adolescent violinist than for an adolescent philosopher.

Person-Centered Variables

Psychosocial variables are key in all of the talent development models. We argue that psychosocial variables play an increasingly important role as one moves through talent development periods. Without the appropriate social skills, moving from expertise to artistry or scholarly productivity is more difficult, and we can predict negative effects on success outcomes. Fortunately, most of these social skills can be taught. Although they are currently part of the curriculum in many of the institutions that prepare artistic and athletic performers, they can be found only rarely in schools and universities developing academic talent.

External Variables

Parental support can be extremely valuable during Stage 1 but is not essential beyond that point. Expert teachers, however, are essential at all stages. As reported by Bloom (1985) and his colleagues, the role teachers play is different at each stage. Without adequate instruction in content and knowledge to achieve expertise, or the necessary mentoring to provide networking opportunities or socialization into a field, it is less likely that potentially eminent individuals can disseminate their ideas as widely as they would otherwise be able to do.

Chance

Over the course of talent development, pure chance becomes less important in predicting fulfillment of talent. Children cannot control the households they grow up in, but adolescents and adults take responsibility for developing their own talent, particularly in Stage 2 and beyond. Of course, larger economic, political, and historical factors can always impede or enhance life plans, whether through war or peace, cultural advantage or disadvantage, recession or economic boom, or new technological developments and possibilities.

FINAL THOUGHTS AND CONCLUSIONS

Although the talent development models cited in this chapter are solidly historical, retrospective, or empirical in nature, none are based on longitudinal data. When longitudinal data have been used in studies of giftedness in childhood (see chap. 3, this volume; Subotnik & Arnold, 1994), the data show that the predictive value of specific variables becomes attenuated over time because of the enormous complexity of cumulative interacting environmental and constitutional factors. To address drawbacks of extended periods of time and continually changing variables, a series of longitudinal studies in each domain needs to be conducted, beginning with the stage closest to the achievement of eminence in that domain. Such studies would allow testing of variables that are key to moving beyond expertise, by exploring why individuals who have mastered the technical and practical skills and knowledge available (experts) are more or less successful at achieving recognition for their path-breaking scholarship or artistry. For example, a study might begin with a cohort of graduating conservatory students who have all met the criteria for graduation at an outstanding level.

Another high-need area for research concerns disengagement from many areas of learning and achievement on the part of potentially talented African American adolescents and young adults. By late adolescence, the developmental trajectories of several domains have advanced beyond competency to expertise. Young people who have not been attracted or sufficiently exposed to these domains because their teachers conveyed low expectations, or none at all (see chap. 8, this volume), or who are not prepared to commit themselves to those domains (see chap. 7, this volume) will have severely limited opportunities to reach their goals. In chapter 7 (this volume), Graham further noted that variables such as self-efficacy and intrinsic motivation are directly related to achievement and that gifted students report high levels of these variables. What is unknown is whether cultural factors influence these variables and whether they heighten the effect of stereotype threat.

Psychologists and educational practitioners who study and serve gifted individuals must pursue the flourishing of demonstrated talent. They must also vigorously promote the development of potential talents among those who show they can and want to pursue this course. At the highest levels of talent development, most of which take place between late adolescence and early to mid-adulthood, it is especially important to focus on providing domain-specific instructional services, practical information on career success, and assistance with improving social and other psychosocial skills. Although a rigorous research base in talent development is very much needed, so much more is now known about expert practices in various domains. The publication of this volume may herald a new sense of urgency to engage in the research needed to understand optimal human performance while also implementing domain-specific best practices for talented individuals of all ages.

REFERENCES

Arnold, K. D. (1995). *Lives of promise: What becomes of high school valedictorians?* San Francisco: Jossey-Bass.

Bloom, B. S. (Ed.). (1985). *Developing talent in young people*. New York: Ballantine Books.

Csikszentmihalyi, M. (1996). *Creativity: Flow and the psychology of discovery and invention*. New York: HarperCollins.

Feldman, D. H., & Goldsmith, L. T. (1986). *Nature's gambit: Child prodigies and the development of human potential*. New York: Basic Books.

Gagné, F. (2005). From gifts to talents: The DMGT as a developmental model. In R. J. Sternberg & J. E. Davidson (Eds.), *Conceptions of giftedness* (2nd ed., pp. 98–119). New York: Cambridge University Press.

Good, C., & Dweck, C. S. (2006). A motivational approach to reasoning, resilience and responsibility. In R. J. Sternberg & R. F. Subotnik (Eds.), *Optimizing success with the other three Rs: Reasoning, resilience and responsibility* (pp. 39–56). Charlotte, NC: Information Age.

Horowitz, F. D. (1987). *Exploring developmental theories: Toward a structural/behavioral model of development*. Hillsdale, NJ: Erlbaum.

Jacobi, M. (1991). Mentoring and undergraduate academic success: A literature review. *Review of Educational Research, 61*, 505–532.

Jarvin, L., & Subotnik, R. F. (2005). Understanding elite talent in academic domains: A developmental trajectory from basic abilities to scholarly productivity/artistry.

In F. A. Dixon & S. M. Moon (Eds.), *The handbook of secondary gifted education* (pp. 203–220). Waco, TX: Prufrock Press.

Katchadourian, H., & Boli, J. (1994). *Cream of the crop: The impact of elite education in the decade after college*. New York: Basic Books.

Matthews, D. J., & Foster, J. F. (2006). Mystery to mastery: Shifting paradigms in gifted education. *Roeper Review, 28*, 64–69.

Piirto, J. (2004). *Understanding creativity*. Scottsdale, AZ: Great Potential Press.

Renzulli, J. S. (2005). The three-ring conception of giftedness: A developmental model for promoting creative productivity. In R. J. Sternberg & J. E. Davidson (Eds.), *Conceptions of giftedness* (2nd ed., pp. 246–279). New York: Cambridge University Press.

Simonton, D. K. (2005). Genetics of giftedness: The implications of an emergenic-epigenetic model. In R. J. Sternberg & J. E. Davidson (Eds.), *Conceptions of giftedness* (2nd ed., pp. 312–326). New York: Cambridge University Press.

Sternberg, R. J. (2005). The WICS model of giftedness. In R. J. Sternberg & J. E. Davidson (Eds.), *Conceptions of giftedness* (2nd ed., pp. 327–342). New York: Cambridge University Press.

Sternberg, R. J., & Wagner, R. K. (1986). *Practical intelligence: Nature and origins of competence in the every day world*. New York: Cambridge University Press.

Subotnik, R. F., & Arnold, K. D. (1994). *Beyond Terman: Contemporary longitudinal studies of giftedness and talent*. Norwood, NJ: Ablex Publishing.

Subotnik, R. F., & Calderon, J. (2008). Developing giftedness and talent. In F. Karnes & K. P. Stephens (Eds.), *Achieving excellence: Educating the gifted and talented* (pp. 49–61). Columbus, OH: Pearson Education.

Subotnik, R. F., & Jarvin, L. (2005). Beyond expertise: Conceptions of giftedness as great performance. In R. J. Sternberg & J. E. Davidson (Eds.), *Conceptions of giftedness* (2nd ed., pp. 343–357). New York: Cambridge University Press.

Subotnik, R. F., Jarvin, L., Moga, E., & Sternberg, R. J. (2003). Wisdom from gate-keepers: Secrets of success in music performance. *Bulletin of Psychology and the Arts, 4*, 5–9.

Subotnik, R. F., Karp, D. E., & Morgan, E. R. (1989). High IQ children at midlife: An investigation into the generalizability of Terman's "Genetic Studies of Genius." *Roeper Review, 11*, 139–144.

Subotnik, R. F., Kassan, L., Summers, E., & Wasser, A. (1993). *Genius revisited: High IQ children grown up*. Norwood, NJ: Ablex Publishing.

Subotnik, R. F., Pillmeier, E., & Jarvin, L. (2008). *The psychosocial dimensions of creativity in mathematics: Implications for gifted education policy*. Manuscript submitted for publication.

Tannenbaum, A. J. (1986). Giftedness: A psychosocial approach. In R. J. Sternberg & J. E. Davidson (Eds.), *Conceptions of giftedness* (pp. 21–52). New York: Cambridge University Press.

Terman, L. M., & Oden, M. H. (1959). *The gifted group at midlife: Thirty-five years' follow-up of the superior child*. Stanford, CA: Stanford University Press.

10

GIFTS AND TALENTS OF ELDERLY PEOPLE: THE PERSIMMON'S PROMISE

JAMES E. BIRREN

There have been dramatic changes in the demographics of age in the past century. In 1900, children were the largest component of the American population, and persons over 60 were the smallest. This trend has been reversed; children now comprise the smallest part of the population and older persons comprise the largest. The birthrate has fallen, and people are living longer and more active lives. In addition, societal transitions from the agricultural age to the industrial age and then to the information age have resulted in considerable ambiguity about life stages and transitions. Lifetime employment has shifted from single careers to multiple careers, often requiring midlife education to meet new employment requirements. All of these changes have led to widespread interest in the talents of older persons and their potential for expanding roles and productivity in the workforce

The purpose of this chapter is to expand the perspective of psychology to include the dynamics of the later years of life. I describe the stages of late life that have been proposed and the diversity of the older population as revealed by longitudinal studies. The abilities of older adults are described in terms of social intelligence, self-regulation, creativity, and wisdom. Unique contributions by elderly persons are described as the products of late-life bloomers, or individuals who express latent talents late in life.

THE CHANGING CONTEXT OF THE DEVELOPMENT
OF ELDERLY PERSONS

Developmental psychology in the past was focused on the early years, although it has now broadened to include the second half of life. Study of older persons is a recent trend in research compared with the study of child development, which began 50 years earlier. It was not until the U.S. Public Health Service began to support research on mental health and aging after World War II that scholarship, research, and education regarding the psychology of adult development and aging emerged as a major subject. As a result, more articles on this subject were published in the 1950s than were published in the previous 100 years.

An exception to this historical trend was G. S. Hall, one of the early child psychologists. His book, *Senescence: The Last Half of Life* (1922), contains his groundbreaking reflections on the transition into late life and his review of the limited literature then available. Hall (1992) divided the life span into five stages, the last of which is a rather bleak phase he called *senectitude*:

> (1) childhood, (2) adolescence from puberty to full nubility, (3) middle life or the prime when we are at the apex of our aggregate of powers, ranging from twenty-five or thirty to forty or forty-five, and comprising thus the fifteen or twenty years now commonly called our best, (4) senescence, which begins in the early forties, or before in women, and (5) senectitude, the post-climacteric or old age proper. (p. vii)

Much later, Erikson (1959) proposed his widely cited eight stages of development over the life cycle.

Although stimulating considerable research, the stage concepts of development seem to have minimized the range of individual differences in the intellectual qualities associated with living productively in the later years of life. Since the views of Hall and Erickson were published, changes in society and in individuals require more flexibility in how developmental stages in the second half of life are described. In his book, *The Mature Mind*, Cohen (2006) commented

> the field of developmental psychology was largely based on theories that looked no further than the onset of adulthood, as though all the important phases of growth were finished by that time. And the popular view of aging is one of loss, as though the developmental clock begins to run backward from adulthood, eventually arriving back at childhood. (p. 29)

Cohen (2006) thus added four phases of adult development to those proposed by Erikson:

> Phase I: Reevaluation, exploration, and transition (midlife reevaluation); mid-thirties to mid-sixties

Phase II: Liberation, experimentation, and innovation (liberation); mid-fifties to early seventics

Phase III: Recapitulation, resolution, and contribution (summing up); late sixties to the nineties

Phase IV: Continuation, reflection, and celebration (encore); late seventies to end of life. (pp. 52–53)

Cohen's (2006) suggested phases or stages reflect the fact that people are living longer and more actively in the 21st century. In 1900, the average life expectancy was 47 years, and the average family tended to dissolve as a result of the death of one of the spouses before the last child left home. More than 30 years have been added to average life expectancy as a result of advances in control of immune diseases, chronic diseases, and understanding the effects of diet and exercise on individuals. Life expectancy is now about 78 for men and women. In fact, more has been added to the average life expectancy in the 20th century than was added from Roman days to 1900 (Svanborg, 1996). This rather rapid advance has contributed to ambiguities about norms for both individuals and society and what to expect from life. A contemporary question that faces individuals and a society whose customs and expectations were established in different cultural eras is how to use the gifts of long and healthy lives to maximum effect.

Growing up and growing old are taking place in new contexts with new roles and new demands. In 1900, orphaned children were a major social problem and institutions were created to care for them. America began as an agricultural nation but has undergone transition to the industrial era and now into the information age. McFarland and O'Doherty (1959) pointed out that "Job opportunities and the pattern of employment are constantly changing and have changed considerably within the lifetime of many workers now approaching the older age groups" (p. 453). They also pointed out that in the latter part of the 1800s over half of the labor force was in agriculture, and after World War II, "only a sixth were so employed" (p. 453). Age 65 was adopted for Social Security benefits when average life expectancy was much shorter than it is now. Grandparents of the boomer generation matured when there was no Social Security, health insurance, insurance for employment health damage, or bank deposit insurance. Developmental psychology of the adult years must now take into account not only changes in the intellectual capacities of individuals but also changes in the context of lives and the dynamics of growing up and growing old.

THE DIVERSITY OF THE OLDER POPULATION

Medawar (1957) gave a comprehensive review of early concepts and theories of aging. From his analysis one may conclude that development was more scientifically understood than was aging and that selective evolutionary

pressures on species operate to produce maximum benefits at the age of reproduction. The genetic picture is that of a "precession" of favorable traits toward
the age of reproduction followed by a precession of unfavorable traits. This
view, if correct, would suggest that there is increasing diversity in human biological characteristics in later life, although little literature supports this point
as of yet. The view of an increasing expression of unfavorable traits in the
later years of life is, however, subject to qualification in that early tribal
groups, which had older members with memories of flood avoidance, successful hunting, and tribal warfare, might have been more likely to survive. The
possibility that long life experience might lead to wisdom and improve tribal
longevity was embraced by the counterpart theory of aging that some late-life
characteristics can influence selective pressure for survival (Birren, 1960).

Other forms of diversity appear at all ages. Presently, homeless and
highly dependent older individuals as well as individuals of all ages suffer
from cognitive and other behavioral impairments resulting from illness.
Raskind and Peskind (1991) after reviewing data on dementing disorders
associated with later life, concluded that the prevalence rate for Alzheimer's
disease was 10.3% among those older than 65 years and 47% for those 85
and older. Do most older individuals show mental deterioration in the later
years and others develop advanced forms of behavior such as wisdom? After
a review of evidence about aging of the nervous system, Vinters (2001)
posed this question:

> Does one 75-year-old person remain psychologically alert, animated, and
> active because of a reserve capacity of "recruitable" brain tissue, while his
> 70-year-old neighbor, lacking this resource, slips into senile dementia?
> And if so, what are the determinants of such a reserve, this plasticity of
> the brain that allows for adaptations and learning after 70, 80, or 90 years
> of activity? (p. 154)

Albert and Killiany (2001) reviewed research on cognitive changes
with aging in relation to brain structure and concluded that

> There is increasing evidence that widespread neuronal loss does not take
> place and produce ever increasing amounts of cognitive decline over
> time. Instead it appears that a variety of neurobiological changes in the
> brain occur as people get older, including functional changes at the
> molecular level, alterations in dendritic branching, and neuronal loss in
> selective subcortical regions. If the changes in the brain with healthy
> aging are, in fact, more subtle than previously thought, it is not surpris-
> ing that imaging modalities that look solely at brain structure and not
> behavioral functions appear not to adequately assess brain-behavior rela-
> tionship. The advent of a new way of simultaneously examining both
> brain structure and function, as is done in fMRI [functional magnetic res-
> onance imaging], thus offers researchers interested in these issues a power-

ful tool for answering questions concerning how the brain changes with age, and how this impacts on cognition. (p. 178)

For scholars interested in life-span intellectual development, an important question remains: How much does active mental functioning influence the structure of the aging brain?

LONGITUDINAL STUDY OF ADULT MENTAL PROCESSES

In their review of longitudinal studies of adult development, Schaie and Hofer (2001) reported that level of education influences the pattern of late-life cognitive changes. Furthermore, the researchers' interpretation of the longitudinal study of nuns is that "low linguistic ability early in life was found to be predictive of lower cognitive functions and Alzheimer's disease in old age" (p. 69; see also Snowdon et al., 1996). Data from these studies, to some extent, answer Vinters's (2001) question about the reserve or plasticity of the brain that allows for adaptations and learning after age 70. Some individuals who live into the later years appear to retain their mental abilities very well, and education and high mental functioning may provide resistance to the pathological decline of mental ability in later years.

An excellent source of evidence about the dynamics of intellectual capacities in older persons can be seen in findings from a 45-year longitudinal study by Schaie (2005; see also Schaie, 1983; Schaie & Hofer, 2001). In this seminal work, Schaie (2005) converted a cross-sectional study into a five-cycle longitudinal investigation that includes not only successive measurements of individuals first studied in 1956, but also new cohorts. This study permits comparisons of change in individuals across age cohorts and makes it possible to examine the relation of psychometric abilities and cognitive functions to personality and health variables such as chronic disease, genetics, and the development of dementia. The data permit inferences about causal relationships between cognitive capacities, physiological measures, different patterns of improvement, and mental maintenance and decline over adult life. In the fifth wave of the longitudinal study, cognitive training was introduced to determine whether such training would increase levels of abilities or reduce or remediate earlier declines (Willis, 2001). Schaie's (2005) conclusions are of broad significance:

> Our studies have shown that there is no uniform pattern of age-related change across all intellectual abilities, and that studies of an overall Index of Intellectual Ability (IQ) therefore do not suffice to monitor age changes and age differences in intellectual functioning for either individuals or groups. There are[,] however, important ability by-age, ability by-gender, and ability by-cohort interactions that complicate matters. (p. 15)

He further pointed out that there are gender differences: "More fine-grained analyses suggested, moreover, that there may be substantial gender difference as well as differential changes for those who decline and those who remain sturdy when age changes are decomposed into accuracy and speed" (p. 15).

Schaie's (2005) findings open discussion about opportunities for making use of the present abilities of older persons and also raises questions about ways to enhance latent or unused abilities. Items about training of older subjects in the longitudinal studies yield striking data:

> Findings from the cognitive training studies conducted with our longitudinal subjects (under the primary direction of Sherry L. Willis) suggested that observed decline in many community-dwelling older people might well be a function of disuse and is clearly reversible for many. Indeed, cognitive training resulted in approximately two thirds of the experimental subjects showing significant improvement; and about 40% of those who had declines significantly over 14 years were returned to their pre-decline level. (Schaie, 2005, p. 17)

It is clear that the dynamics of late-life changes in mental abilities are made complex by disuse, family patterns, socioeconomic factors, genetics, health, and diseases. The influences on cognitive abilities shown in Schaie's (2005) longitudinal data affect the development of individuals' self-identities and the way they evaluate their lives and undertake risks and make complex decisions (Birren & Schroots, 2006).

The existence of documented longer life spans has encouraged the study of centenarians. It will soon be commonly accepted that individuals over the age of 100 years can remain competent and capable of living independently. I was startled some years ago at the University of Southern California when I was introduced to a 102-year-old woman at the Gerontology Center. When I asked her why she came to the center, she said that she was curious about what a university gerontology center did. I then asked her how she came to the center; she said she came on a bus and she was visiting Los Angeles on a trip from Chicago. Two years later I received a letter that the centenarian had died. Her death after a 3-month decline in health was neither painful nor distressing, an example of a long life's ending that may challenge stereotypes about competence and independence in the older population.

LATE-LIFE BLOOMERS

The term *late-life bloomer* has been used to refer to older people who seem to release their intellectual and creative talents late in life. The metaphor of the latent bloomer implies a contrast among flowers that bloom in spring, summer, and fall. Perhaps a metaphor that implies "fruiting" would be more appropriate. The native American persimmon tree does not yield ripe fruit until after the first frost. By analogy, some people do not bring forth the major fruits in their lives until after their hair begins to turn gray.

A best-selling English novelist, Mary Wesley, published her first novel at age 70. She was educated as an economist, spent time in the British War Office during World War II, and later worked in the antique trade. Why was her creative talent latent so long? Wesley often commented that her "chief claim to fame is arrested development" (1986). Redirection in life can lead to previously unexpressed talents and skills. Ethel Percy Andrus, after she retired as a high school principal in Los Angeles, took actions that led to the national availability of health insurance for those over age 65 and went on to found the American Association of Retired Persons.

These examples of *late-life bloomers* lead to the suggestion that earlier life events may set priorities that block the expression of latent talents until they are freed by an encouraging context in the later years. Economic, educational, and other necessities of life may preoccupy an individual's attention during much of adult life or perhaps block the use of exceptional talents. An example of early blocking of the expression of talent was reported in one of my autobiography classes for older adults. A 75-year-old woman said that at age 16 she was a scholarship student at the Juilliard School of Music in New York. In her first year at Juilliard she was called home to St. Louis to help support her family when the family home was destroyed by a tornado. She had a long and productive career as an executive secretary but she never returned to express her talents in music.

Conventional views of the later years are barren of major contributions in the arts, literature, and science. Older people themselves buy into the stereotypes as much as men and women buy into the stereotypes of gender roles. In a question-and-answer session with a group of retirees, I asked whether any of them would like to play a musical instrument. About a third of the 220 attendees held up their hands. I asked about writing, and again about a third expressed an interest. In response to a question about engaging in public speaking, a few people held up their hands. I then asked why they did not pursue such interests. The dominant answer was self-doubt coupled with a fear of losing face if they were in a group that also included young members.

A middle-aged woman I interviewed told me of her uncertainty about pursuing a master's degree. She thought that young students might snicker at her despite the fact that as a young student she had performed at the A level. She did pursue a master's degree, and she performed at the A level there. She went on to earn a doctorate and to become the dean of a major medical school. Self-doubts and reinforcing stereotypes about age may contribute to the reticence of older persons to express their talents and become late-life bloomers. Further study is needed of the factors that lead to blocking or releasing the expression of talents across the life span.

KEY PSYCHOSOCIAL VARIABLES AND AGE

As research on the psychology of the life span continues to expand, new topics have emerged, such as the relationship of age to social intelligence, self-regulation, creativity, and wisdom. Such topics are receiving attention by way of theory generation and empirical research.

Social Intelligence

Living a long life leads to having many interactions with other people. This experience can result in a person withholding a response until one sees more clearly where the other person is "coming from." In brief, many experiences of interacting with other people can lead to better social intelligence, that is, managing oneself and others and forming judgments about other people's intentions. Cohen (2006) summarized his views of the social intelligence of older persons:

> Studies show that older adults use a combination of coping and negotiating strategies that lead to greater impulse control and the tendency to more effectively appraise conflict-charged situations, which results in more effective, satisfying choices of action. This is one reason that age is an asset in many people-oriented occupations such as manager, judge, politician, and diplomat. (p. 121)

This quotation suggests that high levels of social intelligence in the older population are an asset that may be put to more constructive use because many of those who possess it are retired. In 1978, senior peer counseling training was initiated by Evelyn Freeman and her colleagues at the Senior Health and Peer Counseling Center of Santa Monica, California. It was designed to focus and use the talents and experience of older persons to provide counseling to needy peers (Freeman, 1994; see also Bratter & Freeman, 1990). This initiative exemplifies the creation of an organized program to use the social intelligence of retirees for mentoring or coaching. The program that Evelyn Freeman started led to the development of the Association of Senior Counselors. The basic idea was to train and then have older people conduct counseling sessions under licensed therapists and social workers.

Many people need counseling at various stages in life. The release of the social intelligence of retirees makes their experience available to a wide range of younger and older adults. Such use also benefits the retirees because their experience can be used and appreciated at a time in their lives when they may feel their earlier status cast aside by the culture.

Self-Regulation

An important aspect of maturity lies in increased mastery of oneself. With age, individuals can acquire information and experiences that increase their capacity for self-regulation or self-management when making decisions and choosing how to behave. They can develop dispositional self-knowledge as well as support that in others with whom they interact. It is interesting that, for the present discussion, the *Handbook of Self-Regulation*, edited by Boekaerts, Pintrich, and Zeidner (2000) does not address adult development and aging in relation to self-management and self-regulation, although it does discuss the role of self-regulation in students' learning and life. The chapter by Demetriou (2000), in defining the conditions under which self-management expresses itself, listed a principle that is highly relevant to the mature population. Self-regulation "must contain self-modification skills and strategies that can be applied to the present state or activity to direct toward another state or activity" (p. 210). He further emphasized the importance of "how individuals understand and represent themselves and how they take charge of their own functions during critical years of development" (p. 211).

Creativity

Creativity requires divergent thinking and the generation of new ideas. Sternberg and Lubart (2001) defined creativity as "the ability to produce work that is (a) novel, (b) high in quality, and (c) task appropriate" (p. 510). The emotional component of writing poetry appears to manifest itself early in life. In reporting on the work of Simonton (1990), Sternberg and Lubart (2001) pointed out that "poets produced their most frequently cited works at a significantly younger average age than did imaginative prose writers" (p. 511). They also wrote that "Gardner (1993) has made a similar kind of proposal, namely that creative works of younger people tend more to defy previous traditions, where creative works of older people tend to integrate tradition" (Sternberg & Lubart, 2001, p. 511).

Trends in creative works in both artistic and research areas generally show a rise in productivity to sometime in midlife and then a slow decline (Simonton, 1988). In one of the first comprehensive reviews of evidence-based studies of aging, Quetelet (1835/1942) pointed out that

> It will first be necessary to determine the period at which memory, imagination, and judgment commence, and the stages through which they successively pass in the progress to maturity; then having established

the maximum point, we may extend our inquiries to the law of their decline. (p. 74)

It is notable that Quetelet's (1835/1942) analysis of the age at which major contributions were made to French theater reported that tragic themes were developed earlier than were comic themes. Hence, age and emotion may influence the themes of creative writing. Whether contemporary studies would demonstrate a similar pattern is an open question. Sternberg and Lubart (2001) observed in their review that "creative work in basic science, social science, and philosophy often consists of writing memoirs, histories of a field, and text books or records of observations accrued over a life span" (p. 511).

Wisdom

Wisdom, like creativity, requires divergent thinking and the generation of new ideas. But unlike creativity, wisdom relates to the control of emotion, impulsivity, or emotionally driven behavior. If mature people have developed the quality of wisdom, it seems reasonable that they are more likely to be selective about the objectives of their creative energies. Indeed, some early life creative foci might burn out and be replaced with later life goals with broader implications. Transitions in longer adult lives are accompanied by uncertainty and ambiguity and call for divergent thinking, if not for creativity. Models from the lives of parents and grandparents in earlier societies typically do not offer much guidance for today's older adults. Thus, a transition from employment to retirement can evoke uncertainty about what to do with the rest of one's life. When G. S. Hall retired as president of Clark University, he faced this ambiguity and commented, "I surely may indulge myself a little more in many ways but I really want and ought to do something useful and with a unitary purpose" (1922, p. xiii). He further commented,

> As a preliminary event to this, it slowly came to me that I must, first of all, take careful stock of myself and seek to attain more of the self-knowledge that Socrates taught the world was the higher, hardest, and last of all form of knowledge. I must know, too, just how I stand in with my present stage of life. (p. xiv)

This statement reveals a brilliant developmental psychologist groping for insight into how to invest the rest of his life. Hall's statement reflects the ambiguity of late-life transition. It also suggests a personal quest for deep understanding that prompts the use of the term *wisdom*, a topic in psychology that has begun to attract attention relatively recently.

Why the topic of wisdom has been so slow to emerge in psychology and within developmental psychology in particular is in itself an important topic to pursue. Wisdom appears to be a topic particularly relevant to the graying population. The origins of scientific psychology in the 19th century were heavily influenced by advances in physics and chemistry; psychologists studied elemental mental processes in search of the laws of basic processes. The term *psychophysics* was introduced, presumably to denote the hard science orientation of experimental psychology. In a sense, this bottom-up study of the discrete elements of behavior contrasts with the top-down study of personal control processes such as decision making, experience, and wisdom.

Wisdom emerged in about 1975 as a subject for empirical research (Brugman, 2000; Clayton & Birren, 1980; Sternberg, 1990). However, wisdom is an ancient philosophical and religious topic (Birren & Svensson, 2005). In the days of Greek cultural dominance, behavioral traits were regarded as attributes of the gods. One prayed to the gods for desired traits and to avoid the influences of evil gods.

Robinson (1990), in his review of the history of wisdom, concluded that "it was chiefly the aesthetes and artists of the 19th century who preserved the pre-scientific conception of wisdom: a divine gift discovered through an introspective process and manifested in words or works of transcendental truth and beauty" (p. 23). Therefore, as psychology searched for scientific standing in the 19th century, its founders and leaders recognized that any number of ageless issues would have to be ignored, lest the new "science" be corrupted by the older "metaphysics." This argument suggests that wisdom was neglected by psychologists not only because it was complex but also because it was a topic tainted by nonscientific traditions.

Recent approaches to the study of wisdom associate advancing age with experience gained in the many aspects of living. After reviewing the many definitions and approaches to the study of wisdom described in Sternberg's (1990) book on wisdom, Birren and Fisher (1990) concluded that wisdom develops as a balance of cognition, volition, and affect, and it results in wise products in relation to planning, decisions, and advice. In a hierarchical sense, wisdom appears to be one of the most complex qualities of human behavior that leads to benefits for the survival and well-being of individuals and of societies. Wisdom requires that an individual live long enough to accumulate experience in the many dimensions of living and use this experience to make decisions and give advice. Wisdom's implications extend over many facets of behavior, such as being reflective, nonimpulsive, using complex decision-making processes that maximize valued outcomes, knowing oneself and being self-regulating, being immune from competitive struggle, and having time to devote to others.

If these emerging views of wisdom are sound, then wisdom should be available for study in mature persons. Cohen (2006) introduced the concept of *developmental intelligence,* which appears to be very similar to the concept of wisdom. This concept purports that if a highly intelligent older person has the quality of behavior identified as wisdom, such a person would exert more executive control over his or her choices of behavior. Thus, if they are creative, then mature people might deliberate more on the value of their investments of time and effort in creative tasks. However, one must be cautious about assuming the universal existence of wisdom in older people merely because of age and experience in many life events.

It is notable that Atchley (2005) used the word *wisdom* in reference to the implications of his 20-year longitudinal study of 1,400 community residents 50 years and older. The data reveal that seniors drift toward personal relationships and away from organizations, and that they give more of their time to personal service to others than to impersonal work. "Roles that offer opportunities to manifest wisdom include grandparenting, mentoring, participating in informal peer support groups, maintaining close relationships with friends or family, and providing compassionate listening and counseling to upcoming generations" (Atchley, 2005, p. 12). These roles would appear to be behavioral assets of selected older adults that can be cultivated and used.

USE OF ABILITIES IN ADULT LIFE

Ingredients not available to younger decision makers are the experiences of many years of family and work life, personal relationships, economic and health decisions, and the positive and negative outcomes of earlier decisions. In making decisions, educated mature people seek information, talk situations over with family and friends, and reason about possible outcomes. A circle of friends who are competent in many areas of professional and personal life can become increasingly available and valued in later life.

These late-life cognitive abilities can be valuable resources for making wise decisions in daily life. The process of reasoning that underlies wisdom may be described as dialectical, providing alternative or contrasting outcomes for consideration. At the positive end of the older population distribution are individuals who make constructive and productive decisions on the basis of their education and experience. They may more frequently use dialectical or divergent thinking, leading to creative acts or usefully novel ideas.

Freedom from earlier life obligations can release the little used talents of older people. Late-life bloomers' change of focus from work life to more self-directed activities can result in their making distinguished contributions. Developmental psychology has much to gain from a focus on understanding the diversity of the older population: its talents, limitations, and those conditions that encourage the expression of wisdom.

Characterizations of elderly people and their talents need to be evidence based. It is relevant to quote the words of McFadden (2005) reporting at an international meeting on the role of the arts with persons with dementia:

> The conference reflected a growing recognition of the need to move away from a deficit orientation toward people with dementia to working with

their assets and finding out what they can contribute to their own care. This process can be hastened when the public begins to see the profound ways people reveal themselves and comment on their worlds of experience through painting, poetry, storytelling, music, dance, and other forms of creativity. (p. 15)

Many contemporary metaphors attempt to positively characterize life paths in the later years, such as successful aging, vital aging, and productive aging. These metaphors' usefulness in describing the many paths of life await further research on the complex processes of growing up and growing old.

SUMMARY

Increasing attention to the adult years has been stimulated by dramatic increases in life expectancy in the early 20th century. Individuals are living longer and more actively than did their parents and their grandparents. They are also growing up and living in a rapidly changing information society. All of these changes are resulting in considerable ambiguity surrounding life transitions. The stage models used in psychology have to be reconceptualized if they are to accommodate the expanding complexities and possibilities of adult life.

Extensive longitudinal studies of adult behavioral capacities, health, and longevity reveal different patterns of late-life behavior. Individual differences in adults reflect many dynamic and interacting influences, with behavioral variables influencing health and vice versa. The result is increasing diversity in the behavioral capacities of older adults, not only in the number of persons with dementia but also in the number of persons with expanding intellectual capacities.

Many older people have needs for health and personal care, yet there are also those who can contribute to the growth of others and to improving the organization and management of society as a result of their experience, talents, and wisdom. Research points to gains that may be achieved by interventions with mature and older adults, not only to maintain their capacities but also to expand them.

The study of child development generally focuses on normal patterns of child development and ways to optimize children's potential. In the later years, as in childhood, there are pathologies that affect the brain and lead to diminished function. At advanced ages, pathology may be the most frequent pattern in today's population, rendering the concept of normal old age somewhat ambiguous. But something about diversity may be learned from the model of the native persimmon tree that bears its ripe fruit after the first frost. It is intriguing to consider what might be derived from future research into creativity, competency, productivity, and wisdom in older persons. Ways may be discovered to release existing yet underused and underexpressed competency and talents.

REFERENCES

Albert, M. S., & Killiany, R. J. (2001). Age-related cognitive change and brain-behavior relationships. In J. E. Birren & K. W. Schaie (Eds.), *Handbook of the psychology of aging* (5th ed., pp. 161–185). San Diego, CA: Academic Press.

Atchley, R. (2005). In the spirit of service: How we reach out in later life. *Aging Today, 26,* 5.

Birren, J. E. (1960). Behavioral theories of aging. In N. W. Shock (Ed.), *Aging: Some social and biological aspects* (pp. 305–332). Washington, DC: American Association for the Advancement of Science.

Birren, J. E., & Fisher, L. M. (1990). The elements of wisdom: Overview and integration. In R. J. Sternberg (Ed.), *Wisdom: Its nature, origins, and development* (pp. 317–332). New York: Cambridge University Press.

Birren, J. E., & Schroots, J. J. F. (2006). Autobiographical memory and the narrative self over the life span. In J. E. Birren & K. W. Schaie (Eds.), *Handbook of the psychology of aging* (6th ed., pp. 477–498). San Diego, CA: Academic Press.

Birren, J. E., & Svensson, C. M. (2005). Wisdom in history. In R. J. Sternberg & J. Jordan (Eds.), *A handbook of wisdom* (pp. 3–31). New York: Cambridge University Press.

Boekaerts, M., Pintrich, P. R., & Zeidner, M. (Eds.). (2000). *Handbook of self-regulation.* San Diego, CA: Academic Press.

Bratter, B., & Freeman, E. (1990). The maturing peer counseling. *Generations, 9*(4), 49–52.

Brugman, G. (2000). *Wisdom: Source of narrative coherence and eudaimonia.* Delft, the Netherlands: Eburon.

Clayton, V. P., & Birren, J. E. (1980). The development of wisdom across the life-span: A reexamination of an ancient topic. *Life-Span Development and Behavior, 18,* 199–128.

Cohen, G. D. (2006). *The mature mind.* New York: Perseus Publishing.

Demetriou, A. (2000). Organization and development of self-understanding and self-regulation: Toward a general theory. In M. Boekaerts, P. R. Pintrich, & M. Zeidner (Eds.), *Handbook of self-regulation* (pp. 209–251). San Diego, CA: Academic Press.

Erikson, E. H. (1959). Identity and the life cycle [Monograph]. *Psychological Issues, 1*(1), 1–171.

Freeman, E. (1994). Senior peer counseling: Serving a growing and varied population. *Dimensions, 1,* 2–4.

Gardner, H. (1993). *Creating minds.* New York: Basic Books.

Hall, G. S. (1922). *Senescence: The last half of life.* New York: D. Appleton.

McFadden, S. (2005). International conference gets creative edge on dementia. *Aging Today, xxvi*(5), 13–15.

McFarland, R. A., & O'Doherty, B. N. (1959). Work and occupational skills. In J. E. Birren (Ed.), *Handbook of aging and the individual* (pp. 452–500). Chicago: University of Chicago Press.

Medawar, P. B. (1957). *The uniqueness of the individual*. London: Methuen.

Quetelet, M. A. (1942). *A treatise on man and the development of his faculties*. New York: Burt Franklin. (Original work published 1835)

Raskind, M. A., & Peskind, E. R. (1991). Alzheimer's disease and other dementing disorders. In J. E. Birren, R. B. Sloane, & G. D. Cohen (Eds.), *Handbook of mental health and aging* (pp. 477–513). San Diego, CA: Academic Press.

Robinson, D. N. (1990). Wisdom through the ages. In R. J. Sternberg (Ed.), *Wisdom: Its nature, origins, and development* (pp. 13–24). New York: Cambridge University Press.

Schaie, K. W. (1983). What can we learn from the longitudinal study of adult psychological development? In K. W. Schaie (Ed.), *Longitudinal studies of adult psychological development* (pp. 1–17). New York: Guilford Press.

Schaie, K. W. (2005). *Developmental influences on adult intelligence*. New York: Oxford University Press.

Schaie, K. W., & Hofer, S. M. (2001). Longitudinal studies in aging research. In J. E. Birren & K. W. Schaie (Eds.), *Handbook of the psychology of aging* (5th ed., pp. 53–77). San Diego, CA: Academic Press.

Simonton, D. K. (1988). Age and outstanding achievement: What do we know after over a century of research. *Psychological Bulletin, 104*, 251–267.

Simonton, D. K. (1990). Creativity and wisdom in aging. In J. E. Birren & K. W. Schaie (Eds.), *Handbook of the psychology of aging* (3rd ed., pp. 320–329). San Diego, CA: Academic Press.

Snowdon, D. A., Kemper, S., Mortimer, J. A., Greine, L. H., Wekstei, D. R., & Markesbery, W. R. (1996). Linguistic ability in early life and cognitive functions and Alzheimer's disease in late life: Findings from the Nun Study. *JAMA, 275*, 528–532.

Sternberg, R. J. (Ed.). (1990). *Wisdom: Its nature, origins, and development*. New York: Cambridge University Press.

Sternberg, R. J., & Lubart, T. I. (2001). Wisdom and creativity. In J. E. Birren & K. W. Schaie (Eds.), *Handbook of the psychology of aging* (5th ed., pp. 500–522). San Diego, CA: Academic Press.

Svanborg, A. (1996). Postponement of aging. In J. E. Birren (Ed.), *Encyclopedia of gerontology* (pp. 333–340). San Diego, CA: Academic Press.

Vinters, H. E. (2001). Aging and the human nervous system. In J. E. Birren & K. W. Schaie (Eds.), *Handbook of the psychology of aging* (5th ed., pp. 135–160). San Diego, CA: Academic Press.

Wesley, M. (1986). *Harnassing peacocks*. New York: Scribner.

Willis, S. L. (2001). Methodological issues in behavioral interventions research with the elderly. In J. E. Birren & K. W. Schaie (Eds.), *Handbook of the psychology of aging* (5th ed., pp. 78–108). San Diego, CA: Academic Press.

V

LIFE-SPAN PERSPECTIVES: UNDERSTANDINGS AND IMPLICATIONS

11

DEVELOPMENTAL SCIENCE AND GIFTEDNESS: AN INTEGRATED LIFE-SPAN FRAMEWORK

DANIEL P. KEATING

Although there is considerable overlap in the scientific study of gifted-ness and of child development in terms of research traditions as well as par-ticipating investigators, it is important to recognize that there are substantial differences in the history of each research tradition. The historical diver-gence in the core conceptual frameworks guiding each field has led to con-flicting positions at least as often as to a productive connection between them. At the risk of overemphasizing the conflict between these conceptual frameworks, it is important to draw out the distinctions because they illumi-nate many important issues, particularly with relevance to the goal of this volume, an integration of developmental science and the study of giftedness. I thus first provide a brief history of those two approaches, recognizing of course that there is a personal filter through which such a historical analysis must proceed. I take up the implications for a life-span integrative frame-work in the final section.

THE SCIENTIFIC STUDY OF GIFTEDNESS:
FROM CHILD TO ADULT

The first scientific study of giftedness appeared in the form of the five-volume series on the Genetic Studies of Genius (GSG) launched by Lewis Terman in the 1920s (Terman, 1925–1947; Terman & Oden, 1959). Although the terminology sounds a bit strained to the modern ear, it is important to recall that Terman was not referring to the contemporary sense of gene structures as studied, for example, in the Human Genome Project. Rather, he meant *genetic* in the sense of *ontogenetic*, a synonym for *development* in contemporary usage. Nonetheless, Terman was a firm adherent of Darwinian principles, or more precisely the Galtonian interpretation of Darwin as applied to human heritability (Keating, 1990), which undoubtedly influenced Terman's construction and interpretation of his overall project

Similarly, his use of the term *genius* was not as odd in its day as it perhaps sounds today. Although it is clear that he expected some very high performers to emerge when he initiated his longitudinal study of giftedness, he understood that genius arises from a number of different factors (Terman, 1925–1947). Terman's major goal for his genetic studies of genius was to dispel two prevailing myths about genius. The first myth was that individuals who are identified in childhood as very high functioning in the intellectual domain are otherwise dysfunctional. The second myth, "early ripe, early rot," presumed that precocity inevitably led to burnout. The study was primarily concerned with testing the prevailing myths about dysfunctional development in areas other than intellectual giftedness among identified children.

Testing Two Beliefs About Gifted Children

Terman began by identifying a high-IQ group in California, using an initial version of the Stanford–Binet Intelligence Scale that he had developed, using a cutoff of 135, about two standard deviations above the population mean on the norms he had empirically established. This cutoff methodology did not yield a sample of children that was, in fact, representative of individuals above the cutoff score. They were of significantly higher IQ than would have been expected statistically (Keating, 1975), thus biasing the sample toward being a higher IQ sample than the cutoff would suggest. This bias produces a stronger test of Terman's claim that high IQ was not inherently dysfunctional for other domains, but it also raises expectations regarding later levels of achievement if IQ is viewed as a primary predictor.

Terman collected additional data on this sample's personal functioning, social relationships, and family relationships. What he found would not surprise the field today, as it has become conventional knowledge, but at the time it was a quite important finding to recognize that individuals identified in this fashion were not otherwise dysfunctional. In fact, they showed substantial advantages on a fairly wide range of other developmental outcomes, including social competence and popularity (Terman, 1925–1947).

The second major goal was to show that early ability was related substantially to later accomplishment, and Terman proceeded to work on this in two ways. The first and more familiar way was to begin a prospective longitudinal study using his identified sample. The subsequent evidence showed that this sample yielded substantially higher levels of later achievement compared with the full population. This longitudinal pattern was generally supportive of Terman's initial hypothesis that early giftedness would be predictive of subsequent accomplishment. Again, this finding is unsurprising to contemporary researchers in the field or to the public at large, but it was far from conventional wisdom at the time (Terman, 1925–1947).

Research Efforts to Identify High-Level Accomplishment Early in Childhood

Somewhat less well-known today is Terman's second methodology for establishing early high ability as the root of later high accomplishment, reflected in the second volume in the GSG series, a retrospective longitudinal study of individuals who were eminent or at least highly accomplished individuals in various fields (Terman, 1925–1947). This research effort proceeded by identifying such individuals through consensus nominations and then examining their early records from biographical or other available sources. One goal was to generate an assessment of their early promise as well as to generate a specific estimated childhood IQ. As is now known, both the prospective longitudinal study, which would come closer to meeting contemporary research methodology standards, and the retrospective longitudinal study yielded the now commonplace result that early childhood giftedness defined as high IQ was related to substantial levels of adult accomplishment. What is clearly true from the prospective study is that there is considerable variation in adult accomplishment in a population that was roughly similar on the level of giftedness as identified by high IQ, evident as well in a subsequent follow-up of this sample in later life (Holahan, Sears, & Cronbach, 1995). This finding could not have been revealed by the retrospective study because it began only with individuals of extraordinarily high accomplishment.

Much has been made both of the relative lack of extremely high performers, such as Nobel laureates, in the Terman prospective sample, and of the relatively modest accomplishments of large proportions of that sample. In the same vein, many individuals have taken note of the fact that some potential members of the Terman large juvenile study did not in fact make the cutoff and yet went on to have highly distinguished careers. Perhaps the most familiar story (Hulbert, 2005) is that of Luis Alvarez and William Shockley, who despite failing to qualify for the Terman longitudinal study of giftedness went on to become Nobel laureates. One can only speculate whether this success was connected to an increased motivation on Shockley's part that may have led to his substantial accomplishments in the invention of the transistor or, in later life, his preoccupation with eugenics.

The story has an additional twist that would not be out of place in a psychoanalytically inspired novel: Lewis Terman's son, Frederick Terman, provost at Stanford University in 1955, invited Shockley to set up shop near Stanford to pursue his original line of work for commercial technological research and development. The acceptance of this invitation is often credited as the launch of Silicon Valley, which grew very rapidly to become the hub of arguably the most significant technological advances since the Industrial Revolution, speeding the world toward the Knowledge Revolution.

The Social Context of Extraordinary Accomplishment

Out of the early version of Silicon Valley emerged many extraordinarily gifted individuals. Two early students of Frederick Terman, who was a significant innovator in radio engineering in his own right, were William Hewlett and David Packard, whose partnership has remained a significant force in modern information technology research and development. In addition, Robert Noyce and seven other talented recruits in Shockley's new initiative near Stanford left the initiative (because of Shockley's management style) and formed their own start-up company—an innovative management concept in its own right, with enormous historical consequences. This start-up company, Fairchild Semiconductor, would lead the way in the development and exploitation of silicon-based information and communication technology.

This confluence of extraordinary, even history-altering scientific creativity would be hard to attribute to a coincidental accumulation of individuals with exceptional talent. Rather, enormously powerful social affordances promoted these extraordinary advances. The penchant for looking toward individual characteristics of persons for early signs of giftedness or for retrospectively explaining the psychological sources of eminent achievement often leads to overlooking the social affordances that create the context for high achievement.

The Categorical Model

What even a brief overview of Terman's seminal study of giftedness dating back into the 1920s reveals is that the guiding conceptual framework of giftedness embedded in the Terman study was a categorical model (Keating, 1990, 1991). The specific claim was that giftedness is preeminently a characteristic of persons, possessed by only a small percentage of individuals, and that this was a stable trait for those individuals. Terman's claim that a group of early high performers would not show any generalized dysfunction in other areas was supported by his findings and is reinforced by decades of similar findings using multiple approaches and methods (Keating, 1976; Stanley, Keating, & Fox, 1974). His expectation, however, that this group would not only show high accomplishment but also likely produce many of the intellectual leaders of their generation as they reached adulthood was not well supported in the prospective longitudinal study (Terman & Oden, 1959).

The failure to support the second hypothesis—that the highest levels of accomplishment, perhaps even genius, would emerge from an appropriately selected sample—generated two broad lines of inquiry that have continued to interest researchers over the years.

First, there is the possibility that the cutoff criterion for selection was too low. This argument postulated that, if one used a more extreme cutoff score, say 180 IQ, then the probability of finding extraordinary adult accomplishments would be increased. There are two problems with this argument. The lesser one is that Terman's GSG was in fact a more select sample than the cutoff score would indicate, biased upward in terms of mean IQ and with less variance around that higher mean than the cutoff would imply (Keating, 1975). More to the point are the specific cases of Alvarez and Shockley, who were evaluated and not selected at the lower cutoff score but who nonetheless went on to achieve at a more distinguished level than did any members of the sample.

Second, there is the possibility that the selection criterion was too domain specific. Perhaps the IQ-based concept of intelligence is inadequate, and an expanded view, such as that of multiple intelligences (Gardner, 2004), would be more effective. A variant on this idea is to combine the notion of more domain-specific intelligences with the notion of higher cutoffs, such as in the study of child prodigies in particular areas of accomplishment (Feldman, 1993). Yet another possibility is that the hallmarks of eventual accomplishment may be found in some combination of cognitive or achievement indices with "extracognitive" aspects that may be essential to eventual accomplishment, such as creativity, unconscious processes, diligence, the capacity to respond positively to difficulties, social capabilities, motivation, sustained attentional focus, family factors, or cultural influences (Csikszentmihalyi, 1990; Howe, 2004; Olszewski-Kubilius, 2000; Shavinina & Ferrari, 2004; Subotnik & Arnold, 1994).

The difficulty here is that as the list of predictors grows, the capacity to correctly identify individuals (assuming for the moment that it is theoretically possible) diminishes purely for measurement reasons. If one uses multiple criteria, each of which must be met to be in the identified group, fewer and fewer individuals qualify as the number of criteria increases. This is particularly true if the measures of some included criteria potentially conflict. Simultaneously selecting for early childhood manifestations of diligence and creativity, for example, would pose significant measurement challenges. Far fewer individuals would be identified as potentially extraordinary achievers if one used multiple criteria, which would make identification even less sensitive than Terman's univariate IQ-cutoff that failed to locate two subsequent Nobel laureates but included hundreds of others.

The required balance of sensitivity (identifying all of the prospective extraordinary achievers) and specificity (identifying only the prospective extraordinary achievers) raises the stakes considerably. For example, the overwhelming homogeneity of the Terman GSG sample (White and middle class) is at one level a historical footnote, signaling the blinders imposed by the total absence of contemporary political correctness (and for an even starker version of this historical transition, see Terman, 1906). But it is surely incorrect to assume that these blinders no longer function. The risk of using selection criteria that systematically fail to discover prospective talent in some groups is pervasive and persistent. The imbalance of race and ethnicity among individuals selected for gifted education programs remains striking even at present (see chap. 7, this volume). The empirical evidence for successful alternative strategies to select individuals who will subsequently demonstrate extraordinary high achievement on the basis of general performance indicators is far from compelling (Subotnik & Arnold, 1994).

Selecting at very high levels of a specific targeted performance at a later point in development, perhaps as young as early adolescence, may be more promising, particularly if the criterion performance requires the precise skills needed for very high achievement and if the selection level is set high enough. Lubinski, Webb, Morelock, and Benbow (2001) reported on a 10-year follow-up of early adolescents with SAT scores above the 99.99th percentile (i.e., 1 in 10,000); they found very high levels of accomplishment in the pursuit of doctoral degrees from the most prestigious institutions and a high rate of early career awards. In a 20-year follow-up of this group, the same pattern of high achievement emerged, although the degree to which extraordinary accomplishments will emerge remains unclear (Wai, Lubinski, & Benbow, 2005). The selection and training of elite performers entail similar concerns (Subotnik, 2004).

Do Retrospective Histories of Extraordinary Achievers Enhance Early Identification?

The failure of Terman's (or other) prospective studies to identify extraordinary high achievement raises the issue of whether to use retrospective methodologies. In this approach, individuals of clearly extraordinary high achievement are identified (typically by some method of peer consensus of individuals currently working in the same field), and their early histories are then studied for signs of their future accomplishments. This can be done through historical records, such as biographies (as in the second volume of the GSG, cited earlier), or through direct data collection such as proband interviews or interviews with family, friends, mentors, and so on. Perhaps not surprisingly, the collective effect of such studies suggests that extraordinary high achievers have had remarkably diverse backgrounds (Albert, 1992; Howe, 2004; Olszewski-Kubilius, 2000). Clear evidence of below-average intelligence is hard to find in such retrospective samples, but neither is there a characteristic or set of characteristics that yields consistent prediction to extraordinary achievement. There appears to be, on the scientific record to date, no standard formula that can predict extraordinary achievement.

The failure to find a standard formula for the early identification of extraordinary achievement is easy to understand, in hindsight. (Hindsight has an undeservedly bad reputation; looking backward over the historical record has yielded some major scientific breakthroughs, including the theory of evolution.) Extraordinary achievement, or genius, or transformative creativity is by definition a rare event. Predicting forward to rare events is inherently fraught with difficulty because of the sensitivity and specificity demands noted earlier. When the event is multidetermined, as this phenomenon surely is, then the difficulties seem close to insurmountable.

However, despite the failure so far of using prospective studies to find a standard formula for the early identification of extraordinary achievement, retrospective methodologies offer no avenue out of this conundrum. There is not enough commonality among the rare events, that is, among the extraordinary achievers and creators, to generate the formula for its prediction. Even if there were, suspicion would be warranted on the standard grounds of methodology, specifically the unreliability of retrospective accounts. This is why developmental science turned to the far more expensive and tedious prospective longitudinal methodologies.

In this specific instance, there may be more reasons than usual to be concerned about retrospective accuracy. Biographers who take the influence of early life seriously face an almost unavoidable requirement to establish a coherent narrative flow. This narrative imperative requires in turn the selection of events to record, either positive or negative. If direct interviews of the identified individuals are possible, the distortions of quite normal cognitive biases owing to selective memory and to self-enhancement can be studied in addition to conscious selection. It would be the rare genius indeed who would attribute success entirely to external forces rather than to personal characteristics.

This selectivity becomes especially pertinent when such retrospective accounts identify potentially symptomatic, syndromic, or pathological processes as keys to extraordinary achievement, valorizing such elements as alienation, marginalization, loss, or rejection as fundamental ingredients for truly important achievements (see Olszewski-Kubilius, 2000, for a brief review). The romanticized meme of overcoming extraordinary challenges to arrive at extraordinary accomplishments has such a long narrative history—

extending back to the classical period, as in Virgil's *Aeneid*, and even into oral tradition, as in Homer's *Iliad*—that researchers and general readers alike should be wary of scientific theories built on the same meme. When the primary support for such theories is derived from retrospective methods, we should amplify our critical filters.

WHY IDENTIFY EARLY?

If the goal of identifying extraordinary achievement from early life indicators has not been realized, either prospectively or retrospectively, as I have argued, then it may be important to return to primary questions, such as, What is the purpose of early identification of prospective extraordinary achievement? First, there is an inherent scientific curiosity to understand the sources of an interesting and important phenomenon. An additional concern is to protect individuals who show high levels of ability or talent from negative social judgments, although this problem may have diminished somewhat since Terman's early work. Perhaps most significant is the desire to improve the educational circumstances for such children and to promote and optimize their development, or at least not to inhibit it (Keating, 1991).

It is interesting to note that the educational implications of Terman's work were not a primary pursuit for him. His goal was largely to change the public perception of such individuals, and by so doing to remove any particular barriers to their school experience or to their attainment of likely high performance in adulthood—such as the belief that precocity will lead to later problems and should be discouraged. He appears not to have been particularly concerned with a dramatic reform of the educational system so as to benefit gifted children, but rather to reduce the possibility that schooling would get in the way of their eventual destiny.

Educational Reforms for Gifted Student

It was left to Terman's successors in the field of giftedness and gifted education to establish an institutional approach to giftedness. Consistent with the model of giftedness as the categorical possession of a small percentage of children—and note, by the way, that the very terminology of *giftedness* carries an implication of being the passive recipient of some special status—the later generations of researchers and educational reformers following the Terman approach have generally opted for one of two types of educational reform.

The first type of reform involves separate schools or classes for gifted children. This separation, although intellectually consistent with the categorical model of giftedness, has not made great practical headway in public education, largely for political, economic, and logistical reasons. In contrast, many private schools, and many classes within private schools, have been devoted to the gifted. In these separated programs for the gifted, some but not all of which have some ability-based selection criteria, the patterns are familiar. The percentage of White children attending private schools (K–12) in 2000 was almost 13%, whereas the rates for African American, Hispanic or Latino, or American Indian children hovered between 5% and 6% (U.S. Census Bureau, 2000). Asian children were the exception to this trend among minorities, with private school enrollment at about 10%. These percentages reflect some combination of economic, social class, and race, ethnicity, and cultural influences, of course, but they have the effect of reinforcing ability segregation that is evident in school composition effects and in gifted program enrollment statistics (see chap. 7, this volume).

The second most common type of education reform for gifted children in schools was the establishment of enrichment programs based on some version of IQ selection, other test selection (e.g., creativity), teacher nomination, or some combination of these. This educational solution had a number of potential advantages. First, it was an opportunity to address the concerns of many parents of children with high ability or other indicators of giftedness that their children would not be sufficiently challenged academically and thus not be sufficiently prepared for later competition for selective college admissions (Winerip, 2006). This approach addresses student concerns that the conventional curriculum at the conventional pace is boring (e.g., Keating, 1976; Stanley, Keating, & Fox, 1974).

Although this enrichment model has had some success in addressing some parental concerns as well as some inadequacies of the standard curriculum to meet the needs of developmentally advanced children, it does have a number of drawbacks (Keating, 1991). On the academic side, enrichment programs generally fail to provide substantial academic challenge in the core academic areas that such students typically need. That is, challenge arising from participating in an alternate academic arena may address some needs, but it does not usually address the need for educational opportunities to develop high levels of skill in core academic areas. At worst, the benefits from an increased number of field trips or alternative activities, however interesting, do not really address the core intellectual and developmental needs of these students. Nor is it clear, returning to the relevance of specificity and sensitivity of selection for treatment, that such enrichment activities are more beneficial for children identified as gifted than they would be for the general population or for other ability groupings.

As with the separation programs, a concern with the enrichment programs is that when IQ or some variant is used as the selection criterion, individual students who may already enjoy considerable advantages in terms of socioeconomic status or parental educational levels will, in effect, be further privileged by being given additional educational advantages, mirroring the social patterning reported earlier for selective schools. One unintended consequence of this arrangement noted by Graham (chap. 7, this volume) is the increased segregation of such educational opportunities by racial or minority group status.

Summary of the Categorical Model of Giftedness

In summary, the categorical model of giftedness is premised on a belief in a relatively fixed characteristic of children to which the appropriate educational response is some form of segregated special programming. Although not a primary concern of Terman's foundational work on giftedness in the GSG, this pattern is a direct derivative of his original conceptual framework. Its institutionalization in special educational programming, focusing on segregation according to identified high ability (or its surrogates), has become sufficiently entrenched as to seem almost natural, and to engender parental resistance when challenged (Winerip, 2006). It is in this sense that a categorical model is at the core of contemporary theory and practice in giftedness research and education. An alternative and sometimes conflicting perspective is to be found in the emergent interdisciplinary field of developmental science.

DEVELOPMENTAL SCIENCE: THE NATURE AND EDUCATION OF DEVELOPMENTAL DIVERSITY

A contrasting view of the development of high-level talent lies in what I have referred to as "developmental diversity" (Keating, 1990, 1991). This approach starts with the presumption that children differ from each other on many dimensions and that the challenge in educating them is to assess that diversity in its full complexity and to evaluate what developmental supports are required to optimize the development of all individuals, from the academically challenged to prospective high achievers. The implication of this view is that the principles differ little across types of diversity, although the educational content may be vastly different.

Our earliest work in this field was with the Study of Mathematically Precocious Youth (SMPY; Keating, 1976; Stanley et al., 1974), in which we specifically eschewed the notion of giftedness as a global category (based, for example, on IQ) as being of any real use for educational intervention. Rather, the SMPY notion was that extremely high levels of talent could be found in particular domains of academic interests—levels of accomplishment that would be very unlikely to be discovered in a standard giftedness assessment—and that the best approach to education intervention would be to find ways to allow such individuals to continue to develop their talents in a challenging and supportive atmosphere. The particular intervention for a particular child could differ on a variety of dimensions, so long as the options provided the opportunity for the child to continue to move forward in the area or areas in which he or she demonstrated precocious accomplishment.

The ways in which this developmental perspective differs from a categorical perspective can be briefly summarized in a few key principles that have been discussed elsewhere in greater detail (Keating, 1980, 1990, 1991; Matthews & Keating, 1995):

- The goal of identifying at an early stage individuals who are gifted, talented, high ability, or high achieving or demonstrate some important aspect of developmental diversity is principally to find ways to optimize their pathways to further expertise and accomplishment.
- Helping individuals to obtain high levels of expertise and accomplishment is ultimately the goal of such developmental interventions. It is important to avoid seeing the attainment of expertise or content knowledge as somehow competing with advancing the goals of creativity or critical thinking (Keating, 1980). The demands of expertise increase as one progresses in any field of endeavor, and all facets of creativity need to be integrated to keep moving ahead.
- Identifying high levels of developmental diversity to promote development will lead toward more domain-specific rather than more domain-general notions of intelligence or ability (Gardner, 2004). The more extreme the selection process, the less likely it is that the same individuals will be included across different domains (Matthews & Keating, 1995). From this perspective, generalized enrichment is unlikely to hit the developmental target very precisely.
- Supporting development in this way requires increasingly sophisticated understanding of the pathways to expertise (Keating, 1990), defined as the routes along which competence and expertise develop, through an integration of cognitive acquisitions at multiple levels, from executive function to the automaticity of specific skills acquired through effortful practice. There are multiple pathways to the development of expertise, and which sequence works best likely varies across children. The trend toward close study of Instruction × Student interaction has yielded important new insights for education more generally (in early reading, for example, see Connor, Morrison, & Katch, 2004; Connor, Son, Hindman, & Morrison, 2005), and it has of course a venerable tradition in music and other performing arts that could be beneficially emulated in other

domains (Subotnik, 2004). The issue here is not on the form of the educational intervention, such as ability grouping, acceleration, or enrichment; rather, the test is whether the educational content is suitably matched to the individual's level of competence such that his or her pathway to expertise is advanced.

- Approaches rooted in this model are likely to yield substantial enhancements for high levels of ordinary achievement, and the more stringent the selection and the more diversified the developmental scaffolding, the more such enhancements will be observed (Lubinski et al., 2001). But truly extraordinary achievement is likely to remain an elusive goal for prospective prediction, for the reasons noted earlier. Rather, creating as large a population as possible that is highly competent, creating social conditions that allow that competence to be used, and allowing the normal probabilistic and self-organizing principles to operate (Simonton, 2004) are most likely to yield the conditions out of which the extraordinary advances of the human innovation dynamic will be able to flourish at a societal level (Keating, 1999).

- In addition to the optimization of developmental pathways in educational settings, we need to focus on the social opportunities in advanced education through later career options. There are many exits from pathways to high-level expertise, and even successful interventions to promote talent at one level (Shapka & Keating, 2003) may not be maintained at subsequent levels (Shapka, Domene, & Keating, 2006). This need for continuity of support for high-level accomplishment is particularly relevant at the transition to early adulthood but remains important throughout adult development and later life.

The integration of developmental perspectives into the study of giftedness across the life span will need to follow these principles. In addition, it will need to incorporate two particularly important emerging trends in developmental science, both of which are rooted in the growing field of developmental neuroscience.

The first of these trends has been referred to variously as neural sculpting or biological embedding (Casey, Giedd, & Thomas, 2000; Cynader & Frost, 1999; Keating & Hertzman, 1999; Worthman & Kuzara, 2005; Zelazo, Carlson, & Kesek, in press). The core idea here is that in development, especially in early development, the neural system (including the neuroendocrine and neuroimmune systems) is enormously sensitive to developmental experiences. The early shaping of neural networks and response systems contributes in substantive ways to the course of subsequent development and health (Boyce & Keating, 2004). The level of early stimulation is a significant predictor of early ability, as the findings of Colombo et al. (chap. 2, this volume) show. Claims about the effect of early stimulation can be taken to an extreme, of course, as evident in the "scientific legend" known as the Mozart effect (Bangerter & Heath, 2004; Hui, 2006). However, the implications for establishing a strong foundation for later accomplishment, both cognitively and emotionally, are profound. In particular, the role of early experience in the production of social disparities, with attendant consequences for the identification and support of gifted children, requires significant reflection and further scientific inquiry (Boyce & Keating, 2004; see also chap. 7, this volume).

Also emerging from contemporary work in developmental neuroscience, and also having major implications for the understanding of giftedness and its support, is the specific focus on the prefrontal cortex (PFC) and the "executive suite" that it appears to govern (Keating, 2004). A strong case can be made, pending further evidence, that an understanding of the structure and function of the PFC will lead to an understanding of how the cognitive and "extracognitive" features that are essential to high-level achievement become integrated over the course of development. The features include capabilities ranging from (a) high-level cognitive reasoning (Keating, 2004) to the (b) ability to function well under challenges to the stress response system (Dickerson & Kemeny, 2004), to the (c) blend of emotion and attention regulation that is essential to the flow of creativity (Csikszentmihalyi, 1990). This set of findings from neuroscience may be especially relevant to the adolescent transition, during which the role of the PFC is enhanced, both structurally and functionally (Keating, 2004).

AN INTEGRATED LIFE-SPAN DEVELOPMENTAL FRAMEWORK FOR GIFTEDNESS

Pulling together the issues identified in the scientific study of giftedness, the developmental critique of its legacy as a purely categorical model, and contemporary research in developmental science, especially developmental neuroscience, one can begin to see the outline of an integrative life-span developmental model of giftedness. Identifying all the relevant issues for each major developmental period is beyond the scope of this overview, and many of the focal topics are covered in other chapters of this volume. In the concluding section of this chapter, I attempt to identify how this integrative conceptual framework might be applied to two central questions. What is known about the development of high-level ability or talent during a developmental period? What would be recommended to support the advancement of ability and talent, wherever it is found?

Infancy

In the chapter by Colombo and colleagues (chap. 2, this volume), the question is, Can we predict who from infancy who will have high cognitive ability? Their evidence, consistent with related studies, is that it can be predicted by external characteristics (as measured in this case by the Home Observation for Measurement of the Environment [HOME] scale) but not very well from characteristics of the child (as measured by patterns of attention and habituation). In light of these findings, it may be useful to return to a prior question, What is the value of predicting high cognitive ability from infancy? From a categorical perspective, in which a stable trait view of giftedness is assumed, it would be interesting to see what the infant precursors of giftedness look like. But if it is not such a stable trait (as seems evident in the work of Gottfried, Gottfried, & Guerin; chap. 3, this volume), then the goal of pushing back the earliest date of identification may be less meaningful.

From a developmental perspective, it seems more reasonable to want to know the characteristics of early developmental experiences that are most likely to promote subsequent optimal achievement (recognizing that biological endowment may play some role, although the more that is learned about gene function, the more gene–environment dynamic interactions appear to dominate the story). Here, Colombo and colleagues (chap. 2, this volume) report findings that are consistent with emerging perspectives in developmental neuroscience.

The significant role of parenting in cognitive stimulation, novelty provision, and variety of experiences found by Colombo and colleagues is reinforced by the strong findings of Hart and Risley (1995) on the dramatic effects of differential exposure to complex language in early childhood. Taken together, these and similar findings suggest the strong probability that a very large proportion of the variance in predicting high cognitive ability from early infancy is related to the quality and quantity of cognitive exposure during that period. Such findings are consistent with the emerging neuroscience evidence on neural sculpting as well (Boyce & Keating, 2004; Cynader & Frost, 1999). It is not clear that massive, focused stimulation is better than merely high levels of stimulation, and such a claim will require more than the anecdotal evidence currently available. Whether some risk arises from such intensively focused exposures is similarly unclear, but it cannot be dismissed given the potentially important role of extracognitive factors, including emotion and motivation.

An intriguing line of work yet to be done is to explore whether there are significant other early experiences for later high ability. Individual attentional features were not found to be good predictors by Colombo and colleagues (chap. 2, this volume), but whether early experience and early development in areas such as emotion regulation and attention regulation (as scaffolded in early parental interactions) might be implicated remains an open question.

Childhood

Because much of the work in the area of giftedness has focused on this period of development, the discussions earlier in this chapter covered many of the notable features. For example, the increasing domain specificity of ability and achievement begins to emerge during this period (see chap. 4, this volume), which has significant consequences for both identification and intervention (Matthews & Keating, 1995). I argued earlier that fostering domain-specific expertise is a prime requirement for effective programming. Looking backward from the characteristics of high-level adult achievement, however, suggests that more focused attention on extracognitive aspects may be productive. Three of these aspects can be briefly noted here.

First, it seems important to find ways to maintain positive emotion and excitement for learning during the childhood years, almost surely an important precursor of motivation and the welcoming of challenge later in development. Unfortunately, academically advanced students seem to be at considerable risk in this regard and increasingly so as their level of advancement increases (Keating, 1991). Relegating a mathematically precocious student to repetitive "drill and kill" exercises is as dampening of enthusiasm as prohibiting advancement of an apprentice musician to the next level of challenge would be. In other words, pathways to expertise have motivational and emotional components, not just cognitive and expertise-related ones.

Second, and related to the first, is a goal of rapidly moving individuals to the highest levels of expertise as quickly as possible. Not only is this more likely to maintain interest and excitement, but it also has the benefit of automating more expertise so as to free mental effort for the greater demands of creativity and critical thinking (Keating, 2004). In light of the many hours that must be invested to achieve serious expertise in any field, getting as much content automated as quickly as possible is a key goal. This approach of continuously supporting and challenging expertise as it develops is also likely to contribute to a third key goal, self-regulation, which is linked in turn to important aspects such as diligence, persistence, and resilience in the face of challenge. These regulatory aspects have their roots in earlier development, but they need to be consolidated in the same way that expertise needs to be promoted.

Adolescence

A number of the key features of a developmental framework for this period were also noted earlier. Many of the principles are enacted in the ongoing longitudinal study of SMPY participants, who are now in adulthood (Keating, 1976; Keating & Stanley, 1972; Lubinski et al., 2001; Stanley et al., 1974; Wai et al., 2005). Among the core principles were identification of high-level domain-specific talent and the provision of individually appropriate, and optional, educational opportunities in the identified domain of talent. The longitudinal evidence to date appears to support the value of such an approach (Lubinski et al., 2001; Wai et al., 2005). Again, several additional aspects arising from contemporary developmental science enhance this picture.

The first, noted earlier, is the important emerging story regarding prefrontal system integration. This integration can be thought of as a process during which the PFC becomes the governor of behavior through an enhanced, and potentially conscious, executive suite (Keating, 2004). In this sense, adolescents increasingly become their own agents, able both to define and to pursue their own interests with less parental and other external scaffolding. To the extent that subsequent achievement is at least as much a function of extra-cognitive features such as emotion, motivation, diligence, and so on—and the accumulating evidence makes a strong case for this (Csikszentmihalyi, 1990; Howe, 2004; Olszewski-Kubilius, 2000; Shavinina & Ferrari, 2004)—this is the developmental period during which such characteristics are consolidated. Aiding adolescents to choose this more effortful option is in this sense fundamentally important, but to date is primarily a function of teaching and mentoring arts, rather than a function of deep scientific understanding.

A related area of renewed research interest highlights this point. It is known that pubertal shifts are very important for a wide range of developments in the adolescent period, but less is known about how those effects are incorporated into broader functioning, for good or ill (Steinberg et al., 2006). Of particular relevance here are the social forms that exist to "capture the passion" of adolescents. The road to high levels of achievement is often an arduous one, and helping adolescents to create a structured self that incorporates mastery, desire, and persistence is a specific goal that merits more focused effort.

Adulthood and Later Life

A number of significant themes arise from the perspective outlined earlier and from the overview of giftedness in adulthood and later life by Birren (chap. 10, this volume). In many ways, the core features of adult giftedness are the realization of themes laid down earlier in development. It is clear that in adulthood, the acquisition, demonstration, and recognition of expertise become the hallmarks of giftedness, as opposed to potential (Alexander, Murphy, & Kulikowich, in press). This mature level of expert performance requires both building on and going beyond earlier preparation, and there are many exits from the pathway to high-level achievement. In some cases, the exits are attributable to personal choices or to personal characteristics. As noted, the motivational aspects of diligence and persistence—keeping at a difficult problem, overcoming challenge and adversity—perhaps get less credit than they ought.

But too little thought has been given, until recently, to the social affordances, that is, the set of institutionally and culturally structured circumstances that allow talent to be realized and expressed. The role of talent congregation, illustrated earlier in the interlocking stories of Terman (father and son), Shockley, Hewlett, Packard, Noyce, and others, has been less noted in the gifted research literature than have the stories of exceptional individuals. The recent research on group and network high-level creativity has begun to redress this oversight, and future research on the importance of social affordances for the expression of talent and competence is warranted, not only for its effect on individuals but also for its importance to social and economic advancement (Keating, 1999).

This recognition of the interplay of talent and social affordances can also help to address, for some individuals, an unfortunate legacy of the categorical era of giftedness research and practice: the burden of "unrealized potential." If individuals at high levels of childhood ability are expected to demonstrate extraordinary levels of adult accomplishment, then the failure of that to emerge may be viewed and felt as personal. One antidote to this sense of disappointment, of course, is to recognize the fundamental contributions from lives of merely "ordinary high achievement." But in addition, an understanding of the enormous role that social affordances and chance play in the history of extraordinary achievement may go some way to mitigating this unintended effect of a legacy of categorical giftedness.

As Birren (chap. 10, this volume) eloquently and helpfully reminded readers, the later life contributions of gifted individuals should not be overlooked. In some cases, these remain so vivid that they are unlikely to be overlooked. Goethe completed part two of *Faust* in 1832, in his 83rd year of life; Ernst Mayr published a major work on Darwin in 2001, in his 97th year. But the later life contributions of talented individuals that are less noted are nonetheless often highly significant to their fields of work and to their communities. The recent study of wisdom as a domain of expertise closely related to reflection on life's experiences focuses attention on an important but overlooked domain of giftedness—another manifestation of the categorical versus a life-span developmental perspective. Similarly, the degree to which social affordances can be created for the expression of competence is important for the individuals who can enjoy these later life contributions, but even more so for the benefit of society, which can ill afford to lose the benefit of those contributions.

REFERENCES

Albert, R. (1992). *Genius and eminence* (2nd ed.). Elmsford, NY: Pergamon Press.

Alexander, P. A., Murphy, P. K., & Kulikowich, J. M. (in press). Expertise and the adult learner: A historical, psychological, and methodological exploration. In M. C. Smith & T. G. Reio, Jr. (Eds.), *The handbook of research on adult development and learning*. Mahwah, NJ: Erlbaum.

Bangerter, A., & Heath, C. (2004). The Mozart effect: Tracking the evolution of a scientific legend. *British Journal of Social Psychology, 43*, 605–623.

Boyce, W. T., & Keating, D. P. (2004). Should we intervene to improve childhood circumstances? In S. Ben-Shlomo & D. Kuh (Eds.), *A life course approach to chronic disease epidemiology* (pp. 415–445). Oxford, England: Oxford University Press.

Casey, B. J., Giedd, J. N., & Thomas, K. M. (2000). Structural and functional brain development and its relation to cognitive development. *Biological Psychology, 54*, 241–257.

Connor, C. M., Morrison, F. J., & Katch, E. L. (2004). Beyond the reading wars: The effect of classroom instruction by child interactions on early reading. *Scientific Studies of Reading, 8*, 305–336.

Connor, C. M., Son, S.-H., Hindman, A. H., & Morrison, F. J. (2005). Teacher qualifications, classroom practices, family characteristics, and preschool experience: Complex effects on first graders' vocabulary and early reading outcomes. *Journal of School Psychology, 43*, 343–375.

Csikszentmihalyi, M. (1990). *Flow: The psychology of optimal experience.* New York: Harper & Row.

Cynader, M. S., & Frost, B. J. (1999). Mechanisms of brain development: Neuronal sculpting by the physical and social environment. In D. P. Keating & C. Hertzman (Eds.), *Developmental health and the wealth of nations: Social, biological, and educational dynamics* (pp. 153–184). New York: Guilford Press.

Dickerson, S. S., & Kemeny, M. E. (2004). Acute stressors and cortisol responses: A theoretical integration and synthesis of laboratory research. *Psychological Bulletin, 130*, 335–391.

Feldman, D. (1993). Child prodigies: A distinctive form of giftedness. *Gifted Child Quarterly, 37*, 188–193.

Gardner, H. (2004). *Frames of mind: The theory of multiple intelligences.* New York: Basic Books.

Hart, B., & Risley, T. R. (1995). *Meaningful differences in the everyday experience of young American children.* Baltimore: Brookes Publishing.

Holahan, C., Sears, R., & Cronbach, L. (1995). *The gifted group in later maturity.* Stanford, CA: Stanford University Press.

Howe, M. (2004). Some insights of geniuses into the causes of exceptional achievement. In L. Shavinina & M. Ferraris (Eds.), *Beyond knowledge: Extracognitive aspects of developing high ability* (pp. 105–117). Mahwah, NJ: Erlbaum.

Hui, K. (2006). Mozart effect in preschool children? *Early Child Development and Care, 176*, 411–419.

Hulbert, A. (2005, November 20). The prodigy puzzle. *New York Times Magazine.* Retrieved March 15, 2006, from http://www.nytimes.com/2005/11/20/magazine/20prodigies.html?_r=1&scp=1&sq=Hulbert%20prodigy&st=cse&oref=slogin

Keating, D. (1975). Possible sampling bias in genetic studies of genius. *Educational and Psychological Measurement, 35*(3), 657–662.

Keating, D. P. (Ed.). (1976). *Intellectual talent: Research and development*. Baltimore: Johns Hopkins University Press.

Keating, D. P. (1980). Four faces of creativity: The continuing plight of the intellectually underserved. *Gifted Child Quarterly, 24*, 56–61.

Keating, D. P. (1990). Charting pathways to the development of expertise. *Educational Psychologist, 25*, 243–267.

Keating, D. P. (1991). Curriculum options for the developmentally advanced: A developmental alternative for gifted education. *Exceptionality Education Canada, 1*, 53–83.

Keating, D. P. (1999). The learning society: A human development agenda. In D. P. Keating & C. Hertzman (Eds.), *Developmental health and the wealth of nations: Social, biological, and educational dynamics* (pp. 237–250). New York: Guilford Press.

Keating, D. P. (2004). Cognitive and brain development. In R. Lerner & L. Steinberg (Eds.), *Handbook of adolescent psychology* (pp. 45–84). New York: Wiley.

Keating, D. P., & Hertzman, C. (Eds.). (1999). *Developmental health and the wealth of nations: Social, biological, and educational dynamics*. New York: Guilford Press.

Keating, D. P., & Stanley, J. C. (1972). Extreme measures for the exceptionally gifted in mathematics and science. *Educational Researcher, 1*, 3–5.

Lubinski, D., Webb, R., Morelock, M., & Benbow, C. (2001). Top 1 in 10,000: A 10-year follow-up of the profoundly gifted. *Journal of Applied Psychology, 86*, 718–729.

Matthews, D. J., & Keating, D. P. (1995). Domain specificity and habits of mind: An investigation of patterns of high-level development. *Journal of Early Adolescence, 15*, 319–343.

Mayr, E. (2001). The philosophical foundations of Darwinism. *Proceedings of the American Philosophical Society, 14*, 488–495.

Olszewski-Kubilius, P. (2000). The transition from childhood giftedness to adult creative productiveness: Psychological characteristics and social supports. *Roeper Review, 23*, 65–71.

Shapka, J. D., Domene, J. F., & Keating, D. P. (2006, March). *Adolescent and young adult educational and occupational aspirations: An examination of early math achievement as a critical filter*. Paper presented at the biennial meeting of the Society for Research on Adolescence, San Francisco, CA.

Shapka, J. D., & Keating, D. P. (2003). Performance, persistence, and engagement in mathematics and science: Effects of a girls-only curriculum during adolescence. *American Educational Research Journal, 40*, 929–960.

Shavinina, L., & Ferrari, M. (2004). *Beyond knowledge: Extracognitive aspects of developing high ability*. Mahwah, NJ: Erlbaum.

Simonton, D. (2004). Exceptional creativity and chance: Creative thought as a stochastic combinatorial process. In L. Shavinina & M. Ferrari (Eds.), *Beyond knowledge: Extracognitive aspects of developing high ability* (pp. 39–72). Mahwah, NJ: Erlbaum.

Stanley, J. C., Keating, D. P., & Fox, L. H. (Eds.). (1974). *Mathematical talent: Discovery, description, and development*. Baltimore: Johns Hopkins University Press.

Steinberg, L., Dahl, R., Keating, D., Kupfer, D., Masten, A., & Pine, D. (2006). Adolescent psychopathology. In D. Cicchetti (Ed.), *Handbook of developmental psychopathology* (pp. 710–741). New York: Wiley.

Subotnik, R. (2004). Transforming elite musicians into professional artists: A view of the talent development process at the Juilliard School. In L. Shavinina & M. Ferrari (Eds.), *Beyond knowledge: Extracognitive aspects of developing high ability* (pp. 137–166). Mahwah, NJ: Erlbaum.

Subotnik, R., & Arnold, K. (1994). *Beyond Terman: Contemporary longitudinal studies of giftedness and talent.* New York: Ablex Publishing.

Terman, L. (1906). Genius and stupidity. *Pedagogical Seminary, 13,* 307–373.

Terman, L. (1925–1947). *Genetic studies of genius* (Vols. 1–IV). Stanford, CA: Stanford University Press.

Terman, L., & Oden, M. (1959). *Genetic studies of genius: Vol. V. The gifted group at mid-life.* Stanford, CA: Stanford University Press.

U.S. Census Bureau. (2000, August). *School enrollment: 2000.* Retrieved April 15, 2006, from http://www.census.gov/prod/2003pubs/c2kbr-26.pdf

Wai, J., Lubinski, D., & Benbow, C. (2005). Creativity and occupational accomplishments among intellectually precocious youths: An age 13 to age 33 longitudinal study. *Journal of Educational Psychology, 97,* 484–492.

Winerip, M. (2006, April 5). No child left behind? Ask the gifted. *New York Times Magazine.* Retrieved April 6, 2006, from http://www.nytimes.com/2006/04/05/nyregion/05education.html?scp=7&sq=Winerip%20gifted&st=cse

Worthman, C. M., & Kuzara, J. (2005). Life history and the early origins of health differentials. *American Journal of Human Biology, 17,* 95–112.

Zelazo, P. D., Carlson, S. M., & Kesek, A. (in press). The development of executive function in childhood. In C. Nelson & M. Luciana (Eds.), *Handbook of developmental cognitive neuroscience.* Cambridge, MA: MIT Press.

12

A DEVELOPMENTAL PERSPECTIVE ON GIFTEDNESS AND TALENT: IMPLICATIONS FOR RESEARCH, POLICY, AND PRACTICE

DONA J. MATTHEWS, RENA F. SUBOTNIK,
AND FRANCES DEGEN HOROWITZ

Two major objectives motivated us to develop a volume of contributions from developmental psychologists and from experts in gifted education. First, we wanted to better understand how recent advances in developmental psychology might enhance our understanding of high-level achievement and performance and help to translate the science in light of research, policy, and practice in gifted and talented education. Second, we wanted to interest developmental psychologists in a consideration of exceptionally high-end abilities in their conceptual frameworks. These understandings also have implications for clinicians working with clients throughout the life span.

KEY THEMES

Across the chapters in this volume, the authors address four themes central to the talent development process: prediction, domain specificity, diversity, and the contribution of psychosocial variables. Some core questions and conundrums relating to each theme are yet to be fully addressed and can serve as fodder for future research, policy, and practice agendas. Some central examples follow.

Prediction

What are we hoping to predict when we identify giftedness and talent? Those in the field of gifted and talented education, including the authors contributing to this volume, have yet to come to consensus on whether the goal should be (a) to provide exceptional learners in school with appropriate instructional or programming opportunities as they need them, (b) to support talented individuals of all ages in developing their abilities in the name of bettering the world, or (c) to encourage the development of individuals' talent to promote their personal self-actualization. The results of prediction-related research are consequently hard to generalize.

Domain Specificity

Work conducted by Bloom (1985), Feldman and Goldsmith (1986), Lubinski and Benbow (2006), and Simonton (1988) has been instrumental in helping to frame key aspects of the developmental trajectories of various domains, including but not limited to mathematics, music performance, chess, and science. However, efforts to construct naturalistic techniques to assess young children's proclivities for specific domains have not yet come to fruition in spite of the considerable efforts of Feldman as well as Gardner and colleagues (e.g., Krechevsky & Gardner, 1990). What can be learned from prodigies (those who exhibit adult-level domain-specific expertise as children)? Do their demonstrated abilities presage outstanding creative productivity or simply advanced development at a certain point in time?

Even less understood are the indicators of exceptional talent that can flourish in older individuals. Further research might test Sternberg and Lubart's (2001) argument that young people's creative contributions to a domain are more likely to be pathbreaking, whereas contributions made by older creative individuals are more likely to be integrative in nature. In an ideal world, signs of accomplishment or proclivities exhibited by individuals of any age would trigger the provision of more intensive instruction, as well as opportunities for performance and guided practice.

Diversity

If what Winner calls the *rage to master* is associated with great performance and the development of great ideas, how can this kind of passion be elicited from a wider range of people in our society? One example with important policy implications emerges from the observation that so many participants in high school science programs are first-generation Americans. This leads to the question, "What sources of extrinsic motivation and cultural support catalyze the drive needed to develop talent in various domains?"

Furthermore, should societal efforts focus on increasing the number of nonmainstream individuals who are successful leaders and innovators in mainstream fields? Does real pathbreaking begin with mastering mainstream skills and ideas? Or can it start with divergent perspectives and methods derived from cultural experiences outside the mainstream? What are the unique factors that women, for example, or individuals of color or low socioeconomic status bring to the creative process? Can these factors be harnessed with help from teachers, parents, psychologists, and the community? And whether their perspectives are unique or not, how do we broaden the base of individuals whose gifts and talents are developed?

Psychosocial Variables

What propels some people with the same profile of abilities to pursue different domains or challenges at different levels of intensity? If one were to study the area in which the greatest financial investment was made in psychosocial dimensions of talent development, one would look to sport. Members of professional teams and individual athletes participate in psychological strength training as part of their regimen to help endure the challenges faced on the playing field, pitch, or court. Many professional artists also have access to this kind of special training. Are academically talented youth being sold short because they are not provided with the kind of psychosocial interventions promoted by Dweck (2006) and by Subotnik (chap. 9, this volume) and many of the other authors in this volume?

GAPS IN THE RESEARCH LITERATURE

Drawing on the work of the volume's chapter authors, Horowitz (chap. 1, this volume) suggests some of the more obvious candidates for a developmentally informed research agenda in gifted education. Among these are well-designed longitudinal studies—beginning in the early childhood years—that focus on the usefulness of a variety of measures for identifying and predicting exceptionally advanced learning abilities, as discussed in some depth by Colombo and his colleagues (chap. 2, this volume) and by Gottfried, Gottfried, and Guerin (chap. 3, this volume).

According to retrospective studies, the search for talent typically starts with a broad net and gets narrower over time as individuals commit to acquiring needed skills and knowledge in the domain. Also, the community has an important role to play in the timely provision of resources and expertise for high-level talent development. Because longitudinal studies that begin in childhood cannot control for all of these factors, shorter term multimeasure studies of proximal distance to desired outcomes beginning in adolescence or early adulthood would provide valuable contributions to understanding the development of talent (Subotnik & Arnold, 2000).

To study development effectively, whether in longitudinal or shorter multimeasure studies, the chapter authors highlight the need to design and refine assessment tools and strategies for detecting core abilities and skills in different domains, including those associated with home environment.

The studies reported on by this volume's authors make apparent the need to address more systematically the diverse kinds of intelligences that go beyond those used in the traditional academic core subjects and measured by conventional tests of intelligence. More systematic approaches to a wider spectrum of abilities will require good assessment tools and strategies for core abilities and skills involved in different domains of giftedness and talent such as the spatial domain discussed by Liben (chap. 4, this volume) and Winner (chap. 5, this volume).

Another area of investigation concerns the multiple pathways to expertise or developmental trajectories that Keating, Winner, Subotnik, and others discuss (chaps. 5, 9, and 11, this volume). A research agenda aimed at thoughtful explorations of the many possible pathways and sequences that lead to and support gifted-level development holds great promise for providing information that will benefit the field of gifted education. Such work will be particularly valuable to the extent that it yields information on ways that teachers can match educational content to individuals' levels of competence on a dynamic and ongoing basis, and that psychologists can provide services to boost resilience of their clients.

An allied area of exploration concerns findings about developmental variability over time. Because of a regression to the mean effect, it is possible that a child who is identified as gifted at a certain point in time will miss the same cutoff for gifted identification several years later, and that the higher the cutoff, the likelier this result is. However, it is not known whether this is less true in cases in which high-ability learners are provided with appropriately differentiated educational opportunities. Are children who are accelerated in their domain of exceptional advancement, or otherwise provided with an appropriate match for their learning needs, less likely to demonstrate a regression to the mean? Although some findings address this question (e.g., Colangelo, Assouline, & Gross, 2004; Lohman & Korb, 2006; Rogers, 2002), the area requires considerably more investigative attention.

More also needs to be known about the *transitional periods*—infancy to early childhood to middle childhood, to early adolescence, to late adolescence, and through the periods of adulthood—to understand the dynamics of these junctures for (a) sustaining previously demonstrated abilities, (b) triggering developmental discontinuities, and (c) giving rise to the appearance of new gifts and talents. A research agenda that is seriously informed by a developmental perspective must necessarily focus on the complex dynamics of stability and change across the entire life span, including Horowitz's (1985) conception of nodal points in development.

The discussions in this volume make it obvious that a better understanding is needed of the origins and nature of personality characteristics—such as the rage to master, perseverance, and intrinsic motivation—that foster and sustain the development of giftedness and talent.

Another highly promising area of investigation concerns extracognitive factors, including the social identity factors that Graham (chap. 7, this volume) and Worrell (chap. 8, this volume) address, and the psychosocial dimensions of talent development that Subotnik (chap. 9, this volume) describes. What do psychosocial dimensions look like across contexts and across domains, as individuals move from ability through competencies to expertise, and finally to scholarly productivity or artistry in a range of fields? What can teachers, mentors, and parents do to support optimal development across time for different kinds of learners in different domains? And what might interrupt the development of giftedness or talent? Many of the factors and stages identified in Subotnik and Jarvin's work (2005) with musical development apply to other domains, but the nature, order, and relative importance may differ (Subotnik, Pillmeier, & Jarvin, 2008).

In addition, as mentioned by several chapter authors, the availability of increasingly sensitive brain-imaging techniques holds promise for understanding the role of brain function and neural plasticity in the development of giftedness and talent over time in every domain. The rapidly growing use of these tools, when combined with more traditional measures, will likely alter general understandings of the nature of developmental change in different domains and at different periods of the life span.

Most of the research focused on giftedness and talent development has involved children, adolescents, and young adults. However, as Birren discussed in chapter 10 (this volume), an increased interest in the development of creativity, competency, productivity, and wisdom in older persons may well prove highly productive. In addition to better understanding the decline that can come with age, studying the cognitive, psychosocial, cultural, and environmental variables that promote continued learning and development to the level of exceptionality well into adulthood will be informative. Birren's discussion of developmental intelligence—or wisdom—points to the importance of the interpersonal and intrapersonal domains of intelligence, perhaps increasing in potency and possibility as people age. The diversity of the older population offers interesting exploration opportunities for those interested in gifted-level development, especially when one considers the expanding complexities, interacting influences, and dynamic possibilities of adult life that Birren describes.

Besides these individual developmental factors, the final suggestion for future research attention that emerges from the contributions to this volume is to explore the nature of social and cultural contexts that advantage and disadvantage the appearance and maintenance of exceptional capabilities across the life span, and across race, gender, and socioeconomic circumstance. Keating (chap. 11, this volume) tells a story of connectivity that illustrates the role of the social milieu in fostering creative productivity, as well as the importance of understanding how such environments might best be supported in schools. Keating recounts how Luis Alvarez and William Shockley—neither of whom met the selection criteria for Terman's longitudinal study of giftedness—went on to become Nobel laureates for their invention of the transistor and work in elementary particle physics, and sparked the social and business phenomenon that became known as Silicon Valley, the nexus of the technological advances that have transformed the world. This hive of intellectual activity is noteworthy not for the intellectual genius of any one participant, but rather for the transformative creative productivity of a lot of smart people working in a social milieu in which their individual and collective creativity thrived.

We recount the Silicon Valley story here as an illustration of a social milieu perhaps actually generating giftedness, constituting a social rather than individual perspective on what giftedness is and how it develops. It is reminiscent of Putnam's (1993) description of the civil society in northern and central Italy in the Middle Ages, in which a widespread engagement in community led to a successful participatory democracy as well as to the extraordinary achievements in the arts and sciences that became the Renaissance. The brilliant accomplishments of Leonardo da Vinci, Machiavelli, Michelangelo, and many others may never have come to pass had there not been the history of investments in social capital, norms of reciprocity, and networks of civic engagement that Putnam documents. Historical analyses illustrate the role that political, economic, and social forces—both positive and negative, depending on the domain—played during periods of great creative productivity (Simonton, 1984) and document how individual, community-based, and institutional connections can work to support or undermine gifted-level achievement. Similarly, Csikszentmihalyi (1996) has discussed the effects of historic, economic, political, social, and cultural contexts during societal periods of high creativity.

According to Sternberg (1998), acting wisely involves the application of intelligence and creativity to achievement of the common good. Renzulli (2002) asked, "Can a better understanding of people who use their gifts in socially constructive ways help us create conditions that expand the number of people who contribute to the growth of social as well as economic capital?" (p. 34). He went on to write about ways that educators can cultivate the social capital, norms of reciprocity, and networks of civic engagement that Putnam (1993) identified as essential to civic society. The findings reported here by Colombo et al. (chap. 2, this volume) and by Gottfried et al. (chap. 3, this volume), and the analyses provided by other authors, come together with

Putnam's, Simonton's, Sternberg's, and Renzulli's observations in suggesting that there are many benefits from better understanding the social affordances and inhibitors of gifted development.

In summary, then, the future research directions identified in this volume are derived from gaps in the developmental literature on giftedness and talent in the areas of prediction, domain specificity, diversity, and psychosocial variables, particularly

- studying development longitudinally, beginning in the early childhood years;
- generating shorter term, multimeasure studies of proximal distance to desired outcomes, beginning in adolescence or adulthood;
- designing and refining assessment tools and strategies for core abilities and skills in different domains including those associated with the home environment;
- conducting systematic studies of the process of talent development in different domains, including the spatial domain;
- exploring the multiple possible pathways and sequences that lead to gifted-level development;
- studying developmental variability over time, including the effect of appropriately differentiated curriculum and instruction on the stability of gifted-level achievement over time;
- better understanding the transitional periods—early childhood, early adolescence, and late adolescence—and the role of these periods in the complex dynamics of stability and change across the life span;
- exploring the origins and nature of personality characteristics and psychosocial variables that foster and sustain the development of giftedness and talent in different domains;
- investigating the extracognitive factors that can support or inhibit giftedness and talent development as these change over time and across domains;
- learning about the role of brain function and neural plasticity in the development of giftedness and talent;
- learning about the cognitive, psychosocial, cultural, and social variables that promote continued learning and talent development into older adulthood; and
- better understanding environmental supports and interferences (i.e., the social and cultural affordances and inhibitors of gifted development) across the life span and across race, ethnicity, gender, and socioeconomic circumstance.

IMPLICATIONS FOR POLICY

Many of the authors in this volume focus on the urgent need to expand the notion of giftedness to make it more inclusive in a number of ways. One way is by expanding the number of domains to be cultivated while working in collaboration with outside-of-school agencies such as talent-search organizations, museums, art and music schools, nature programs, and hospital laboratories. In their consideration of the spatial domain, Liben (chap. 4, this volume) and Winner (chap. 5, this volume) argue for the value to society and to individuals of a more systematic understanding of this domain as expressed in a number of fields in the arts and sciences, as well as the need for educational attention to spatial development, including spatial giftedness. Furthermore, Liben ties her commentary to Winner's and Feldman's research on how children are attracted to more formal and rule-governed domains. From a policy perspective, this kind of domain organization may make the spatial domain as well as others more accessible to young people. Liben argues that the spatial domain needs a more comprehensive investment of research on spatial thinking and education and spatial giftedness to establish the basic structure of the domain.

For their part, Graham (chap. 7, this volume) and Worrell (chap. 8, this volume) address minority underrepresentation in gifted programming and argue for a broadened approach to identifying and supporting gifted development.

Worrell (chap. 8, this volume) and Keating (chap. 11, this volume) advise a public health approach of broadening the possibilities for optimal cognitive development, whereby schools implement policies that are designed explicitly to support high-level learning in all children, with a special focus on the early years. They argue that rather than focus specifically on increasing representation of minorities in gifted programs, public policy should focus on creating a large and diverse population of highly competent individuals. This approach should begin at preschool by supporting the acquisition of basic numeracy, literacy, and computer skills, as well as mastery of the symbol systems in other domains, so that opportunities to learn and grow are spread more broadly across the population. Programs to do this would be just the beginning of a much more intensive and extensive talent development process, but they are important catalysts to opening up high-level achievement possibilities to an expanded range of people.

Many of the contributors to this volume discuss the importance of teacher education and professional development. In addition to academic content knowledge, mastery of child and adolescent development, and practice with differentiating curriculum for individual learners, teachers need a deep and practical understanding of current findings on cognitive and social psychology, including the importance of habits of mind and mind-sets, to work effectively with gifted learners and performers. They need support, for example, in finding ways to foster the growth mind-set—an understanding of learning as developing incrementally over time with appropriate opportunities for the hard work (Good & Dweck, 2005) and disciplined practice (Ericsson, Roring, & Nandagopal, 2007) that are critical to high-level learning and achievement in all domains.

Another implication for policy consideration that emerges from this volume involves the way in which school systems provide parents and early childhood educators with the information they need to nurture gifted-level development. Colombo et al. (chap. 2, this volume) and Gottfried et al. (chap. 3, this volume) describe important new findings that bear on this matter. Matthews (chap. 6, this volume) as well as many of the other authors in this volume review additional discoveries about the early environmental conditions that support optimal cognitive development and increase the possibilities of gifted-level development over time. It is becoming clear, for example, how important it is that parents and early educators respond to young children's bids for activities and stimulation and provide broad intellectual and cultural exposure, stimulation, and opportunities to acquire mastery. Early childhood education and educational policies should find ways to address the need for parent education. On the other end of the age spectrum, Birren (chap. 10, this volume) demonstrated that a great source of talent goes undeveloped among older persons.

Programs of systematic research on any of these questions and topics require sustained sources of financial support by way of research grants and graduate student training programs. Sadly, however, there has been minimal sustained federal funding for research and research training on the development of giftedness and talent at state or federal levels in the United States, or among private funders, including individuals and foundations. Needed now is a policy that recognizes the value of a deeper understanding of how giftedness and talent develop across the life span and across domains, cultures, and context. Along with a commitment to supporting students who appear to be at risk for normal development, serious research efforts should be invested in understanding the factors involved in children being "at promise" for high-level achievement, as well as the interventions that are most effective in developing those achievements.

Also needed are sustained sources of financial support that focus on developing and delivering programs for those individuals of all ages who have already demonstrated gifted and talented development, as well as a better understanding of the developmental trajectories and learning needs of those students who are exceptionally advanced relative to their age peers. A hopeful sign that things may be moving in this direction can be found in the America Competes Act of 2007, which funds initiatives directed at establishing specialized high schools of mathematics and science and promotes more intensive instruction for teachers in mathematics and science.

Implicit in a broadened approach to gifted identification is an understanding that entry points to gifted programming should be flexible and open. Early identification, although very important for children with learning problems and developmental delays, generates many false positives and false negatives when applied too rigidly to giftedness, as discussed by Gottfried et al. (chap. 3, this volume) and Matthews and colleagues (Matthews & Foster, 2006; see also chap. 6, this volume). Gifted learning options should remain available as needed across the years of schooling, with educators implementing a special education model whereby assessment is as ongoing for giftedness as it is for learning problems. An example of this approach can be seen in the province of Ontario, Canada, where school boards are responsible for meeting the exceptional learning needs of all students, including those with advanced or gifted-level abilities. The province mandates annual evaluations for students who are identified as gifted and also for students who develop gifted learning needs as time goes by. It holds school boards accountable for acting on the evaluations and providing appropriately differentiated curriculum as needed. The Ontario policy allows for a wide range of programming and placement options, including grouping students of similarly advanced ability and interests when maximal benefit is derived from interacting with an academic or talent peer group, such as in science research, music, sport, and mathematics.

One challenge in instituting such a policy in American public schools—particularly in urban areas with weak or underfunded schools—is that too often gifted programs are highly sought after by parents of students who may not need special services but are concerned about a substandard quality of education in regular classrooms. This observation leads us to a policy recommendation that ties back into our recommendation for a public health approach whereby all students are provided with learning opportunities that support their optimal cognitive development, beginning at preschool. As needs are addressed and do not require further special services, provision of such services can end. Gifted programs should be used for meeting exceptional learning needs rather than as selective temporary repairs of ailing education systems.

Another important policy decision follows from recent funding for specialized and magnet schools. Such schools provide opportunities for greater specialization in specific domains such as mathematics and science. Although anecdotal data and school-based studies suggest that these schools play a significant role in supporting the pipeline for scientific research, controlled evaluation studies have not yet been conducted on specialized or magnet schools, or on summer enrichment programs (Subotnik, Edmiston, & Rayhack, 2007).

In summary, then, the implications for policy identified in this volume point to

- expanding the notion of giftedness to make it more inclusive with regard to domains, including by working in an integrated way with out-of-school resources to enhance talents in academic and nonacademic areas;

- implementing a broadened approach to identifying and supporting giftedness and talent, by focusing on domain-specific talent over the course of development;
- taking a public health approach by broadening the possibilities for optimal cognitive development in all learners, particularly in the early years;
- supporting teachers in acquiring a deep and practical understanding of current findings on child and adolescent development, teaching and learning and exceptional abilities, through teacher education and professional development;
- providing parents and educators with information and support designed to foster children's positive responses to Graham's questions (chap. 7, this volume) of "Can I?" and "Do I want to?";
- creating sustained sources of financial support for systematic research programs, including research grants and graduate student training programs that investigate children "at promise" for giftedness, as well as interventions designed to develop recognized talent;
- creating sustained sources of financial support that focus on developing and delivering programs for those individuals of all ages who have demonstrated such promise for gifted and talented development;
- ensuring opportunities for ongoing admission to gifted programming, as needed;
- using gifted programs for meeting exceptional learning needs, rather than as selective temporary repairs of ailing education systems; and
- when possible, encouraging the disciplines, through their scholarly societies, to develop easily accessible resources and structures that enable those who might pursue careers or interests in those domains to know more transparently how the associated knowledge and skills fit together successfully.

IMPLICATIONS FOR EDUCATIONAL PRACTICE

The strongest implication for precollegiate educational practice is the need to move beyond a simple categorical approach of understanding high cognitive ability. From a developmental perspective, the pathways to exceptional adult achievement are complex, diverse, and domain-specific, varying across individuals, developmental periods, contexts, and cultures, with continuities and discontinuities that are not fully understood. Educators should therefore be providing appropriate curriculum and programming matches for exceptionally advanced learners, creators, and performers, recognizing that what is provided will vary across domains and change over time with development. It means making sure that children and adolescents continue to learn, grow, be challenged, and have opportunities to perform and create in their areas of interest and exceptional ability. Furthermore, unless directly associated with developing specific talent, generalized enrichment that could be beneficial for all students—activities such as trips to museums, cultural experiences, more access to better computers—may reasonably be viewed as elitist when experienced only by those labeled *gifted*.

Another implication of a developmental perspective is that the range of areas in which giftedness might be identified and supported is broadened. For example, the spatial domain, as argued by Liben (chap. 4, this volume) and Winner (chap. 5, this volume), merits further investigation. The social–emotional domain, including wisdom, motivation, and many other important dimensions of human ability, yields other candidate areas for attention and gifted development, as discussed by Birren (chap. 10, this volume) and by Gottfried et al. (chap. 3, this volume).

Many of the authors in this volume advocate broadening the approach to gifted identification by incorporating searches for talent in specific domains. There is no clear consensus, however, among our authors or in the field more generally on whether attempts to broaden gifted identification by increasingly inclusive standards within a domain will be counterproductive to serving students whose exceptionally advanced needs are the field's reason for being. From a developmental perspective, the most appropriate identification practices assess individuals' exceptional advancement relative to their age-peers at a given point in time and use content-valid methods to do so. In an optimal situation, educators have access to assessment information on students' domain-specific achievement, reasoning, interest, and persistence.

It is not enough to gain useful information about students' learning needs. We must also find ways to use this information to plan and adapt curriculum, as discussed by Keating (chap. 11, this volume), Matthews (chap. 6, this volume), and Worrell (chap. 8, this volume). In light of concerns about underrepresentation of certain minority groups in gifted programming (as discussed particularly by Graham and Worrell in chaps. 7 and 8, this volume), it is worth noting that this approach, which is appropriate for all students, has proven effective with academically promising minority students.

There is an important caveat here: Although broadening assessment information should be inclusive rather than exclusive, this does not imply forsaking those students who demonstrate exceptional ability on the basis of current (narrower) approaches to gifted identification. Quite the reverse. Those students who excel in intelligence and academic achievement test scores clearly have advanced learning needs that must be met, no matter how they perform in any alternative approaches. It does not make sense, for example, to create a multiple-measures approach that might exclude from gifted-level mathematical programming a child with 99th-percentile achievement on mathematical reasoning and computation tests but whose disinterest in response to classroom mathematics instruction leads to a low score on a teacher observation checklist.

Broadening assessment means starting by identifying as gifted those who clearly and simply demonstrate gifted learning needs, and also working outward from there, looking for and facilitating signs of possible present or future giftedness in diverse others. As indicated in our first educational implication—that appropriate programming is that which fits individual learning needs—a one-size-fits-all "gifted program" will not be able to address both kinds of needs very well. Such a program is not enough to close the achievement gap, but it is a good start, a first step toward more inclusive educational support for giftedness and talent development.

A developmental approach means moving away from a categorical perspective by which some children are identified as gifted (once and forever) at an early age and others are deemed by default to be fixed in the not-gifted category (also forever). In practice, this translates into making entry points to gifted programming flexible and open, on the basis of transparent and relevant criteria.

A developmental approach also means moving toward the public health approach advocated by Worrell (chap. 8, this volume) and Keating (chap. 11, this volume). In practice, this translates into finding ways to ensure that all children master the basic academic competencies sufficiently well that they are not obstructed from developing and demonstrating gifted-level abilities down the road.

Any shift in educational policy rests on teacher development. An essential component of a developmental approach to supporting giftedness and talent is that educators be provided with the training and support they need to both demand high standards for their students and also provide unconditional support for their efforts and potential.

A recurrent theme across chapters in this volume is the need to support both educators and students in understanding the incremental nature of all learning, such that they adopt what Dweck and her colleagues (e.g., Good & Dweck, 2005) have called a *growth mind-set*, particularly when it comes to academic ability. Such a mind-set involves focusing on individual students' current learning needs, by subject area, providing appropriate differentiation for those with advanced instructional or performance needs. Educators cultivate a growth mind-set when they use assessment information to focus on implications for immediate learning, rather than on students' limitations or potential for future achievement. Teachers who adopt a growth mind-set are more effective in encouraging their students' continued engagement in the learning process, and thereby in fostering gifted development.

A final and critically important implication of a developmental approach to understanding giftedness and talent is an affirmation of the importance of extracognitive or psychosocial factors—the hard work, persistence, and effort that are prerequisite to all truly creative work and high-level achievement. A recommendation that weaves its way throughout the chapters of this volume is that educators work together to ensure that all students learn the value of sustained periods of engaged time and task commitment in the learning process.

In summary, then, the implications for educational practice identified in this volume point to needs that involve

- providing appropriate curriculum and programming matches for exceptionally advanced learners, creators, and performers, making sure they continue to learn and grow and be challenged in their areas of interest and exceptional ability;
- broadening the range of areas in which giftedness might be identified and supported, such as the spatial and social–emotional domains, understanding that some development in these domains will take place outside of school;
- broadening the approach to gifted identification by assessing students' domain-specific achievement, reasoning, interest, and persistence;
- using assessment information to plan and adapt curriculum;
- continuing to serve those students who demonstrate exceptional ability on the basis of current approaches to gifted identification while concurrently seeking opportunities to support talent development in others;
- making entry points to gifted programming flexible and open, on the basis of transparent and relevant criteria;
- ensuring that all children master the basic academic competencies sufficiently well that they are not obstructed from developing and demonstrating gifted-level abilities;
- providing educators with the necessary training and support;
- supporting educators and students in understanding the incremental nature of learning, and in adopting a growth mind-set; and
- affirming the importance of extracognitive or psychosocial factors—the hard work, persistence, and effort that are prerequisite to all truly creative work and high-level achievement.

IMPLICATIONS FOR PSYCHOLOGICAL PRACTICE

Many of our recommendations for research, policy, and educational practice need the support of psychological practitioners who work with talented individuals in schools, clinical practice, and the workplace. Such support includes

- considering alternatives to intelligence testing at very young ages for purposes of gifted identification and programming;
- expanding practice to include exploration of clients' domain-specific interests and abilities;
- providing psychological strength training to support individuals in managing competition and periods of adversity;
- promoting the development of social skills, which have been shown to be a key component of talent development in advanced stages; and
- exploring and addressing with clients their doubts and hesitations regarding "Can I?" and "Do I want to?"

CHALLENGES MET AND CHALLENGES AHEAD

In the course of the conference that stimulated this volume and working with the contributing authors, we have been struck by the fruitfulness of bringing together psychological scientists who have spent their careers focused on the study of normative development with psychological scientists who have spent their careers investigating giftedness and talent. We appreciate the way that the developmental psychologists who participated in this project rose to the challenge we offered them to explore early markers of exceptional behavior and to consider high-end performance as it intersects with their own research programs. In a similar way, we anticipate that those specialists in gifted and talented education who have not focused specifically on developmental issues in their work with the here-and-now responsibilities of understanding, identifying, and facilitating giftedness and talent will profit from this expansion of the field and its intersection with developmental science.

We hope that the benefits gained by the readers of this volume will ultimately lead to the improvement of learning and life opportunities for the young and the old, for those individuals whose diverse gifts and talents are displayed early and late. We are encouraged by the possibilities of developmentally oriented research to increase our understanding of giftedness and talent in a variety of domains, in diverse cultures and communities, and across the life span. And although the benefits of all that we have discussed, if realized, will enhance the lives of individuals, they will also enhance those societies that find ways to more effectively nurture into fruition the gifts and talents of their members.

REFERENCES

Bloom, B. S. (Ed.). (1985). *Developing talent in young people*. New York: Ballantine Books.

Colangelo, N., Assouline, S., & Gross, M. (Eds.). (2004). *A nation deceived: How schools hold back America's brightest students: Vol. II. A Templeton national report on acceleration*. Iowa City: University of Iowa.

Csikszentmihalyi, M. (1996). *Creativity: Flow and the psychology of discovery and invention*. New York: HarperCollins.

Dweck, C. S. (2006). *Mindset: The new psychology of success*. New York: Random House.

Ericsson, A., Roring, R. W., & Nandagopal, K. (2007). Giftedness and evidence for reproducibly superior performance: An account based on the expert performance framework. *High Ability Studies, 18*, 3–56.

Feldman, D. H., & Goldsmith, L. T. (1986). *Nature's gambit: Child prodigies and the development of human potential*. New York: Basic Books.

Good, C., & Dweck, C. S. (2005). A motivational approach to reasoning, resilience, and responsibility. In R. J. Sternberg & R. F. Subotnik (Eds.), *Optimizing student success in school with the other three Rs: Reasoning, resilience, and responsibility* (pp. 39–56). Greenwich, CT: Information Age.

Horowitz, F. D. (1985). *Exploring developmental theories: Toward a structural/behavioral model of development*. Hillsdale, NJ: Erlbaum.

Krechevsky, M., & Gardner, H. (1990). The emergence and nurturance of multiple intelligences. In M. J. A. Howe (Ed.), *Encouraging the development of exceptional abilities and talents* (pp. 222–245). Leicester, England: British Psychological Society.

Lohman, D. F., & Korb, K. A. (2006). Gifted today but not tomorrow? Longitudinal changes in ability and achievement during elementary school. *Journal for the Education of the Gifted, 29*, 451–484.

Lubinski, D., & Benbow, C. P. (2006). Study of mathematically precocious youth after 35 years. *Perspectives on Psychological Science, 1*, 316–345.

Matthews, D. J., & Foster, J. F. (2006). Mystery to mastery: Shifting paradigms in gifted education. *Roeper Review, 28*, 64–69.

Putnam, R. D. (1993). *Making democracy work: Civic traditions in modern Italy*. Princeton, NJ: Princeton University Press.

Renzulli, J. S. (2002). Expanding the conception of giftedness to include co-cognitive traits and to promote social capital. *Phi Delta Kappan, 84*(1), 33–58.

Rogers, K. B. (2002). *Re-forming gifted education: How parents and teachers can match the program to the child*. Scottsdale, AZ: Great Potential Press.

Simonton, D. K. (1984). *Genius, creativity, and leadership: Historiometric inquiries*. Cambridge, MA: Harvard University Press.

Simonton, D. K. (1988). Age and outstanding achievement: What do we know after a century of research? *Psychological Bulletin, 104,* 251–267.

Sternberg, R. J. (1998). A balance theory of wisdom. *Review of General Psychology, 2,* 347–365.

Sternberg, R. J., & Lubart, T. I. (2001). Wisdom and creativity. In J. E. Birren & K. W. Schaie (Eds.), *Handbook of the psychology of aging* (5th ed., pp. 500–522). San Diego, CA: Academic Press.

Subotnik, R. F., & Arnold, K. D. (2000). Addressing the most challenging questions in gifted education and psychology: A role best suited to longitudinal research. In K. Heller, F. Monks, R. J. Sternberg, & R. F. Subotnik (Eds.), *International handbook of giftedness and talent* (2nd ed., pp. 243–252). Oxford, England: Pergamon Press.

Subotnik, R. F., Edmiston, A., & Rayhack, K. (2007). Developing national policies in STEM talent development: Obstacles and opportunities. In P. Csermely, K. Kormevic, & K. Sulyok (Eds.), *Science education: Models and networking of student research training under 21* (pp. 28–38). Amsterdam: IOS Press.

Subotnik, R. F., & Jarvin, L. (2005). Beyond expertise: Conceptions of giftedness as great performance. In R. J. Sternberg & J. E. Davidson (Eds.), *Conceptions of giftedness* (2nd ed.). New York: Cambridge University Press.

Subotnik, R. F., Pillmeier, E., & Jarvin, L. (2008). *The psychosocial dimensions of creativity in mathematics: Implications for gifted education policy.* Manuscript in preparation.

AUTHOR INDEX

Numbers in italics refer to listings in the reference sections.

SUBJECT INDEX

Categorial model. *See also* Indentification; Labeling; Not-gifted
Categorical model, 192–1943
    developmental perspective *vs.*,
        199–200
    individual differences in developmental trajectories, 9
    mastery model *vs.*, 9
    selection criteria in, 193–194
    summary of, 198
Challenge
    adult, 158
    motivational, 117
Challenging courses. *See also* Academic challenge
Chance, 205. *See also* Coincidence; Luck; Theory of coincidence
    in talent development, 157, 158, 159, 160
    talent fulfillment and, 168
Charisma
    in transition from expertise to artistry, 166
Chess, 158
Childhood
    in developmental model, 203
    in integrative developmental model, 203
Childhood transition into adolescence
    challenges of high ability learners, 90
    cognitive plasticity and, 90
Children
    gifted *vs.* others, 79
Class clown, 95
Co-education, 97. *See also* Mixed-sex; Mixed-sex education; Same-sex; Same sex education
Cognitive ability
    late life, 182
    longitudinal study in older persons, 175–176
Cognitive capacity, 99
Cognitive changes
    in Alzheimer's *vs.* wisdom, 174
    gender differences in, 176
    in relation to brain structure, 174–175

Cognitive development
    neurosciences and, 13
Cognitive plasticity, 90. *See also* Neural plasticity
Cognitive psychology
    interest in prediction and explanation, 76–77
Cognitive skills, 103
Coincidence, theory of, 157–158. *See also* Change; Luck
Competency
    to expertise, 93, 159, 163–164
Competition, 223
Conduct disorders, 95
Constitutional factors. *See also* Biological embedding; Neural sculpting
Context. *See also* Cultural context; Social context
    in development of elderly persons, 172–173
    social and cultural, 11–14, 213–214
Context talent development, 157
Continuities. *See also* Discontinuities
Core academic subjects, 102
Core competencies, 93
Core educational programming, 133
Creative productivity, 214
Critical thinking, 94–95
Cultural attitudes, 96
Cultural context, 214. *See also* Context; Social context
    and creativity, 213–214
    and diversity, 11–14
Cultural ecological theory, 6
Cultural identity
    achievement and, 145
Cultural learning styles
    for African Americans, 139–140
Culture-fair
    identification, 96
    practices, 96
Curriculum. *See also* Educational programs; Optimal match; Range of options
    match, 92, 93
    planning, 220

Depression, 95, 137
Development
  adult, 172–173
  domain-specific, 103
  early adolescent, 215
  early childhood, 191–192
  of elderly persons, 172–173
  life span, 201–205
Developmental asynchrony. *See also*
    Asynchrony; Uneven development
Developmental discontinuities, 212. *See*
    also Continuities; Discontinuities
Developmental diversity, 198
  domain-specific *vs.* domain-general,
    199
  nature and education of, 198–201
  need for continuity of support, 200
  vs. categorical model, 199–200
Developmental intelligence, 213
Developmental neurosciences. *See also*
    Neuroscience
  brain function and neural plasticity,
    213, 215
  effect of developmental experiences
    on neural system, 200–201
  focus on prefrontal cortex in, 201
Developmental niche, 14
Developmental perspective
  challenges, 223–224
  educational practice, implications
    for, 219–223
  gaps in research literature, 211–215
  key themes and, 209–211
  policy implications, 216–219
  research agenda for, 14–16
  vs. categorical model, 221
Developmental psychology
  of adult years, 172–173
Developmental science, 200–201, 213,
    215
Developmental theory
  constitutional and environmental
    variables in, 4–5
  continuity and discontinuity in, 6–7
  individual differences and, 6, 11
  systems theory and, 6
  transitional points, 7

Developmental timing, 93
Developmental trajectories, 101
  domain-specific and cross-domain,
    103
Developmental transitions
  early adolescence, 212
  early adulthood, 212
  late adolescence, 155
  timing of, 93
Differentiated
  academic programming, 92, 93. *See*
    also Differentiated curriculum;
    Differentiation; Educational
    programming
  curriculum, 98, 218
  educational programming, 93
Differentiated instruction, 98
Differentiation. *See also under* Differen-
    tiated
Diligence, 204. *See also* Effort; Hard
    work; Perseverance; Persistence;
    Tenacity; Willingness to over-
    come obstacles
Disciplined practice, 93
Discontinuities
  developmental, 6–7, 212. *See also*
    Continuities
Discrimination. *See also* Stereotypes
  microaggression, 118
  perceived, 117–118
    consequences of, 118
Disengagement
  in adolescents, 95, 115
  in advanced students, 100
  in African American adolescents,
    115
Disidentification
  in African American adolescents,
    115
Disparities
  academic, 111
  cultural, 96
  economic, 96
  social, 201
Diverse developmental trajectories. *See*
    also Developmental pathways;
    Developmental trajectories

extrinsic, 165, 210
in gifted learners *vs.* others, 78
of gifted students, 111–112
intrinsic, 52, 54, 162, 165, 213
minority student, 96
in pathways to expertise, 203
research in, 111, 112–113
Multiple criteria. *See also* Multiple
measures
Multiple intelligences, 6. *See also*
Domain-specific development;
Domain specificity
neglect of, 11–12
Multiple measures, 96, 221. *See also*
Multiple criteria
Multiple pathways to expertise, 203
Mystery model, 9

National Geographic Bee, 66–68
described, 66–67
relation of
to gender, 67
to mapping and geography, 67
spatial concepts of
Euclidean, 62–63
projective, 62–63
topological, 62
spatial structure of
viewing angle, 62
viewing azimuth, 62
viewing distance, scale, 62
National Research Council, 100–101
Native American, 197. *See also* American Indian
Neural
imaging, 213
networks, 200–201
plasticity, 213, 215. *See also* Cognitive plasticity
sculpting, 200. *See also* Biological
embedding; Constitutional
factors
Neuroendocrine patterns, 90
Neuroendocrine system, 200
Neuroscience. *See also* Developmental
neurosciences
Normal curve, 91

Not-gifted. *See* Categorization; Identification; Labeling

Older population. *See also* Elderly persons; Late adulthood; Late life
cognitive ability of, 175–176
diversity of, 173–175
Optimal match, 102, 103. *See also*
Appropriate learning match;
Educational match; Match;
Range of options
Organismic-experiential interactions, 91

Paradigm shift
Parents, 39. *See also* Family; Home environment
Passion. *See also* Drive; Engagement;
Rage to master; Zeal
Peer
acceptance, 120–122
group, 101
interactions, 95
relationships, 101
Peer culture
identity and, 119, 120
peer admiration in, 120–122
Peer relationships
in adolescence, 101
Perceived discrimination, 117–118
Perceived social position, 92
Perseverance, 100, 213. *See also* Diligence; Effort; Hard work; Perseverance; Tenacity; Willingness to
overcome obstacles
Persistence, 162. *See also* Diligence;
Effort; Hard work; Perseverance;
Tenacity; Willingness to overcome obstacles
Personal agency
in adolescence, 100
Personality characteristics
research literature and, 213
Photographs
spatial and aesthetic qualities of,
68–69
Plasticity
cognitive, 90

cultural learning styles and, 140
giftedness and, 140
Racial
group membership, 92
identity, 92
socialization, 124
underrepresentation, 95
Rage to master, 98, 210. *See also* Drive,
Engagement, Passion, Zeal
in gifted children, 78, 83
Range of options, 102, 218. *See also*
Appropriate learning match;
Educational match; Optimal
match
Reference group orientation, 92
Regression
early prediction and, 49, 52
effect, 91
to the mean, 91
Relevance, 100
cultural, 123
Research
developmental, 14–16, 212, 215
longitudinal, 190–191, 211–212, 215
multi-measure, 212, 215
prospective, 82, 191, 194
retrospective, 191–192, 194–195,
211
Research agenda
for developmental approach
application of new techniques, 15
attention to framing of, 15–16
focus on promise, 16
new approaches using standard
technique, 14–15
role of personal/psychological
factors, 15
Research literature gaps
brain function and neural plasticity,
213, 215
context, social and cultural, 213–214
developmental variability over time,
212, 215
environmental variables, 213
extracognitive factors and, 213
knowledge of transitional periods,
212–213

longitudinal studies, 211
need to design and refine assessment
tools, 212
personality characteristics, 213
shorter term multimeasure studies,
211–212
summary of, 215
Resilience, 46, 124, 203
Resources
educational, 141
Retrospective studies, 191–192, 194–195
of expertise, 98–99
Rewards
in transition from ability to competency, 163
Risk taking
in transition from expertise to
artistry, 166

Scaffold
scaffolding, 204
scaffolded opportunities to learn, 96,
100
Scholarly productivity, 165
Scholarly productivity/Artistry, 165
Schools, 97
specialized, 217, 218
Secondary school, 158. *See also* High
school
Self-confidence
in transition from competency to
expertise, 164
in transition from expertise to
artistry, 165–166
Self-efficacy, 97
achievement and, 145
Self-fulfilling prophecies, 135–136
Self-knowledge
in transition from competency to
expertise, 164
Self-promotion
in transition from competency to
expertise, 164
Self-regulation, 203. *See also* Attention
regulation; Emotion regulation
in older adults, 179
Sensitive periods, 89, 101

Sex differences, 94, 95, 97. *See also*
Gender
in academic engagement, 97
Sexual
changes at adolescence, 204
development, 97
Silicon valley, 101, 192, 214
Single-sex. *See also* Co-educational;
Mixed-sex
mathematics, 97
science, 97
Social affordances, 15
interplay of talent and, 204–205
Social capital, 214
Social context. *See also* Cultural context; Social environment; Social
milieu
in adolescence, 101
and creativity, 213–214
of extraordinary accomplishment,
192
and identification of adolescent giftedness, 92
Social-emotional domain, 220
Social environment, 101. *See also* Cultural context; Social context;
Social milieu
Social identities, 47, 92
achievement and, 143–145
Social intelligence
of older adults, 178–179
Social milieu, 101. *See also* Cultural
context; Social context; Social
environment
influence on creativity, 214
influence on output, 101
Social skills, 223
in transition from competency to
expertise, 164
in transition from expertise to
artistry, 165
Social variables, 159
Socioeconomic status
achievement and, 144–145
interindividual diversity and,
95–96

Socioeconomic underrepresentation.
See also Societal inequities;
Underrepresentation
in students' opportunities to learn,
95–96
SP/A. *See* Scholarly
productivity/Artistry
Spatial domain. *See also* Domains
education and research on, 216
need for
more coherence, 71–72
more respect, 72
Spatial education, 71, 216
Spatial giftedness
in adults, 69–70
National Research Council
report on, 69, 70
brain imaging for markers of, 83
core spatial abilities and, 82, 83
longitudinal research in trajectories
and development of, 71
need for understanding of components, 82–83
prospective study of, 82
relationship between core abilities
and socially constructed
domains, 83–84
research in origin of, 83
research to measure, 71
retrospective study of, 82
Spatial-graphic giftedness
core abilities
requirements for each domain, 81
vs. socially constructed domains,
80—81
Spatial-graphic representation. *See also*
Maps and map users
in cartography, 61–66. *See also* Maps
and map users
definition of, 60–61
environmental, 62–68
implications for research and practice, 70–72
maps and map users, 62–66
in National Geographic Bee, 66–68.
See also National Geographic
Bee

ABOUT THE EDITORS

Frances Degen Horowitz, PhD, is a professor and president emerita at the Graduate Center of the City University of New York. She is an elected member of the American Academy of Arts and Sciences, a fellow of the American Psychological Association (APA), and a fellow of the American Association for the Advancement of Science. A developmental psychologist, she is the author of more than 130 articles, monographs, and books in the field of child development, with an emphasis on infant behavior and development and developmental theory. Among numerous leadership positions in the field of psychology and child development, she has served as president of the Society for Research and Child Development and president of APA's Division 7 (Developmental Psychology). She coedited, with Marion O' Brien, the book *The Gifted and Talented: Developmental Perspectives* (1985) and was an editor of the *Monographs of the Society for Research in Child Development.*

Rena F. Subotnik, PhD, is the director of the Center for Gifted Education Policy at the American Psychological Association (APA). The center's mission is to generate public awareness, advocacy, clinical applications, and cutting-edge research ideas that will enhance the achievement and performance of children and adolescents with special gifts and talents in all domains (including academic disciplines, performing arts, sports, and professions).

She is a coeditor of an upcoming series titled *Levers of Change* and has a volume in preparation with APA Books titled *Methodologies for Conducting Research on Giftedness.* She has also coedited *Optimizing Student Success in School With the Other Three R's: Reasoning, Resilience, and Responsibility* (2006); *The Scientific Basis of Educational Productivity* (2006); *International Handbook of Giftedness and Talent* (2nd ed., 2002); *Remarkable Women: Perspectives on Female Talent Development* (1995); and *Beyond Terman: Contemporary Longitudinal Studies of Giftedness and Talent* (1994). She is also the primary author of *Genius Revisited: High IQ Children Grown Up* (1993).

Dona J. Matthews, PhD, has been teaching, writing, counseling, consulting, and conducting research on gifted development and education since 1985. From 2003 to 2007, she was the director of the Center for Gifted Studies and Education at Hunter College, The City University of New York, where she worked with New York City (NYC) teachers and the NYC Department of Education on policies and practices relating to giftedness. She is currently a visiting professor at the Ontario Institute for Studies in Education, engaged in several writing projects and working with families and schools on issues relating to gifted education. In addition to dozens of journal articles, she is a coauthor of *Being Smart About Gifted Children: A Guidebook for Parents and Educators* (2005) and a coeditor of the *Routledge International Companion to Gifted Education* (2009).